Administering Affect

Administering Affect

Pop-Culture Japan and the Politics of Anxiety

Daniel White

Stanford University Press

Stanford, California

Stanford University Press
Stanford, California

Printed in the United States of America on acid-free, archival-quality paper

Library of Congress Cataloging-in-Publication Data

Names: White, Daniel, 1980– author.
Title: Administering affect : pop-culture Japan and the politics of anxiety
    / Daniel White.
Description: Stanford, California : Stanford University Press, 2022. |
    Includes bibliographical references and index.
Identifiers: LCCN 2021049474 (print) | LCCN 2021049475 (ebook) | ISBN
    9781503630680 (cloth) | ISBN 9781503632196 (paperback) | ISBN
    9781503632202 (ebook)
Subjects: LCSH: Popular culture—Political aspects—Japan. | Cultural
    diplomacy—Japan. | Anxiety—Political aspects—Japan. | Japan—Cultural
    policy. | Japan—Politics and government—1989–
Classification: LCC DS822.5 .W44 2022 (print) | LCC DS822.5 (ebook) | DDC
    306.0952—dc23/eng/20211013
LC record available at https://lccn.loc.gov/2021049474
LC ebook record available at https://lccn.loc.gov/2021049475

Cover illustration: J-POP Summit 2017 Main Visual / MITSUME, © 2022
Cover design: Michel Vrana

For Arlyn and Patti White

Contents

	Acknowledgments	ix
	Notes on Language	xi
	Introduction: Pop-Culture Japan and the Circuitry of Affect	1
1	Soft Power: An Affective History of the Politically Possible	31
2	Nation Branding: The Hypernormalization of Cool Japan	61
3	Anime Diplomacy: Characterizing Obligatory Nationalism	86
4	Kawaii Diplomacy: Ambassadors of Cute and the Gendering of Anxiety	115
5	Administering Affect: Anxiety and the Everyday	144
	Conclusion: Melancholic Belonging and the Future of Pop-Culture Japan	173
	Notes	195
	References	215
	Index	241

Acknowledgments

This book is a collaboration. Indeed, at times I felt my task was not to write but simply to connect others' perspectives so they could better flourish together than apart. I put my name to the part of this book that integrates my interlocutors' voices, that theorizes their implications, that spends a little too much time on details, and to any of the book's subsequent shortcomings. For the rest, I credit all those who made this book whole. Getting there has incurred enormous debts, and my gratitude to all those who contributed their time and insight to it is overwhelming.

This book began while I was at Rice University's Department of Anthropology. I owe its early formulation to all those faculty and friends there who fostered it: Michael Adair-Kriz, Ala Alazzeh, Dominic Boyer, Lisa Breglia, Tarek Elhaik, Eugenia Georges, Cymene Howe, Chris Kelty, Hannah Landecker, Steven Lewis, George Marcus, Nahal Naficy, Valerie Olson, Nichole Payne-Carelock, Stacey Pereira, Elizabeth Rodwell, Ayla Samli, Carole Speranza, Stephen Tylor, Elizabeth Vann, Maria Vidart-Delgado, Amanda Ziemba, and many others. James Faubion requires a special note of gratitude but one that is impossible to convey. He embodies a rare combination of genius in intellect, skill in pedagogy, and care in collegiality without which neither this book, nor I, would likely have made it.

Many colleagues have shaped this work over its long journey. Several have read and commented on different versions of the book. Others have contributed guidance and inspiration. I thank Anne Allison, Tamotsu Aoki, Eyal Ben-Ari, Kukhee Choo, Kyle Cleveland, Joel Cohn, Ian Condry, John Ertl, Patrick Galbraith, Blai Guarne, Paul Hansen, Sachiko Horiguchi,

Marilyn Ivy, Koichi Iwabuchi, Hirofumi Katsuno, James Laidlaw, David Leheny, Gracia Liu-Farrer, Catherine Lutz, John McCreery, Aaron Miller, John Mock, Hirokazu Miyazaki, Yael Navaro, Shunsuke Nozawa, Gregory Poole, Glenda Roberts, Ryan Sayre, Mitch Sedgwick, David Slater, Kathleen Stewart, Satsuki Takahashi, Yasushi Watanabe, David Willis, Christine Yano, and especially Emma Cook, Andrea De Antoni, and all the members of the Emosense research group who have inspired my thinking.

I also owe an enormous debt to all those faculty members and colleagues at subsequent institutions who have supported my teaching, research, and other activities that helped produce this book. Thank you to colleagues at the University of Hawaiʻi, Waseda University, Hosei University, the Free University of Berlin, Doshisha University, and the University of Cambridge. Colleagues like Shiaw Jia Eyo, Hirofumi Katsuno, Diana Khor, Yu Niiya, Glenda Roberts, Christine Yano, and many others have gone out of their way to cultivate and care for this work and everything that sustained it. I am forever grateful. I also especially thank Elvin Hatch and Allan Grapard at UC Santa Barbara for the many hours they graciously dedicated to my early thinking in anthropology and Japan studies.

I am deeply indebted to Marcela Maxfield, Sunna Juhn, Dylan Kyung-lim White, and the staff at Stanford University Press. Their professionalism is astounding, reassuring, and will no doubt guide my publishing practices henceforth.

My fearless partner, Hiroko, has served as an enduring model for me of care, grace, patience, flexibility, adaptability, and warmheartedness when such faculties have so often fallen short on my end through the stress of academic production. I hope one day to emulate her heart, even if only in part.

Most importantly, I thank my parents, Arlyn and Patti White, who have enabled this project and the much longer history that conditioned it. I can think of no better experts in the heartfelt management of unruly affect.

Portions of chapters 4 and the conclusion have been published respectively as chapters in two edited volumes as "How the Center Holds: Administering Soft Power and Cute Culture in Japan," in John Ertl, John Mock, John McCreery, and Gregory Poole eds., *Reframing Diversity in the Anthropology of Japan* (Kanazawa University Press, 2015); and "The Globalization of Melancholic Affect: Escaping Soft Power through the Literature of Murakami Haruki," in Paul Hansen and Blai Guarne eds., *Escaping Japan: Reflections on Estrangement and Exile in the Twenty-First Century* (Routledge, 2018). A short excerpt from chapter 1 also appears in "Notes Toward an Affective Anthropology of International Relations," *GIS Journal* 3 (2017). I thank these publishers for allowing me to feature overlapping fieldwork material here.

Notes on Language

Japanese words are written in Hepburn romanization. Japanese names are given in the traditional Japanese style of family name first and given name second.

All names of interlocutors are pseudonyms except where permission was granted to the author or where similar information is elsewhere published. Any instances of names resembling actual individuals are coincidental.

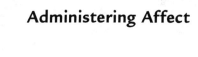

Administering Affect

Introduction

Pop-Culture Japan and the Circuitry of Affect

They were called the Ambassadors of Cute (*kawaii taishi*): three young women selected by Japan's Ministry of Foreign Affairs (MOFA) and presented to the press in February 2009. Their mission, according to the ministry, was "to transmit the new fashion trends of Japanese pop culture to the rest of the world and to promote an understanding of Japan through their respective cultural projects, carried out by the Japanese Embassies and the Japan Foundation" (MOFA 2009). Each ambassador represented one particular trend of Japanese cute (*kawaii*) fashion. Kimura Yū, age 27, represented Harajuku-style fashion (*Harajuku-kei fasshon*), named after a trendy area in one of Tokyo's most popular shopping and entertainment districts. Aoki Misako, also age 27, modeled the more established and eccentric Lolita fashion (*Rorita fasshon*), named after the nymphetic subject of desire in Nabokov's famous 1955 novel. Finally, actor and fashion coordinator Fujioka Shizuka, age 21, featured so-called high school girls' fashion (*joshi kōsei fasshon*), styled after school uniforms of female high school students in Japan. Dispatched to Japanese embassies and cultural festivals in countries such as France, Russia, and Brazil, the Ambassadors of Cute represented one of several projects serving what MOFA called "pop-culture diplomacy," a new paradigm in public policy that was officially launched in 2006 but that continues through the start of Japan's third decade of the new millennium. In this respect, and from the perspective of the program's mostly male administrators, the Ambassadors of Cute were more than cultural communicators. They were representatives of a new Japan.

For many of the project's organizers in MOFA, the Ambassadors of Cute were a success. Building on perceptions of the growing popularity of Japanese popular culture abroad, the program increased publicity for Japan's content industries represented in goods such as anime, manga, characters, TV drama, and pop music and promoted images of what the government began calling "Cool Japan" in a national branding campaign. For other administrators, however, as well as many members of the public who heard about it, the program was less inspiring. During a conversation I had with the head of MOFA's Public Diplomacy Department at the time, the director conceded he had received some criticism: "One female member of parliament voiced concern . . . that there may be some misunderstanding in a recipient country if a young girl walks around with a very short mini-skirt." Regarding this critique, the director acknowledged that from the perspective of "soft power," a new idiom of Japan's public diplomacy, reception was key: "When we send or deliver this soft power culture [abroad], the most important thing is that it is well received by the recipient country." He also noted in defense, "It is only one girl who shows her legs." In addition to this member of parliament, some female officials working on cultural policy in Japan confessed concern that the Japanese government seemed to be relying too heavily on young cute women to represent Japan's national culture. One university educator writing and advising on cultural policy expressed to me her skepticism over whose Japan the Ambassadors of Cute represented. She added later, "I never know what those bureaucrats are thinking!" If for some of Japan's national cultural administrators, the Ambassadors of Cute embodied the hopes of cultural resurgence in a time of geopolitical anxiety, for others, the ambassadors triggered anxieties over what it now meant to be identified as Japanese.

Administering Affect examines the emergence, emotional appeal, and management of a new national figure in the twenty-first century that I call "Pop-Culture Japan." Like the swirling signifiers on the front of this book, stamped with Takahashi Hiroyuki Mitsume's energetic art, popular culture in Japan includes a cornucopia of commodities, practices, styles, ideas, ethics, and desires.[1] And while Pop-Culture Japan draws on this eclectic mashup of popular culture, it is nonetheless a different animal altogether. Far more uniformly constructed and affectively consistent, Pop-Culture Japan represents a hopeful vision for Japan's cultural resurgence after nearly three decades of economic stagnation and geopolitical anxiety. It is manufactured not within the subcultural terrain of Mitsume's youthful art, in the capacious creativity of anime and manga, or even in the ever-evolving varieties of popular fashion, but rather in more conventional and conservative sites of Japan's government administration. Importantly, because those sites reflect selective views on what counts as the nation's popular culture,[2] Pop-Culture Japan is also fundamentally a political figure, embedding particular views and sentiments over others. For example, while its advocates are disproportionately older and male, its representative images, such as the Ambassadors of Cute, are more often young and female, inscribing a politics of gender into a narrative of national resurgence. Pop-Culture Japan thus represents a dominant figure of state administration as well as a contested figure of national cultural politics.[3]

In my use of the term, "Pop-Culture Japan" refers to an assemblage of pop-culture diplomacy projects and government-sponsored imagery, soft power ideology, national branding strategies, and, above all, an affective concern among state administrators over the international status of the nation that I call "geopolitical anxiety."[4] Together, I argue that these heterogeneous pieces contribute to mark a political paradigm shift over the last two decades in the way national Japanese culture was imagined by state administrators and, as a consequence, felt by both foreign and domestic consumers of media commodities produced in and about Japan. Grounded in sixteen months of fieldwork among administrators of Japan's national culture at a critical point in this history, from 2009 to 2011, and looking historically backward and forward from this period in order to tell a comprehensive story, *Administering Affect* analyzes how administrators of Japan's national cultural policy and diplomacy increasingly turned their attention to the uses of popular culture to modulate the feelings that both foreign and domestic publics associated with Japan. In analyzing government motivations for and practices of managing popular culture, this book asks how pop-culture diplomacy, soft power ideologies, and nation branding strategies otherwise known as "Cool Japan" emerged so powerfully in twenty-first century Japan, and, despite ample criticism of those policies from both inside and outside Japan, why they continue to this day. Additionally, because I think the answer to this question reveals important insights about how affect and emotion can structure a state's public policymaking in ways that are difficult to articulate and thus have not received ample attention in scholarship, the book ultimately traces accounts of Pop-Culture Japan to address a broader anthropological question on the relation between political administration and personal feeling.

The anthropological question driving this book is, How do the worlds that state administrators manage become the feelings others embody but often imperfectly know? In 1927 the American philosopher John Dewey famously offered one explanation that suggests what is at stake in this question. He argued that a "public"—a collection of people such as a community, village, or even a nation-state—coalesces around consequences of social life that are "felt" but "cannot be said to be known" (Dewey, [1927] 1954, 131). The organization of a group of people that share a common consciousness, he claimed, requires the articulation of the problems they suffer. Because, through an extension of this logic, the status of a group's flourishing depends on how well its problems are articulated, it is important who is most entrusted with this task. Ideal candidates should be articulate, empathetic, and, above all, sensitive to the causes of collective suffering. For Dewey, artists were likely the best suited for this task, given that "the function of art has always been to break through the crust of conventionalized and routine consciousness" (183). They were certainly better than the mass media, which were increasingly and, for Dewey, disconcertingly dominating public opinion in 1920s America during the time of his study. In any case, because a public's problems could so quickly become everyone's problems, especially where the imagined public was the nation-state at large, the stakes invested in sensing its problems and articulating them well were extremely high.

If the ideal candidates for narrating a nation-state's problems were the artists, and the least ideal—at least at the time, when their susceptibility to mass publicity and profit incentives seemed insurmountable—were the mass media, then who were the *actual* articulators? Who, in most cases, was most prominently sensing the nation's problems and offering solutions? Although Dewey disagreed with one answer that was offered, so much so that his disagreement is still debated today (Marres 2005; Whipple 2005; Schudson 2008),[5] there is evidence to suggest that in the context of the United States in the 1920s, as well as in many contexts of geopolitics today, it is the nation-state's administrators.

This might come as an unwelcome surprise. After all, since when were bureaucrats and technocrats known for their sensitivity? In a classic account of bureaucratic organization, the sociologist Max Weber ([1922] 1978, 975) claimed that it was the "objective discharge of business" according to "calculable rules and without regard for persons" that characterized the legal authority of the modern bureaucratic state, an entity distinct from and immune to the affective vagaries of "charismatic" and "traditional" types of authority ([1922] 1978, 215).[6] Nearly one hundred years later, this perspective has not changed all that much. Updating Weber's study of national bureaucracy, anthropologist Michael Herzfeld (1992) argued that while "Western" bureaucracy does not lack the symbolic and emotional characteristics we find in "culture" at large, if it has a signature affective disposition, it is "indifference." Such assessments do not inspire much hope for realizing Dewey's flourishing democratic public in the form of a politically reorganized state.

Despite their common appeal, I think these assessments on the insensitivity of state administrators might be wrong. Or, at best, they are incomplete. Having spent sixteen months among Japan's government administrators of the state's national cultural assets, I found bureaucrats to be incredibly sensitive figures.[7] I do not mean that the "real" people behind the bureaucratic desk were just as sensitive as everyone else once they left the office at night. I mean that bureaucrats became especially sensitive, albeit in a particular way about particular things, in their role *as* administrators. This is not to say that bureaucrats in Japan are especially sensitive because of an all-pervasive sensitivity characteristic of so-called Japanese culture. Rather, I suggest that around the turn of the new millennium in Japan, geopolitical shifts of power in East Asia created the conditions where Japan's administrators of its national culture became hypersensitive to perceptions of Japan's declining political prestige in the world. Consequently, for reasons this book will explain, they became especially sensitive to feelings of anxiety that seemed inextricable from, in the famous aphorism of Benedict Anderson ([1986] 2006, 6), the "style" in which the national community was imagined.[8] Subsequently, the world that these administrators sensed and subsequently built policies for was physically *felt* by many others in Japan's national community who also imagined themselves a part of it. I name this style of feeling among administrators as well as the administrative practice of targeting, modulating, and impacting public feeling through policies and programs *administering affect*. This book tells the story of this style and strategy of administering affect by describing a diplomatic shift in policy by which the threatening world that state administrators perceived became the anxious sentiments they sought to manage and, in some cases, even consequently circulated among multiple publics in Japan. I begin this story by introducing how such anxieties emerged with and ultimately integrated three discursive components that I argue are constitutive of Pop-Culture Japan: pop-culture diplomacy, soft power ideologies, and nation branding.

Sensing Anxiety through Pop-Culture Diplomacy

It was only after several months of interacting with Japanese bureaucrats that I began to sense the anxiety. I had returned to Japan in 2008 in the midst of what mass media would later call the second lost decade (*ushinawareta jūnen*), referring not only to lost opportunities for economic growth after the collapse of Japan's bubble economy in 1992 but also to lost possibilities for revitalization of all kinds, political and personal. I began fieldwork in 2009 among several government agencies whose officials were charged with curating and communicating to the world the nation's "culture," which was in the midst of transformation from one marked by tradition (Buddhist temples, calligraphy, and court music) to one by contemporary pop and "cool" commodities (anime, manga, and kawaii fashion). Through conversations and interviews with administrators, attendance at government committee meetings, and an internship at the Japan Foundation, a key agency managing the nation's public and cultural diplomacy, I observed how politicians and bureaucrats began discussing programs aimed at boosting the nation's geopolitical status by cultivating resources of popular culture. This shift in perspective was largely inspired and framed through a new political idea called "soft power," a concept coined by Harvard political scientist Joseph Nye that described how a nation could cultivate appeal and influence abroad through its policies, values, and, most important for Japan's national caretakers, its "culture." More than a political strategy, however, the term also operated among Japan's bureaucrats like a conduit for political insecurity, channeling anxiety into a variety of creative policy outlets.

Entrusted with caring for the nation's image and cultivating a positive attitude toward it abroad, my interlocutors had reason to be anxious. China was predicted to surpass Japan to become the second largest economy in the world, which it did in late 2010, and Japan's own economy had been stagnating since the collapse of its asset price bubble in 1992. Furthermore, other regional neighbors like South Korea were proving increasingly formidable economic competitors. In the midst of these perceived geopolitical threats, a consensus grew among officials that recently popularized strategies of nation branding and the cultivation of soft power might be a way to reclaim Japan's declining political and economic prestige within the field of culture. As the geopolitical became increasingly tethered to national culture, and national culture tugged on the nerve endings of personal belonging, political stakes in the global economy manifested as risks to individual identity. Officials felt this pressure. A sense of desperation inspired imaginative policy ideas that drew from the latest trends of Japanese youth culture, circulated abroad and then recycled and adapted by bureaucrats. Fashionable young women (the Ambassadors of Cute described above) were dispatched to overseas embassies and cultural expos; the beloved manga character Doraemon, a robot cat from the future, received honorary diplomatic credentials from the Minister of Foreign Affairs; an international manga award was created to inspire foreigners to participate in what was framed as a quintessentially Japanese art form; and the ambassador to Iraq in 2008 was reassigned in 2009 to the Public Diplomacy Department, where he found himself attending and advocating for the political expediency of cosplay conventions.[9] In 2006 Japan's Ministry of Foreign Affairs officially named these activities part of Japan's pop-culture diplomacy (*poppu karuchā gaikō*) and described them as aims to "to further the understanding and trust of Japan" (MOFA 2017).

These creative policy responses hinted at an anxiety engendered by a sense of geopolitical pressure among state bureaucrats and politicians, and they tied deeply to a growing belief that the cultivation of soft power through pop-culture diplomacy could address it. When this anxiety was refracted through a domestic lens, however, it seemed to mix with an anxiety pervading society at large, characterized by the decline of Japan's economy and a sense of labor-based social and psychological unease that Anne Allison (2013) has called "precarious." Conscious of their role as storytellers of national crisis, administrators from Japan's public broadcaster (NHK) proclaimed that the country faced a national "syndrome" and in 2011 proposed a series of programs in order to address the situation:

NHK TO LAUNCH "OVERCOMING 'THE JAPAN SYNDROME'" CAMPAIGN

January 6, 2011 (Tokyo)—NHK is to start months of intensive coverage about Japan's national malaise rooted in years of economic and social stagnation, naming it "The Japan Syndrome."

The campaign will be led by "Next Japan," NHK's flagship project providing comprehensive reporting and analysis of long-term issues surrounding Japan.

Masaru Shiromoto, head of "Next Japan" project, said "anxiety clouds over the society as Japan faces unprecedented demographic change and global competition. We will address the issue head on and search for a remedy to climb out of this situation." (NHK 2011a)

NHK's press release described a widespread anxiety (*fuan*) inflicting Japanese society and, importantly, gives it a name: "The Japan Syndrome." Interestingly, the title is not NHK's but is borrowed from an article in the November 20, 2010 issue of *The Economist*, "The Future of Japan: The Japan Syndrome."[10] Thus, in a rhetorical act staged repeatedly throughout Japan's modernity, the NHK announcement makes a diagnosis of national anxiety by appealing to a proverbial Western authority. For NHK and the government bureaucrats newly interested in the potential of popular culture to lift Japan from its depression, the remedy for anxiety required leveraging geopolitics to domestic healing. While pop-culture diplomacy grew out of a sense of urgency among administrators over Japan's slipping status in the world, administrators also saw their geopolitical anxieties reflected in society at large. Projecting their fears into the public sphere, administrators transformed a diverse and ambiguous set of affective insecurities among everyday people into a common narrative of national anxiety. Subsequently, inspired by emerging discourses of soft power recently circulating among political elites, they also saw the nation's popular culture as a possible vehicle for transforming widespread anxiety into national hope.

The Administrative Appeal of Soft Power

The concept of "soft power" is central to understanding how Japan's bureaucrats applied pop-culture diplomacy to address domestic anxiety. Like the phrase "The Japan Syndrome" used in NHK's program announcement, "soft power" was also a concept imported from Western intellectuals. Responding to concerns in the 1980s that the United States was losing its political and economic prestige, Harvard political scientist Joseph Nye set about investigating the legitimacy of these claims. "After looking at American military and economic power resources," Nye recalled years later, "I felt that something was still missing—the ability to affect others by attraction and persuasion rather than just coercion and payment" (2017, 2). Nye called this ability to attract others "soft power" and argued that it was rooted in a country's culture, its political ideals, and its policies (2004, x). Most importantly, he argued, soft power operates independently from "hard" power, which is based in military and economic strength. Nye introduced this concept in a prominent article in *Foreign Policy* and in his book *Bound to Lead*, both in 1990. Due to the term's rapid popularization, he outlined his theory more explicitly in a book in 2004, *Soft Power: The Means to Suc-*

cess in World Politics. In the early 2000s "soft power" became a buzzword that captured the attention of Japan's politicians and state administrators. They widely cited Nye's claim that "Japan has more potential soft power resources than any other Asian country" (2004, 85). They fast-tracked new policy measures and nation-branding projects. And they launched government committees to realize soft power's potential. In Japan today, even after nearly two decades of discussion that sometimes waned but always waxed again, soft power serves as a normative if still awkwardly applied concept of modern government, politics, diplomacy, and even industry.

Soft power is also by all measures a normative concept in geopolitics. Contributing to its appeal in places outside the United States today is the perception that given America's long-ranging war on terror, its unilateral style of international politics, and its loss of legitimacy since both its 2016 and 2020 presidential elections, soft power is up for grabs. This has enabled the rise of soft power contenders, especially in Asia (Bhutto 2019). For example, India is seen as making a strong bid for soft power through resources such as its technology and communications service sectors, its massive-scale democracy, its widely popular and prolific film industry referred to with mixed feelings as "Bollywood," and, as advocated enthusiastically by Prime Minister Narendra Modi, its traditions of yoga and Ayurveda.[11] South Korea has also been touted as a new soft power nation, especially in the wake of a global wave (*Hallyu*, or *hanryū* in Japanese) of rising appeal in the 1990s for its own popular culture commodities of K-pop, TV drama, and film. More immediately worrying to Japan's bureaucrats, however, is China, and what has been called its "charm offensive" (Kurlantzick 2007). China made impressive displays at both the Beijing Olympics in 2008 and the Shanghai World Expo in 2010; its economy averaged almost 2 percent growth from 2010 to 2019;[12] it received early praise for its response to the global pandemic of COVID-19 in 2020, if with reservations over its belated transparency and authoritarian style of management; and its Confucius Institutes, which offer generous funding for Chinese language and culture classes, have rapidly expanded over the past ten years and now operate in 149 countries.[13] Hanban, the administrative agency of the Confucius Institutes, is set on further expansion, with China's last two presidents, Xi Jinping and Hu Jintao, fully embracing a combined hard and soft power approach to global politics (Hubbert 2019; Hubbert and Powers 2020).

This growing interest in soft power suggests that the field of culture has become a coveted site for political investment and global competition.

Through their ability to turn cultural production into political capital, soft power discourses reflect a growing trend in what George Yúdice (2003, 1) has called "culture-as-resource":

> Culture-as-resource is much more than commodity; it is the lynch-pin of a new epistemic framework in which ideology and much of what Foucault called disciplinary society (i.e., the inculcation of norms in such institutions as education, medicine, and psychiatry) are absorbed into an economic or ecological rationality, such that management, conservation, access, distribution, and investment— in "culture" and the outcomes thereof—take priority.

Contributing to an ideology of culture-as-resource, the idea of soft power has reframed policy debates on what in decolonization literature was once called "cultural imperialism" (Tomlinson 1991, 1999), recasting political uses of culture in a more ethically acceptable frame and protecting against accusations of propaganda. For example, if Hollywood under the frame-work of cultural imperialism was a malignant force of what Wim Wenders referred to in *Kings of the Road* as the Yanks' "colonization" of the "sub-conscious" (Ashkenazi 2005, 351), under soft power it is an exemplary resource for a modern and responsible employment of power that appeals to freedom of choice within open markets. The increasing naturalization of soft power today as an indispensable component of diplomacy puts culture at the forefront of geopolitical competition, reflecting Yúdice's assessment that "we can expect the economy and the polity to be globalized to the extent that they are culturalized" (2003, 29). In this respect, soft power not only offers hope for cultural administrators but also serves as a warning to those who would ignore it.

Although the idea of soft power has thus become commonplace in global politics, those seeking to develop or critique it have also raised practical questions regarding its application: What is and is not soft power? Who has it and who doesn't? In what resources is it based? And to what degree is it dependent on hard forms of military and economic power?[14] Although these questions dominate soft power debates today, they are not the ones this book addresses. Instead, by observing the adoption of soft power as a governing framework within Japan's offices of national cultural administra-tion, I seek to understand not what soft power is or how it can be applied but rather what it *does* at the level of everyday bureaucratic practice. My contention and the central argument of this book is that the theory of soft power in Japanese government agencies functions most importantly as a discursive mechanism through which anxious concerns for Japan's present became manufactured into hopeful sentiments for its future.[15] In this sense, I argue that Japan's bureaucrats serve as dominant but not broadly representative nor accurate "articulators," in Dewey's terms, of the nation's malaise. Because this part of my argument depends on my demonstration of a feeling of anxiety that I claim underlies soft power frenzy in Japan among state administrators, it demands further explanation. I think it can be delivered most clearly by illustrating how affect sustains what I call the "soft power contradiction."

Early in my research I was struck by a contradiction that seemed to characterize soft power discussions in Japan. In short, the amount of energy and optimism over soft power's potential seemed incongruous with the lack of evidence suggesting it could, in reality, be cultivated. In fact, the prospect of wielding soft power faced several practical problems. First, within government agencies strategizing soft power in Japan, definitions of it were multiple, contradictory, and vague. Even in the academic literature on soft power this is notoriously and admittedly the case.[16] Second, among both government officials and academics, there was consensus that soft power could not be easily quantified in measurable indexes, a particularly acute problem for bureaucratic agencies that are required to demonstrate clear relationships between programs and outputs in order to justify publicly funded budgets.[17] Third, what indicators *might* exist for measuring soft power's positive effects will likely become visible only far into the future. The benefits of educational exchange programs, for example, can best be evaluated only ten to twenty years after their implementation, when students reach positions in industry or politics prestigious enough to effectively influence colleagues and form partnerships with members of the host country. Fourth, hard economic evidence from those content industries cited as resources for Japan's soft power demonstrates not an increase but rather a stagnation and in some sectors even a decline in revenue (Kawamata 2005; Kawashima 2018; Oyama 2019; METI 2020a).[18] Finally, optimism over Japan's popular culture content industries (anime, manga, music, games, film), the sectors of the economy most optimistically perceived to generate Japanese soft power, is offset by the common observation that consumers who adore a nation's cultural goods are often not equally enamored of its policies (see Anholt 2007; Iwabuchi 2007; Dinnie 2008; Aronczyk 2013). While Chinese and South Korean consumers may like Japanese manga, for example, this does not necessarily aid the Japanese government in realizing its political agendas, which, as issues like Yasukuni Shrine and territorial disputes illustrate, often elicit outright hostility from foreign publics.[19] Further, where national governments seek to involve themselves with cultural commodities, the results are often counterproductive. In short, as observed by many critics of Japan's Cool Japan campaigns, a nation's bureaucrats are usually not the most appealing advocates of counterculture.

Given this set of challenges embedded in the concept of soft power, it is easy to see how its popular endorsement in Japan draws from an affective source of enthusiasm to sustain it. Through its ability to transform a present sense of anxiety into a future project of hope, soft power proved effective in generating optimism even in the face of practical challenges to it. As the term *soft power* became slowly inscribed in various bureaucratic organizations, it manifested this contradiction more poignantly. Government agencies with specific and standardized procedures found it difficult to incorporate such a vague concept into practical administration. However, the circulation of the concept itself increasingly routinized its idiomatic use within bureaucratic spaces. In this way, as soft power became naturalized within government administrations, it was at the very same time revealing its *unnatural* adaptability to them. What resulted were not only curious new programs of pop-culture diplomacy but also concerted efforts to rebrand the nation as contemporary, convivial, and cool.

Branding Pop-Culture Japan

It was in the context of decreasing economic confidence and increasing attention to soft power discussions that a punchy article from American correspondent Douglas McGray became the banner flag for what came to be called "Cool Japan," a term officials in MOFA's Public Diplomacy Department borrowed from the short-lived and widely scorned Cool Britannia campaign from the UK's Labour Party in the 1990s. Writing in the American journal *Foreign Affairs*, McGray (2002, 44) proclaimed:

Japan is reinventing superpower—again. Instead of collapsing beneath its widely reported political and economic misfortunes, Japan's global cultural influence has quietly grown. From pop music to consumer electronics, architecture to fashion, and animation to cuisine, Japan looks more like a cultural superpower today than it did in the 1980s, when it was an economic one.

McGray's article, first published in English in 2002 and translated into Japanese in the popular literary magazine *Chūō kōron* (Central Review) in 2003, became a stable narrative through which to understand Japan's uneasy position at a regional fault line in shifting global power relations. As McGray describes, with Japan's economic stagnation, a rapidly growing China, and a United States increasingly aloof to the interests of Japan, the nation was struggling. On the other hand, Japan's popular culture, what McGray called a resource of "Gross National Cool," is loved around the world: its content industries tripled in size from 1993 to 2003 (although stagnating later), making it at the time the second highest exporter of cultural goods in the world (METI 2005). Even more, as often noted by Japanese government officials, it ranked second of twenty-three countries in a BBC World opinion poll measuring perceptions of a nation's "positive influence" (BBC World Service 2008). By framing popular commodities from Japan as part of the nation's gross domestic product of national cool, McGray's article tied popular culture to cultural power and presented them both in an appealing and easily communicable package.

In the years following McGray's article, the idea of Japan's Gross National Cool became commonplace in bureaucratic circles with surprising speed. David Leheny writes, "'Gross National Cool' captured the Japanese elite imagination in a way that few other recent American articles have" (2018, 103). Matsui Takeshi is even more forthright, claiming the article inspired a "Cool Japan craze" among Japan's "elite central bureaucrats" (*chūō kanryō*) (2014, 82, 85). My own assessment suggests if not a "craze" then at least a dramatic and energetic shift of attention. In 2003 McGray was invited to Japan for a symposium by the business newspaper the *Nikkei Shimbun* (Leheny 2018, 103). Shortly thereafter, a joint MOFA–Japan Foundation report directly cited McGray and advocated for the value of "gross national cool" (*Nihon no kokumin sōseisai*) and "national cool" (*nashonaru kūru*) as important "political and economic contributors to resources of soft power" (MOFA 2003, 45; Kawashima 2018, 28). In 2004 the Cabinet Office's Intellectual Property Headquarters published a report noting "Cool Japan" (*Kūru Japan; kakko ii Nippon*) as a key part of its content industry strategy for the "age of soft power" (Kantei 2004, 2). Also in 2004, the Public Diplomacy Department was created within the Ministry of Foreign Affairs, which was largely responsible for creating the nation's pop-culture diplomacy initiatives (Iwabuchi 2015). In 2005 an important study outlining Japan's content industries and circulated among officials at METI also cited McGray and described the article as "commend[ing] Japan's role as a new superpower in the field of culture in the 1990s compared to its power in the economic field in the 1980s" (Kawamata 2005, 107).[20] The list goes on. In 2006, two books were published focusing on Japan's "pop power" (Nakamura and Onouchi 2006) and Cool Japan (Sugiyama 2006), the former coauthored by a former bureaucrat from Japan's Ministry of Internal Affairs and Communications (MIC). In the same year, the nation's public broadcaster started broadcasting the program *Cool Japan* (*Kūru Japan hakkutsu! Kakko ii Nippon*), which still airs to this day in 2021. Finally, in 2013, Cool Japan was inscribed into law with the Cool Japan Fund, providing an initial government investment of 30 billion yen (roughly 290 million US dollars) that created a direct institutional link between soft power ideology and the funding of content producers that could realize the ambitions feeding Pop-Culture Japan.[21]

The idea that Japan's cultural resources could augment the nation's Gross National Cool thus created an opportunity to inspire and reinvent the nation at a time when old national narratives had run out of energy. As David Leheny writes, after two decades of economic decline, "Cool Japan existed because Uncool Japan collapsed; now Cool Japan would need to show that it was, after all, still Japan" (2018, 107). This appeal to culture held promise that a new Japan could be built on something tied not exclusively to the "precarity" (Allison 2013) of its economic development but rather to cultural expressions more authentically its own. Nation-branding strategies would thus prove fundamental to enacting this transformation.

Most conveniently, by framing pop-culture commodities as products of the nation, emerging techniques of nation branding could be applied to maximize the political impact of the culture industries. Arising in the early decades of the twenty-first century as an extension of consumer advertising applied to geopolitics, nation branding entails the modulation and management of the images, meanings, and, by extension, the feelings associated with commodities of cultural consumption (Anholt 2007; Dinnie 2008; Aronczyk 2013). Critical to my analysis of the relevance of nation-branding strategizing to affect theory, which I return to below, is that it stakes a claim in the gap between what consumers feel about cultural commodities and what they *know* about what they feel about them. As a framework that renders consumers of overseas publics into political resources, nation branding suggests the possibility of capitalizing on the affective attachments consumers build between themselves and their commodities, promising to turn practices of consumption into feelings of national fandom. As Christine Yano writes in the context of Hello Kitty and what she calls "pink globalization," "The emotive forces coalescing around 'art' objects make them sites of personal and collective negotiations of identity" (2013b, 20). Drawing from Jean Baudrillard, she argues that objects such as Hello Kitty "may be interpreted as a mirror . . . [that] sends back not real images, but desired ones" (20). I suggest this is as true for consumers as it is for state administrators seeking to leverage consumption to political ends. While administrators may not engage in projects of pop-culture diplomacy with the strategic mind of an advertiser, the adaptation of nation branding to diplomacy nonetheless normalizes the habit of thinking of consumers in political terms.

Nation branding thus offers administrators an explanation for con-sumers' desires and affective attachments that posits these as amenable to management. Nation-branding thinking suggests to administrators that fans desire Hello Kitty, manga, or anime not for the fantastically imagined worlds that commodities inspire or the unique qualities of their characters (*kyarakutā*), but because these commodities possess a charm rooted in a characteristically "Japanese" culture.[22] By extension, administrators reason that if a consumer shows affection for anime, a commodity imbued with the charm of Japanese culture, that consumer might also show affection for other products of Japanese culture, which, precisely because they are "Japa-nese" things, possess the same charm and enchantment. Nation branding thus serves as a mechanism for translating a consumer's affective affinity for a product into an emotional attachment for Japan. This ability for nation branding to translate one kind of feeling into another reveals its importance not only for understanding Pop-Culture Japan but also for evaluating key anthropological questions about how discourse and affect mutually interact in engendering political shifts in consciousness.

Emotion, Affect, and the Circuitry of Sentiment

While pop-culture diplomacy, soft power, and nation branding serve as the discursive mediators of a political paradigm shift among Japan's politi-cal elites, it is the affective dimensions of this assemblage that makes Pop-Culture Japan such a powerful new figure of the nation for administrators. This point requires clarification on what I mean by *affect*, how it differs from emotion, and why I think this very act of distinction can serve as both a critical tool of theory and an ethnographic object of study.

While the ethnographic record has produced an established body of work from the 1970s to the 1990s on how emotions as well as *theories* of emotions differ according to the cultural, discursive, and linguistic settings in which they arise, more recent discussions on "affect" have pushed studies of emotion into new terrain.[23] Although the multiple threads of affect theory entail numerous and complex genealogies,[24] by highlighting one contested feature of this literature relevant to the "unknown consequences" and "perceived emotions" of Dewey's public, we can better understand how the splitting of a dynamic process of *feeling* into somatic sensations, or *affects*, and conceptual representations of those feelings, or *emotions*, becomes a strategic act exercised both within the politics of nation branding as well as in affect theory at large. Identifying this overlap between the aims of anthropologists and the political elites they sometimes study also reveals complicities that can be productively leveraged to anthropological critique.

A central concern to scholars of affect is how to understand the relationship between two different aspects of feeling: one *somatic*, concerning the body and its sensations, and the other *semiotic*, concerning representations of those sensations. In one of the most often cited contemporary articulations of a much older debate, the philosopher Brian Massumi has proposed calling the somatic dimension *affect* and the semiotic one *emotion*.[25] In his 1995 article "The Autonomy of Affect" and later in his 2002 book *Parables for the Virtual*, Massumi defined affect as nonconscious modulations of "intensity" moving through and between bodies. Emotion, on the other hand, is "qualified intensity," the "socio-linguistic fixing of the quality of an experience which is from that point onward defined as personal" (1995, 88). He further describes emotion as the "conventional, consensual point of insertion of intensity into semantically and semiotically formed progressions, into narrativizable action-reaction circuits" (88). Put simply, affect is the physiological modulation of feeling, while emotion is its symbolic capture in socially recognized symbols: words, narratives, and consensus-based representations.

This somatic-semiotic gap that Massumi posits between affect and emotion reflects the gap that nation-branding strategists make between consumers' feelings toward commodities and the meanings they assign those feelings. However, it is worth drawing attention to some concerns over Massumi's model before returning to how it might be applied in an untra-

ditional way to understand nation branding. While many cultural theorists have welcomed the introduction of "affect" to highlight nonconscious
and non-linguistic aspects of feeling outside a Freudian framework of the
unconscious,[26] equally as many have criticized what they see in Massumi's
definition of affect as a sidelining of affect's social and cultural grounding. For example, powerful critiques by scholars like Ruth Leys (2011) and
Emily Martin (2013) have claimed that emphasizing an ontological split
between the body's affects and discursively expressed emotions reproduces a
biological-based approach to affect that universalizes emotion. Other critics
have noted Massumi's failure to explain how social aspects of gender (Ahmed
2004b; Thien 2005; Boler and Zembylas 2016), race (Ramos-Zayas 2011;
Berg and Ramos-Zayas 2015), and place (Navaro-Yashin 2009, 2012) can
code and socialize affect even at the level of nonconscious and automatic
responses. Still others have criticized citational practices surrounding Massumi, arguing that to the degree that affect theory inspired by Massumi
pushes critique into what some call "non-representational" terrain (Thrift
2008), it also risks the "ruination" (Navaro-Yashin 2009) of previous schol-
arly genealogies on the social and discursive construction of emotional
worlds. Finally, and most challenging to the methodological application
of Massumi's distinction in ethnography, is his claim that affect cannot be
captured in narrative—or, more accurately, that the most effective analysis
of affect requires recognizing its imperceptibility, "as long as," in Massumi's
words, "a vocabulary can be found for that which is imperceptible but
whose escape from perception cannot but be perceived" (2002, 36). This
philosophical and poetic puzzling of affect as that which always escapes
its articulation has frustrated those researching and writing about affect
from the field and has invited experimental alternatives in response that,
while powerful in their insight and virtuosity, can also appear theoretically
abstract. I think there is another way.

In order to understand how discourses of Pop-Culture Japan impact
in both a somatic and semiotic register, I propose to focus not on how affect
is ontologically distinct from its semiotic fixing in emotion but rather on
how affect and emotion are mutually and interactively constructed. Affect
theorists such as those cited above demonstrate that *affect*, or socially constructed automatic feelings triggered in and between bodies, can shift and
move discourses in unexpected ways. They also make clear that *emotions*, or
feelings fixed in discourses, representations, and the conventions of social
"arrangements" (Slaby, Mühlhoff, and Wüschner 2017), condition affect's

automaticity. So how can we figure the relationship between affect and emotion to account for both distinctiveness and interactivity? How can we think about affect as something nonconscious and immediately responsive but also socially conditioned? And finally, and most ethnographically, how can we understand how bureaucrats and the people whose policies they affect come over time to feel variously passionate or put off by Pop-Culture Japan in ways that are embodied, surprising, immediate, and deeply personal?

I argue that we can think about the relationship between affect and emotion in terms of *circuitry*, which contains components of feedback, transduction, and, importantly but counterintuitively, gapping—each of which I elaborate below.[27] In drawing these components from observations in fieldwork, I suggest in conversation with other thinkers of and with "recursivity" in anthropology (Holbraad 2012; Laidlaw and Heywood 2013; Holbraad and Pedersen 2017) that our starting point for theorizing sentiment should be to apply an ethnographic rather than an exclusively philosophical lens to the relationship between affect and emotion. As illustrated in my discussion of soft power and nation branding above and as I demonstrate in subsequent chapters, it is not only academics who theorize emotion but also, and increasingly, state administrators. I argue that in their development of policies to help realize soft power and build a new national figure of Pop-Culture Japan, administrators of Japan's national culture exercise implicit understandings of the relationship between affect and emotion and exploit and demonstrate certain affordances in this relationship that can shed light on anthropology's own theoretical engagement with sentiment, sensation, and feeling.

The first component of sentiment that I explore is the most critical. As it may at first appear contradictory, however, I take some extra space to articulate it. I call it *gapping*, or more formally, the *affect-emotion gap*. As I described in my discussion of nation branding above, the splitting or "gapping" of feeling into affect and emotion is not only something that theorists do, although not without contention, but something that state administrators do as well. In numerous instances of both theoretical and political discourses, experts render vaguely construed affects (e.g., an unsettling but unnamed anxiety) knowable and manageable through discursive strategies of labeling (e.g., "national malaise rooted in years of economic and social stagnation," or "the Japan syndrome"). I argue that focusing ethnographic attention on this contextual "gapping" of feeling into affect and emotion can serve as both an ethnographic object of analysis and a tool for affect theory critique. Most importantly, it can illustrate how both the citational practices around prominent works of theory like Massumi's as well as the branding practices surrounding Cool Japan are similarly subject to relations of institutional power and political contest and similarly depend on the productive ambiguity of affect.

To this end, I offer a working definition of the *affect-emotion gap* as the dynamic slippages between what subjects feel and what they conceptualize and make "known" of what they feel that are often made into sites of political, economic, and ethical investment and management.[28] Because each side of the affect-emotion gap never neatly maps onto the other, which can cause somatic-semiotic dissonance, I suggest that it is richly productive of discourse. I argue that this productivity is critical to building the mediated assemblage of Pop-Culture Japan through which affects independently move—and *move* administrators in turn. Placing this figure of the affect-emotion gap squarely within its social context, I further suggest that it is not a natural, biological, or psychological gap between feeling and the act of labeling feeling—and thus generating knowledge out of it—that activates its productivity but rather the formulation in discourse of this gap as something that should, could, and in many cases, must be reconciled. This renders the affect-emotion gap a fundamentally social and politically contested object. This also makes the affect-emotion gap a dynamic entity, as affect and emotion become connected through recursive practices of feeling on one hand and practices of describing and narrating feeling across an epistemological gap on the other.

This connective and constitutive property of affect and emotion highlights the second implicit understanding of the relationship between affect and emotion I observed in administrators. I call it *feedback*, or, drawing on Margaret Wetherell (2012), a "looping" effect.[29] The looping effect of the affect-emotion gap describes the interactive operation of affect on emotion and emotion on affect, which facilitates what Teresa Brennan (2004) called the "transmission of affect." Put simply, the more that bureaucrats describe and "attend" (Csordas 1993) to stories of Japanese popular culture as loved by foreign publics, such as the news of Miyazaki Hayao winning the 2003 Academy Award for Best Animated Feature for *Spirited Away* (*Sen to Chihiro no kamikakushi*), the more sensitized they become to feeling hopeful for the political power of Japan's pop culture. Ideological descriptions of Pop-Culture Japan thus prime one's capacities to feel affect, and affect empowers Pop-Culture Japan in an operative feedback loop. While this dynamic operation of affect and emotion is evidenced ethnographically, it was also articulated by early feminist thinkers of emotion well before the so-called affective turn. Feminist philosopher Alison Jaggar wrote in 1989, "There is a continuous feedback loop between our emotional constitution and our theorizing such that each continually modifies the other and is in principle inseparable from it" (170). Jaggar's insight suggests how the affect-emotion gap can be applied, to reiterate, as a powerful tool of both ethnographic inquiry and affect theory critique.

The final component creating the sentimental circuitry of Pop-Culture Japan is *transduction*. I use this term to refer to the capacity for affect to be transformed, translated, and transmogrified into emotion, and emotion into affect. In this way, figuring a gap between affect and emotion serves as a mechanism for translating one kind of energy (e.g., somatic) into another (e.g., semiotic).[30] By appealing to discourses of soft power, nation branding, and pop-culture diplomacy in building an image of Pop-Culture Japan, administrators transduce affects of anxiety into an emotionally strategic project of manufacturing hope for Japan's future. In this sense, administrators illustrate how affect can be transformed into emotion and how emotion can, in turn, condition and subsequently trigger affect.

These three aspects of the relationship between affect and emotion—its gap, its connective looping, and its transduction—constitute a sentimental circuitry of affect and emotion that at once integrates and vitalizes Pop-Culture Japan as a powerful operative assemblage for state administrators. This anthropological rather than philosophical line of inquiry into emotion illustrates how methods of managing feelings manifest as political problems—or in other words, how projects of knowing become projects of power as narrative strategies seeking to neatly align emotion with affect, and thus close the affect-emotion gap, are applied to economic and political gain.[31] This is not to suggest something necessarily sinister or manipulative about such projects; it is only to say that those narrative investments in the discourses backed by the most resources and infrastructure disproportionately build those worlds, bring them into being, and demand of them their ongoing management. It is in this sense that we can draw on the sentimental circuitry of affect and emotion to help us better understand practices within Japan's state bureaucracies that I call *administering affect*.

Administering Affect

I invoke the term *administering affect* to illustrate how anxiety becomes a bureaucratic target, technique, and unintended consequence of promoting Japan's national popular culture. First, as a *target* of administration, I refer to administrators' own sense of anxious urgency over Japan's geopolitical prestige that is strategically transformed into hope for Japan's resurgence through soft power. Critically, the way administrators do this incorporates another aspect of administering affect as target, which refers to the commodity desire of foreign publics that nation branders hope to transform into affectionate feelings for Japanese culture at large. Second, as a *technique*, administering affect (or what I sometimes call "administrative affect" to disambiguate this dimension from the others) refers to a style and method of administrative practice among bureaucrats whereby consciously attending and nonconsciously attuning to anxiety creates an affective habit or "enskillment" (Ingold 2000) of administering well, determined in coordination with one's colleagues. Finally, administering affect as *consequence* refers to administration as a distributive property—for example, as the capacity to administer and circulate anxious affect through the effects of policy.

Drawing on these three aspects of administering affect, in the following chapters I describe how anxiety becomes at once a target, technique, and consequence of bureaucratic administration that has led to the creation of Pop-Culture Japan as a newly imagined and hopeful figure of the nation. More specifically, I argue that by investing in the fantasies of the culture industries as a political strategy, the creation of Pop-Culture Japan has served as a therapeutic mechanism to transform administrators' geopolitical anxieties into hopes for the nation's cultural resurgence; however, in the process, Pop-Culture Japan has also consequently circulated anxieties among broader publics in Japan by appealing to images of national culture that are hypercommodified, highly gendered, and that allude to Japan's historical ascendancy in Asia. This argument builds on other scholars of the pop-culture/soft power nexus in Japan, such as Koichi Iwabuchi (2007, 2015), Kukhee Choo (2009, 2013), Nissim Otmazgin (2008, 2013), and several others.[32] Most of all, my argument draws from David Leheny's (2018) expert explanation for how around the start of Japan's new millennium modes of political attention to feeling exercised through highly sentimental stories of national unity and nostalgia helped construct the image of Japan as an "empire of hope." *Administering Affect* adds to this discussion an ethnographic analysis of the role that bureaucratic sensitivities played in fixing anxiety to hope in a mutual relationship of productive combustion: an anxious present driving hope for the future; unanswered hope aggravating anxiety in the present.[33]

In evaluating the usefulness of the term *administering affect* to articulate a dynamic process of affective translation, one might ask why it is necessary to focus so much attention on anxiety, what it precisely means, and whether this is a newly emergent phenomenon. To be clear, while the figure of Pop-Culture Japan may be new in Japan's political history, the administrative anxiety that in large part fuels it is not (Leheny 2006b). Various storylines of anxiety—insecurity in relation to Western countries, the self-Orientalization identified as a product of it, and the reactionary focus on Japanese uniqueness that largely characterizes the genre of national character studies (*Nihonjinron* or *bunkaron*)—have become conventional themes in studies of modern Japan (Befu 2001). Often in Japan's modern history, the adopted remedies for such diagnoses of anxiety were framed in reference to nostalgia. In her monumental work *Discourses of the Vanishing*, Marilyn Ivy (1995) argues that anxiety associated with a sense of loss emerges with Japan's transition to modernization, which evoked a "double movement whereby that which was marginalized by the advent of nationalist modernity in the Meiji period (1868–1912)—peasant practices, superstitions, the folkloric— was in the same movement objectified as most essentially traditional" (25). National culture, in Ivy's view, becomes fixed to a past that must be repeatedly recalled to affirm it. Ivy articulates her point artfully: "For the loss of nostalgia—that is, the loss of the desire to long for what is lost because one has found the lost object—can be more unwelcome than the original loss itself" (10). This characteristically "Japanese" nostalgia identified by Ivy operates on the logic of Freud's fetish, addressing a "symptomatic" anxiety over loss of the national body's past (11).

Building on the critical luminosity of Ivy's work, I wonder if her characterization of nostalgia might also be updated, and subsequently help clarify what I mean by *anxiety* and why I emphasize it. While a shift in cultural policy that emphasizes Japan's popular culture has not in the eyes of administrators come at the expense of its traditional culture, it has nonetheless created historical ruptures in cultural continuity that become increasingly challenging to reconcile. Ivy's analysis locates anxiety's antidotes in the past, in a sentiment of nostalgia for traditions lost. Pop-Culture Japan, on the other hand, is future-oriented, anticipating a new Japan out of the ashes of now three "lost decades." While taking nostalgia into consideration, I

suggest that it is precisely the playful, popular, and future-oriented imagination of a pop-culture nation—always optimistic yet always just out of
reach—that is in part so conducive to sustaining a sensitivity to geopolitically generated anxiety among administrators.

Cast between nostalgic habits of imagining a lost Japan and hopeful
expectations of a Japan to come, *anxiety* in my study refers to that palpable
but imperfectibly identifiable impetus to change an uncomfortable present.
It refers not to a singular emotional experience but to a variety of discomforting affects that my interlocutors in Japan at different times call *fuan*,
fuanshin, and *fuantei* and that I variously refer to as *anxiety*, *uncertainty*, and
instability and *insecurity* in order to highlight anxiety's multiple dimensions,
contexts, and articulators. In this manner, *anxiety* refers to a dynamic and
interconnected set of sensations that are connected by what the philosopher
Ludwig Wittgenstein ([1953] 2009) called a "family resemblance," while
also drawing on critical theorizations of anxiety.[34] Most important among
these theorizations are those that emphasize anxiety as an affect that marks
an uncomfortable situation and motivates escape. Summarizing her many
years of study on national sentiment in the United States, Lauren Berlant
(2011, 4) has claimed that the "present is perceived, first, affectively." One
reason for this is that the conditions that create the sense of a moment
are too complex to manifest as anything other than feeling. Any narrative
explanation appears too simple. From this perspective, affects of anxiety
are not evidence of a cognitive failure to grasp a multifaceted reality but
rather of an "intelligence beyond rational calculation" (Berlant 2011, 2).
One problem with this "intelligence," however, is that it is just as socially
constructed as our means of rational calculation, if nonetheless capturing
more of its complexity. Thus, sometimes those affects that manifest as a
hope for something otherwise can work against us, a condition that Berlant
(2011, 1) calls "cruel optimism." While Berlant's concept proves useful for
generalizing anxious conditions in theory, I want to ground the particular
experiences of anxiety I encountered in Japan in fieldwork.

Although the story of the intersection of cultural diplomacy, soft
power, and nation branding, as well as of the anxious sentiments that connect them, has often been referred to in ethnographies of Japanese popular
culture, it has not been fully told from the perspective of administrators.
Ethnographic accounts of Japanese toys (Allison 2006), hip-hop (Condry
2006), anime (Condry 2013), TV drama (Lukács 2010), characters (Tobin
2004; Yano 2013b; Galbraith 2019), and popular culture at large (Iwabuchi

2002) provide intimate portraits of how engagement with Japanese popular culture at home and abroad structures identity and sociality through the consumption of commodities. As these works acknowledge, the government's investment in Cool Japan is an important part of their stories.[35] However, alluding to the government as only a minor character and focusing on specific consumption habits rather than on administrative practices, they leave room to construct a more comprehensive narrative from the point of view of state actors. Such a story would show not only how government actors in intimate spaces of planning committees and policy deliberation put soft power policy into action, but it would also illustrate how government efforts to transform Japanese subculture into national culture affected how citizens were newly and often uncomfortably interpellated as subjects of a newly emerging pop-culture nation. *Administering Affect* offers this missing story of how the circulation and contested articulations of anxious affect became a target of cultural administration as well as a broader consequence of its execution.

Masculinity, Methodology, and Modes of Fieldwork

Drawing on my discussion on the circuitry of affect and emotion above, I analyze in *Administering Affect* how Pop-Culture Japan was manufactured in policy as well as in the imagination of administrators. Because many of the administrators engaged in the management of national culture that I studied were men, I incorporate into my methodological approach attention to how the imagination, practices, and images creating Pop-Culture Japan represent asymmetrically gendered and masculinized representations. Inspired by other ethnographic works addressing the politics of gender and, specifically, masculinity in Japan (Roberson and Suzuki 2003; Cook 2016; Saladin 2019), I consider how historically male-dominated institutions of state administration reproduce and exercise certain masculine histories of the nation through administering pop-culture policy. What often results from this gendered dimension of Pop-Culture Japan is the selective promotion of young, *kawaii*, feminized images that correspond less to the diversity of gender play in popular Japanese culture and more to a historically masculinized interpretation of it. Given this gender asymmetry in the imagery of Pop-Culture Japan, I evaluate to what extent the styles of administrative affect I attend to among administrators exhibit particularly male-specific forms of affect, while also acknowledging that masculinity is multiple, mutable, contextual, and mutually constructed with and against similarly dynamic forms of feminine and nonbinary gender expressions (Cook 2016, 5–8).

In the course of excavating affect among mainly but not *only* male administrators, I pay attention to two primary kinds of fieldwork encounters in order to make the feelings and sentiments I found invested in Pop-Culture Japan legible. First, I note moments where administrators engage in the active gapping of feeling and meaning, such as by claiming to have observed overseas fans passionately engaged in cosplay and explaining those passions as evidence of an affinity for "Japanese culture." Second, I also note moments of gapping in administrators' own accounts, where the stories they tell show discordance with the sentiments they express. These moments come in logical contradictions, abrupt changes of topic, instances of silence, stifled sentences, and suggestive bodily comportments whose meaning can never be verified but whose sensations can, over time and habituation, be sensed and "transmitted" (Brennan 2004).[36] In this way, I engage in "practices of feeling with the world" (De Antoni and Dumouchel 2017) and the interlocutors I momentarily share it with in ways that I find ethnographically instructive. While it is impossible to verify what interlocutors "actually feel," one can note patterns of emotive expressions and the stories attributed to them across a flexible gap of interpretation. Paying attention to this linking of affective feeling and descriptions of emotion reveals patterns of embodying and managing feeling—or, in other words, a *style* of administering affect.

Focusing on this style of administering affect in state agencies, which differs from styles of managing feeling in other sectors of Japanese society, challenges the notion of a fixed "structure of feeling" (Williams 1977) that is naturally coterminous with the boundaries of the Japanese nation-state. Neither does my own fieldwork nor that of other recent anthropologists of the state suggest that feelings operate in this culture-bound way, even if we accept that wide-ranging communal feelings can be stoked by stories of national unity and uniformity. Rather, the state has "many faces," to borrow a phrase from Yael Navaro-Yashin's (2002) insightful study of the politics of secularism in Turkey. It exists not as a common space of binds and ties, even if people at times create spaces of commonality through stories of those ties, but rather like a "meshwork" (Ingold 2011, 64–65), an interwoven network of threads that connect and affect one another in asymmetric ways that cluster certain feelings here and others there. This is not to say that one cannot write an account of those clusters that seem to affect most widely and generate sentiments that move many members of a nation. Again, David Leheny's (2018) *Empire of Hope* is a testament to how a study of the dominant narratives of the nation can be effectively done and why doing it is so important. However, I find it effective to zoom into a particularly salient production site within the meshwork, the site of central government administration, where substantial resources of capital, power, and media institutionalization have the power to manufacture story lines that disproportionately capture attention, build political infrastructures, and subsequently impact the hearts and minds that administrators target.

My study thus focuses on those agencies most responsible for the creation of Pop-Culture Japan: Japan's Ministry of Foreign Affairs (MOFA), the Agency for Cultural Affairs (ACA), the Ministry of Economy, Trade and Industry (METI), and most importantly, the Japan Foundation. I refer to officials in these agencies as "cultural administrators." Although there is no commonly used term in Japanese for designating officials working specifically within the field of culture, national officials are referred to as *kōmuin*, *kanryō*, or, more informally, as *yakunin*, meaning roughly and respectively "official," "bureaucrat," and "administrator."[37]

Over the course of sixteen months of fieldwork, I circulated through the offices of these agencies conducting interviews, sitting in on committee hearings (some of which were open to the public by registration, some of which required invitations), and observing the everyday practice of administering affect. I observed its temporal flows, its rhythms, its moods, and its bodily expressions, such as a slowly building tension, a stressful withholding, or a moment of relief. I also visited symposiums on cultural diplomacy and soft power, attended licensing shows for the marketing of Japan's pop-culture goods, and participated in academic public diplomacy and history courses taught by government officials at Japanese universities. In the most single-sited period of what was otherwise multi-sited research, I conducted a one-month internship with officials at the Japan Foundation, working closely with colleagues administering the Ambassadors of Cute program. As many other anthropologists of labor and professional spaces in Japan will confirm, however, the most important scenes of interaction often come outside the office.[38] I regularly interacted with colleagues in restaurants, bars, and, to my surprise, jazz clubs, where high-ranking officials, always mindful of their professional position, nonetheless opened up and shared more private feelings (*honne*) about pop-culture diplomacy that sometimes supported and sometimes contrasted with their public viewpoints (*tatemae*). Because of the sensitive nature and proprietary status of much of what I observed,

I often rely on public accounts that feature sentiments resembling what I observed in private. But as I aim to capture a style of administrative affect productive of Pop-Culture Japan rather than an authoritative catalogue of its policies and history, I hope such accounts will in most cases prove just as illustrative.

As my goal was not only to document the embodied sensitivities of cultural administrators working with soft power but also to trace the effects of Pop-Culture Japan beyond administration, I also followed the trails of administration into the sites of everyday life that policy touched. I analyzed media coverage on soft power, interviewed artists and writers who felt affected by it, and spoke with as many "everyday" citizens as I could on Japan's pop-culture policy efforts. As these stories of Pop-Culture Japan mix with other narratives of economic insecurity, precarity, and other negative moods circulating in Japan, what arises is not a single narrative but rather a negotiated and contested politics of anxiety. By *politics of anxiety*, I refer to the ways in which the affective consequences of imagining the nation and one's relation to it are made into explicit and sometimes contested projects of emotion management on both a national and personal level. Following stories of anxiety and national culture from administration into the everyday, I attempt to trace the affective distribution networks of and responses to Pop-Culture Japan. While such a strategy may sound at first diffuse, haphazard, and ambitious, as my fieldwork trails were guided by encounters in administration, following them eventually gave shape to an emerging network of affect's management and distribution—in other words, of its administration. As George Marcus (1998, 90) famously says of it,

> Multi-sited research is designed around chains, paths, threads, con-
> junctions, or juxtapositions of locations in which the ethnographer
> establishes some form of literal, physical presence, with an explicit,
> posited logic of association or connection among sites that in fact
> defines the argument of the ethnography.

While Marcus's paths may be of the fieldworker's own pursuit, they are not of the fieldworker's own making. And by following where they lead, a felt sense of things emerges that serves as the relational logic that holds discourses together and sustains their affective potential in an assemblage. Applying this affect-oriented perspective to Dewey's notion of how a pub-lic emerges around a shared feeling that is sensed but only imperfectly known allows for an empirical view of the state that captures its shifting and "circulating immaterialities and affects" (Dittmer 2017, 16). Sensations of anxiety emerge from this picture not only as the effects of geopolitical arrangements but also as the driving forces of state apparatuses (e.g., committees, programs, policies, departments, budgets, personnel) that respond to them.

This institutional dimension of Pop-Culture Japan proves powerful at integrating political narratives with personal feelings. Where talk of soft power, pop-culture diplomacy, and nation branding emerged among interlocutors, I found it was often accompanied by stories of historical and national loss as much as by stories of personal anxiety and insecurity. Such stories evidenced a poignant capacity among officials to sensitively register national concerns as personal anxieties when imagining Japan and, through soft power thinking, "transduce" (Massumi 2002, 80–81; Ingold 2013, 102–5) those loosely formed affects of anxiety into formalized sentiments of hope for a more optimistic future. In this way, Pop-Culture Japan as a new national figure serves as a dominant discursive mechanism for understanding, channeling, and distributing anxious administrative affect through policy. The aim of *Administering Affect* is to shed light on how this geopolitical anxiety perceived by state administrators is experienced by officials, distributed through policy, and variously felt, managed, and contested by those it impacts.

Outline of Chapters

In the following chapters, I build up piece by piece the assemblage in which a politics of anxiety emerged and ultimately inspired the development of Pop-Culture Japan. Chapter 1 focuses on soft power, the first discursive pillar of Pop-Culture Japan, and how its ideological framing gave birth to pop-culture diplomacy as a strategy for cultivating state power through culture. Chapter 2 takes up nation branding strategies, the second component of Pop-Culture Japan, such as the Ministry of Economy, Trade and Industry's neo-Japanesque project and NHK's television program *Cool Japan*. The next two chapters address Pop-Culture Japan's third pillar: pop-culture diplomacy. Chapter 3 examines anime diplomacy through examples such as the nomination of the manga character Doraemon to Anime Ambassador and the promotion of anime culture by MOFA officials at overseas consulates. Chapter 4 analyzes Pop-Culture Japan's girl-centered imagery through a cultural diplomacy program promoting the Ambassadors of Cute. Chapter

5 follows soft power discourses outside bureaucracy and into sites of the everyday, analyzing how anxiety was manufactured by state administrators and circulated among publics through institutions of the state. The concluding chapter reflects on the future of Pop-Culture Japan through fiction writers such as Murakami Haruki and others who have imagined alternative national imaginaries, either through escape, reinvention, or an unresolved sensation that I call *melancholic belonging*.

1

Soft Power

An Affective History of the Politically Possible

The story of Pop-Culture Japan begins with soft power. However, while I have summarized the intellectual history of the term in the introduction and while other scholars have documented its official inscriptions in Japanese state policy,[1] in this chapter I want to tell a different story altogether. Rather than catalogue recent policies, papers, and committees in which soft power appears, I aim to describe a recent history and social organization of administrative affect that makes soft power's adoption in Japan possible. In other words, I attempt to narrate a feeling coming into being. Doing so requires setting some historical context. However, because I aim to offer a history of how soft power popularity became possible—if not inevitable—in Japan and because I think this possibility depends on a structure of feeling more than a sequence of events, my historical context-setting may appear, at first, unorthodox.

Standard academic summaries of postwar Japan that set the context for ethnographic work on popular culture often go something like this. Japan emerged from the Pacific War (World War II) impoverished. As the emperor's status suddenly declined from divine to demure, as US military personnel occupied Japanese territory, and as Japan's constitution was rewritten in America's interests, economic despair was coupled with moral defeat. When through processes of reconstruction and liberalization, Japan's economy eventually began to boom, so did morale. A period of high economic growth (*kōdo seichō*) through the '60s and '70s led to an "economic miracle" and booming 1980s. A small group of enormous corporations (*zaibatsu*), which interconnected real estate, banking, construction, and consumer manufacturing, accelerated Japan's growth and fostered along with it a system of lifetime employment and social and psychological security often called "Japan Inc."[2] Such accelerated growth, however, fueled by increasingly risky spending and arbitrage, particularly in real estate, dramatically inflated prices and created an asset price bubble that officially collapsed in 1992. The economic recession and deflated morale that followed was named the "lost decade," characterized by the loss of lifetime employment, the attenuation of male self-esteem on which it was based, and a general sense of national malaise. Despite further efforts to regenerate Japan's economy through further liberalization policies, Japan's economy has continued to stagnate through two, three, and now potentially even four lost decades. If Japanese society after World War II seemed enduringly postwar, today it is seen by many as enduringly post-bubble.

Similar historical sketches, albeit less caricaturized than the one above, often serve in Japan ethnographies as useful starting points to frame a sense of social insecurity that manifests as a state-sanctioned, economic-rooted broken promise.[3] Most importantly, they help explain how technological growth in the 1970s and '80s and economic recession in the 1990s accelerated a transformation from a manufacturing to a service economy that produced more flexible, individual, and ultimately more precarious conditions for labor (Genda 2005; Miyazaki 2006, 2009; Lukács 2010, 2020; Allison 2013).[4] In turn, such conditions also engendered opportunities for creators, content producers, and artists to generate the eclectic worlds of fantasy and play that have captured the attention not only of Japan's government officials but also, in a recursive process, of Japan studies researchers who have made popular culture a core focus over the last three decades—a critical reflexive point I return to in chapter 5.

As important context-setting strategies in ethnographic work on Japan, historical summaries like these provide key events and labels—Pacific War, economic miracle, asset-bubble collapse, lost decade, precarity—which orient scholars and integrate scholarship into a cohesive field. These events also serve as shorthand signposts for national storytelling enacted by administrators, signaling how scholars and politicians engaged with Japan's popular culture share practices of authoring history for their respective ends of critical analysis and cultural policymaking. And while these easily canonized frameworks serve the important purpose of context-setting, they also show the limits of this kind of historical storytelling in ethnography. Especially where affect is concerned, I wonder if these summaries take for granted the sense of malaise, anxiety, and insecurity they often describe as an inevitable product of a state-sanctioned economic broken promise. This chapter uses more personal historical anecdotes and stories to communicate a feeling rather than a structure of that broken promise, especially as it was perceived and magnified by state administrators and politicians. It reasons that the sequence of events often told of Japan's postwar economic, social, and spiritual struggles leading to its soft power endeavors does not actually explain soft power's appeal because it leaves out that appeal's affective dimensions in the context of domestic and geopolitical insecurity.

I thus propose that telling an affective history of the politically possible, despite its challenges, is indispensable for understanding not only how soft power operates in practice but also for understanding why it and the fantasy of Cool Japan have persisted for nearly two decades despite so many critics' proclaimed confusion over what soft power and Cool Japan in detail are, as well as pronouncements over Cool Japan's inevitable end.[5] This alternative story of soft power's possibilities in Japan would necessarily attend to the sensitivity of bureaucratic bodies that are anxiously attuned to the nation's status relative to other nations—primarily regarding the United States but also including regional neighbors like China and South Korea. How, I ask, in practice and in discourse, is this administrative anxiety actually cultivated? And how did it encourage the enthusiastic adoption of soft power stories since the start of Japan's new millennium? I begin by suggesting that one answer to these questions and one way to empirically link the political to the personal is to observe how state officials, media, and intellectuals talk about states in ways similar to how they talk of persons.

Personified and Embodied States

While public speeches from state bureaucrats often appear as formal, measured, and by all measures rather mundane affairs, especially in Japan, where such events are heavily scripted and rehearsed, sometimes the bureaucratic register can rise to the melodramatic. Such moments, which I outline below through a mix of accounts from historical records and my own fieldwork, serve as a useful means by which to trace how historically intensifying but still amorphous sensations finally take conceptual shape. These moments occur most powerfully when speakers for the nation speak *of* their nation as they would of a close friend, loved one, or, in a classic trope of national belonging, a family member. As such, they reveal the affective power of anthropomorphically framing states as having the agency of human—and often gendered—bodies.

In a presentation at Japan's prominent International House during my fieldwork in 2010, an American diplomat whose name I intentionally withhold offered his assessment of the current US-Japan relationship:

> The relationship between the US and Japan too often, I think, resembles a husband and wife. Sometimes when there is instability in a relationship one partner will ask the other, "Do you still care about me?" "Do you still need me?" It's not a healthy relationship. Japan sometimes does this. I think Japan needs to stop being so concerned with what the US thinks and start telling it what Japan wants.

While this example represents the most candid and perhaps most unapologetically gendered version of a US-Japan relationship imagined through an interpersonal register, it is not uncommon. In fact, the creator of the "soft power" concept, Joseph Nye, also alluded to the analogy of marriage in explaining soft power: "Soft power rests on the ability to shape the preferences of others. At the personal level, we are all familiar with the power of attraction and seduction. In a relationship or a marriage, power does not necessarily reside with the larger partner, but in the mysterious chemistry of attraction" (2004, 5).[6]

I heard similar instances in which the nation is anthropomorphized in talking to Japanese state administrators, who often referred to "Japan's" ability to "communicate," "speak," or "express itself." During a break at a conference on soft power organized for US and Japanese government administrators, hosted in Tokyo in 2009, a former Japanese ambassador to the United States told me, "It is very difficult for Japan to express itself. . . . However, even if we do not express ourselves as well, we are often evaluated for what we are speaking about, and our message is appreciated."[7] Prominent US officials visiting Japan have made similar comments. In the same conference former US deputy secretary of state Richard Armitage said:

> In terms of public diplomacy, I am afraid that the United States is often accused, and many times correctly so, of confusing public diplomacy and loud speech. If we only speak more loudly, people will understand us. I could make the opposite point that if we were only quiet a little bit and listen to people, that might make for more

effective communication. The criticism for Japan, however, is just the opposite of that for the United States. I think that for far too long Japan has spoken too softly.

A year later, Obama's first ambassador to Japan, John Roos, expressed yet another similar sentiment in speaking to a small audience at a major university in Tokyo: "Sixty years now after the US-Japan Security Alliance, I want to hear what Japan wants today. What does Japan need?"

The observation that diplomats, journalists, and analysts of international relations personify nations and their relationships to other states is neither new nor exceptional.[8] And to the degree that such forms of speech act as a shorthand for describing a complex conglomeration of often competing agencies and offices of a state, one could argue that the rhetorical device is simply a necessary heuristic for getting on with the political work of administration in and of the nation-state. But I suggest that it is precisely this practice of speaking of nations in terms of personal motivations, personality types, and tendencies that also importantly enables the "transmission of affect" (Brennan 2004) within administrative structures. In other words, such habits enable diplomats and officials to *feel* and make others *feel* as a matter of administrative practice and "habitus" (Bourdieu 1977) and to be affected by what a state, as an imagined subject and agent, is perceived to *do* to other states.

Closely connected to this idea of the *nation-as-person* is the idea of the *nation embodied*. In a variety of ways, nations are not only personified but also embodied in subjects. Heads of state, for example, are regularly represented through media depictions as the very embodiment of the nation-state itself: grand metonyms in the flesh. In turn, media organizations depict heads of state interacting with each other as if their personal relationship directly reflected the relative status of nations. This leads to interesting situations where nations can, for example, personally "offend," "disrespect," or "suffer humiliation."

Consider a prominent historical example that Japanese officials even today regularly cite as illustrative of personal injuries to the nation. In anglophone historical literature, *Nixon shock* refers to the decision of the US government in 1971 to untether the US dollar from gold; in Japan, however, *Nixon shock* (*Nikuson shokku*) refers to the revelation of Nixon's decision to visit China in 1971 without directly informing Japan, which was often explained to me by my bureaucrat interlocutors as a personal blow to

Japan. In 1996, Kusuda Minoru, the former chief secretary to Japan's prime minister during the Nixon shock, Satō Eisaku, offered an account of the day they learned of Nixon's intentions:

> It was on Friday, July 16, 1971, Japan time, on a day when the regular cabinet meeting was being held. Usually these cabinet meetings start at 9:00 a.m. Just before the end of the meeting, a message came from the Foreign Ministry to the official residence of the Prime Minister. The contents of the message said National Security Advisor Henry Kissinger went to Beijing from July 6th to July 7th, whereupon Kissinger told Chou En-lai that President Nixon wanted to visit China.
>
> This message had been relayed from the Secretary of State Rogers to the Japanese Ambassador in Washington, Ushiba, and then to Vice Foreign Minister Yasakawa in Tokyo. It had not been communicated through the US-Japan hot line, one that had been installed upon an agreement at the Satō-Nixon meeting in November 1969.
>
> As soon as I received the news, I rushed to the Cabinet meeting room, but the meeting for the day had been adjourned, so I went to the Prime Minister's office and reported the news to Prime Minister Satō. The Prime Minister's instantaneous expression was very hard to describe. It seemed as if he were fighting a thousand emotions in one frozen minute in time. His verbal reaction was only one word of acknowledgment, "*sō ka?*" or literally translated, "Is that so?" He fell silent afterwards. (Kusuda 1996)

In academic and mass media discourses of international relations, prominent political figures are depicted as not only representatives but also *representations* of the nation; in turn, when these political figureheads act, their actions carry symbolic weight that feels somatically heavy for the political and administrative caretakers of the nation.

In 2009, the new prime minister Asō Tarō's first meeting with Barack Obama was covered with especially high interest in the press, with news agencies eagerly speculating over what kind of impression Asō would make on the enormously popular and charismatic American president. News anchors specifically evaluated Asō's "presence" (*sonzaikan*), a common point of discussion concerning US-Japan meetings at least since the iconic imagery of General MacArthur's visit with Emperor Hirohito in 1945 (figure 1.1).

Figure 1.1 Emperor Hirohito and General MacArthur, Tokyo, September 27, 1945. Source: US Army photographer Lt. Gaetano Faillace. Wikipedia Commons.

Their assessments after the meeting were overwhelmingly negative. Asō, it seems, did not make a very good impression—nor, worse, any real impression at all. In the wake of Asō and Obama's meeting in 2009, I Googled "Asō" and "Obama" in Japanese and clicked "images." The one in figure 1.2 was the second to appear.

Figure 1.2 Barack Obama and Asō Tarō in the White House. Source: Pete Souza, photographer, White House. 2009. Wikipedia Commons.

In widely circulated images like these, the nation manifests in the imaginary of publics through the mediated flesh of its leaders. Images and commentary from media—in particular from Japan's public broadcaster NHK—translate and transduce that manifestation further, channeling the scene into sentiments of embarrassment or shame.

Such sentiments can run deep—even into habituated patterns of thinking that seem to carry on below the level of conscious awareness. In further comments offered by Kusuda (1996) in his retelling of Nixon's personal slight to Japan, he alludes to dreamscape:

> There is no denying that there was a joke circulating among Japanese diplomats that one of them had had a nightmare that one morning he would wake up and find US and China had established relations and failed to tell Japan. This nightmare had become a reality, and so I hope you can understand the sense of astonishment and consternation among the government, the business world, the academia, and the media.

While recognizing the idiosyncratic use of *nightmare* in Kusuda's statement, I nonetheless thought about his statement in relation to a moment of fieldwork in which a high-ranking official also made a reference to dreams. Toward the end of a long meeting in 2009 with officials from the Agency for Cultural Affairs in Japan's Ministry of Education, I found my attention wandering. However, I was soon startled by a loud, animated voice that proclaimed, "Last night President Obama appeared in my dreams!" The voice was that of the agency's commissioner. I refocused just in time to register the commissioner's story. It seemed Obama had appeared in his dreams to motivate the committee. Real change, the commissioner cajoled, was possible even for Japan's bureaucracies. "*Ganbarimashō!*" he ended enthusiastically—a phrase I would usually translate as "Let's give it our best" but given the timing of the meeting during a high point of Obama fever, I might more appropriately translate as "Yes we can!"[9]

What can the anthropologist of affect, in contrast to the psychoanalyst, make of Obama's appearance in this official's dream? Here, Obama, so much the promise of a hopeful America in the flesh, was in dream image an example of hope for Japan as well. The nation—in human body, then in dream figure—seemed to take on an almost magical power to affect, to transcend space and time in visiting the commissioner's dream world as a kind of haunting or hallowing host.[10] The juxtaposition between the monotony of administration and the reference to dreaming felt odd. But then again, I had begun to experience the same feeling at other instances in which reason and romance intersected during my fieldwork in administrative settings. This experience is consistent with Don Handelman's description of what he calls the state's regular "torquing of passion and reason," a major function of bureaucracy whose ultimate objective is to negotiate the mutual demands of nation and state:

> The modern state depends on torquing together the sides of this divide. The vector of bureaucratic logic shifts the State towards the mathematical, towards lineal topologies of separating and fitting together parts with the exactitude of sameness and difference, while governing these machinic processes through rationality, clarity, precision, control. By contrast, the vector of totalizing effervescent emotion shifts the State towards the modern national, towards the romantic sublime (Weiskel 1976), combining a secular metaphysics of transcendence with nationalism, generating the intense arousing of emotion, their over-abundant penumbra of effervescence spilling over, uncontainable within lineal classification. . . . The State must

join the two sides of the divide, yet does so without being able to predict emergent outcomes. (2007, 134)

As discussed in the introduction, bureaucratic logic is classically understood as sidelining strong emotion; however, as Handelman shows, administration establishes a fluid and mutually constitutive relationship with practices of national imagining that are motivated and sustained by affect. "Bureaucratic logic may constrict, strangle, choke off the emotionalism of the national," Handelman explains, "and the enthusiasm of the national may overflow and swamp the neat borders and divisions made through bureaucratic logic" (2007, 135). While classic sociological accounts may artificially partition affect from bureaucratic "reason" in theory, the two appear mutually implicated in practice.

The Insecurity of National Administration

Thinking of international relations as a kind of *interpersonal* relations amplifies a sense of geopolitical insecurity that manifests as personal anxiety. For national administrators, to think with the narrative of soft power thus activates a set of anxious affects structured along asymmetric lines of imagined geopolitical power. Because the capacity for those "powerlines" to affect others depends upon the perception of national and cultural difference, to the degree that cultural difference is evoked and emphasized, the intensity of those affects is increased. This is the ironic consequence of the dominant trope of "Japanese uniqueness" regularly exercised in national political rhetoric: as discourses of cultural uniqueness are increasingly offered as answers to perceptions of national power imbalances, the anxiety evoked by the appeal to difference intensifies. The language of soft power thus activates a perception of difference that is intimately entangled with feelings of anxiety as it posits Japan in relation to a United States that is increasingly turning its interest to Japan's primary competitor, China. Operating in this register of national difference and competition, as national administrators do, is to be continually affected by an anxiety over Japan's slipping position in the configuration of contemporary geopolitics.

Consider how the soft power discourse channels anxiety through stories of Japanese uniqueness and perceptions of its rising pop-cultural popularity around the world. Nakamura Ichiya is a former bureaucrat from Japan's Ministry of Internal Affairs and Communications (MIC). He serves

on a number of committees and research groups connected with support-
ing Japan's content industries such as the Content Policy Research Group
(Kontentsu Seisaku Kenkyūkai) and the Pop Culture Policy Project (Poppu
Karuchā Seisaku Purojekuto). Onouchi Megumi is a media arts producer
and a researcher at Japan's International Foundation for Information Technology (Kokusai IT Zaidan). Together they published a book titled *Japan's
Pop Power: The True Image of World-Changing Content* (*Nihon no poppu pawā:
Sekai o kaeru kontentsu no jitsuzō*, 2006). Its opening line could hardly better
demonstrate the anxious context out of which hope for Japan's resurgence
springs through its content industries: "Japan's economy may have escaped
the lost decade [of the 1990s], but it does not have the confidence that it
has found the path to steady growth" (1). Within this grim assessment,
however, there is hope: "Industry builds culture, and culture is a mechanism
for building industry, so how about tapping into the light of the so-called
'power of the culture industries' [*sangyō bunkaryoku*]? The power of the
culture industries is clearing the path to a new age" (1).

As justification for their hope, Nakamura and Onouchi present, again,
Douglas McGray's article as the tool for realizing soft power:

> At the level of evaluation, since the publication of Douglas Mc-
> Gray's article "Japan's Gross National Cool" in the magazine *Foreign
> Policy*, Japan's entertainment industries have been garnering atten-
> tion. Gross National Cool is a concept likened to Gross National
> Product and serves as an index of a country's power based on the
> fashionable cultural power, or its "cool." (2006, 16)

The authors follow McGray's logic by which subculture trends are translated into a measure of a country's potential power and cite this popular
passage from McGray's article, also mentioned in the previous chapter:

> Japan is reinventing superpower—again. Instead of collapsing
> beneath its widely reported political and economic misfortunes,
> Japan's global cultural influence has quietly grown. From pop music
> to consumer electronics, architecture to fashion, and animation to
> cuisine, Japan looks more like a cultural superpower today than it
> did in the 1980s, when it was an economic one. (2002, 44)

McGray posed the theme of Japanese soft power as a question, asking
whether Japan would be able to turn its culture into a source of power. For
him, power was about message. In the caption to a photo in McGray's article

showing a male Japanese teenager, hair dyed bright blonde and speaking on a cell phone, McGray ungracefully quips, "Cool phone! But does he have anything meaningful to say to the world?" (52). The authors of *Japan's Pop Power*, however, are less concerned about McGray's critique of Japan's messaging and treat the article as confirmation of Japan's potential soft power resources. More important to them is subsequently identifying the sources for generating Japan's resurgence. McGray's term Gross National Cool thus serves as a useful means for sustaining their hope for Pop-Culture Japan, even if the possibilities for measuring it empirically prove elusive.

Another work, *Cool Japan: The Japan the World Wants to Buy* (*Kūru Japan: Sekai ga kaitagaru Nihon*) (Sugiyama 2006), follows a narrative structure similar to that of *Japan's Pop Power*. Like Nakamura and Onouchi, its author, Sugiyama Tomoyuki, who was at the time of publication the president of Japan's Digital Hollywood University, views Japan's content industries as a source of hope in an anxious time:

> The rejuvenation of "Made in Japan" (*meido in Japan*) is a new industry that is economizing culture and technology to a high degree. This new industry is no doubt gaining traction within a contemporary Japan that feels an anxiety over the fate of its national economy and dwindling population [*shoshi kōreika*—literally, "decreasing birth rate combined with an aging population"]. (5)

Sugiyama's book cites McGray's piece as well, calling it the "impetus starting this new benefit to citizenship" (*shiminken o toku hajimeta no wa*). McGray's article helped commentators like Sugiyama normalize "Cool Japan" as a lens through which to view culture as a resource for generating national renewal through soft power: "The fate of Japan's future is dependent on the ability to activate the resources of 'Cool Japan'" (Sugiyama 2006, 5). Ultimately, Sugiyama expresses hope: "Since the beginning of the twenty-first century, manga and anime, which have attracted high praise of Japan's pop culture abroad, are enormously popular. . . . I feel a bright future for Japan's content industries" (3).

These hopeful sentiments, often rooted in anecdotal evidence for the popularity of Japan's popular culture overseas, might be easy to dismiss as a peripheral soft nationalism typical of popular nationalist literature in Japan (*bunkaron*). However, the degree to which the phrases "soft power" and "Cool Japan" enter into government policy reports and white papers (*hakusho*), outlined in this book's introduction, reveals a network of shared sentiments that pervade bureaucracy. These examples are representative of a discourse linking soft power to Cool Japan that circulates widely if asymmetrically among administrators thinking through Japan's future, tuning administrators' bodies to resonate to an anxious sensitivity through what Thomas Csordas (1993) calls a "somatic mode of attention."[11] The more that soft power is cited in conjunction with hopeful stories of Japan's resurgence in the cultural field for what it lost in the economic one, the more that administrators exercise and cultivate a sensitivity to anxious affect. Even for those administrators that may be skeptical of the possibility for popular culture to cultivate soft power, the increasingly common uses of the terms "soft power" and "Cool Japan" in everyday governance render the phrases into triggers to which the bureaucratic body cannot help but attend.[12] Repeatedly cited and discussed, these triggers reproduce an administrative habit of evaluating Japan's status in relation to Western consumers of popular culture. In order to understand how such affect-producing habits of comparison become routinized, it is worth reflecting on their history within the context of Japanese bureaucracy more generally.

Affective Histories of/in Japanese Bureaucracy

Historians of Japan's bureaucrats (*kanryō*) have long noted the disproportionately central role bureaucrats have played in managing the state relative to politicians. While this reputation is warranted, it can also misleadingly portray bureaucracy as a uniform system that endured unchanged through Japan's modernity. In reality, the history of Japan's bureaucracy is better characterized as a story of contest, both externally in relation to politicians and internally between adjacent agencies. As Sheldon Garon (1987, 230) argues, the social-policy-focused bureaucracy that we think of as characteristic of the contemporary Japanese state "acquired its dynamic and relatively autonomous character after World War I." Despite this fact, the imaginary of Japan as a kingdom of bureaucrats (*kanryō taikoku*) persists within the consciousness of historians, as articulated by Shimizu Yuichirō:

> In Japan, politics has long been described as a "kingdom of bureaucrats," an "administrative supremacy," and "empty of politicians." Japan's bureaucracy may indeed be a faceless juggernaut of power, but it is also a capable one. This has been the image conveyed of Japan's bureaucracy. (2013, 1)

What should be added to Shimizu's characterization is that the "kingdom of bureaucrats" has been composed, from the Meiji period to this day, primarily of men, a point I return to most specifically in chapter 4.[13] Central to the historical development of Japan's male-centric bureaucratic system and, as I argue, to the administrative style of anxious affect that is cultivated along with it are two dominant themes that have become tropes of national history: the comparison of Japan's modernization with that of the West and the role of the state as a creative adopter and adapter of the West's administrative structures.

As studies analyzing the Japanese state and its bureaucracy have documented (Garon 1987; McVeigh 1998; Shimizu 2013; Soga 2016), the imagined "West" and, most notably, the United States emerge repeatedly as figures against which Japan's political elites have measured Japan's "modernization." These accounts begin with the Meiji Restoration (1868) and frame Japan's state administrators, who emerge in this era (Shimizu 2020), as making a concession to exogamous forces seen to threaten the very survival of a newly unified Japanese state. Such narratives of the nation rendered it nearly impossible to imagine "national culture" outside of a culturally comparative framework that was always already entangled with contests over power. Naoki Sakai (1997, 48) has documented how this inescapable cultural imaginary is embedded in intellectual works of history of the Meiji Period (1868–1912) that arise in tandem with histories of Western thought. Such historiography sets up for Sakai what, following René Girard, he identifies as a "mimetic desire" (Sakai 1997, 48) that indelibly obliges administrators of the nation's development to measure their progress based on Western models. Because *soft power* is a term attributed to a Harvard professor and prominent US government advisor (Joseph Nye), and it is modeled after the UK's Cool Britannia campaign, the concept recalls and rehearses a long but ever-present history of cultural comparison between Japan and Western nations characterized as advanced nations (*senshinkoku*).[14]

Historians of the Meiji Restoration and Japan's modernization have thus paid ample attention to Japan's approach to importing organizational structures of administration from the West. Most dominant among these portraits are characterizations of Japan as either the clever copier of Western traditions or the creative editor and adapter of Western systems to Japanese contexts (Westney 1987, 4). Both views represent varying interpretations of the fact that Japanese systems were consciously and rationally modeled after a variety of Western ones: "the navy on the British; the army first on the

French and then on the German . . . the communications systems on the British; the police on the French; the banking system on the American; the legal system first on the French and then on the German" (Westney 1987, 5). In the genre of Japan's homegrown *bunkaron* literature (again, "theories of Japanese character"), it is the latter perspective—Japan as innovative adapter—that wins out.[15] Numerous works in this genre laud Japan's ingenuity at incorporating elements from other traditions and making them its own—tea ceremony from China, Buddhism from India, technology from the West, food from everywhere. This praise of Japanese adaptability turns adaptability itself into a national character trait. As Westney writes, "Copying is less estimable than inventing; imitation is less honorable than innovation." And "the Japanese of the Meiji period, like their descendants today, felt belittled by the Western image of their nation as an assiduous copier of other people's innovations" (5). Although I see this concern as limited to Japan's political elites rather than generalizable to Westney's "Japanese" at large, the image of Japan as adapter as opposed to copier nonetheless enabled administrators to strike a balance in characterizing the nation-building project of Meiji as one based on both Western technology and "Japanese spirit."[16]

Rehearsing Japanese History in the Present

Just as nation-states are often framed in anthropomorphic terms, enabling and augmenting the transmission of affect, national histories and the simplified narratives in which they are sometimes expressed can evoke powerful personal feelings. Patterns of national storytelling in the past can thus be reproduced and rehearsed in the present, engendering a heavy sense of history in administrative practice. A young male Japanese official at the Japan Foundation whom I call Tanaka articulated to me in conversation how history permeated his understanding of the national culture he was tasked with managing. He later expanded on his thoughts to me in writing, whose English I edit slightly for fluency but whose punctuation and idiosyncrasies I maintain:

> If you look at the history of Japan, you realize that Japan has never created a system which enforces the common rule or built the common foundation for even regional countries to follow. It became more obvious and somewhat interesting to look at the con-

trast between Japan's rapid success after the Meiji Restoration and WWII, yet Japan has never enjoyed the status of hegemony. Japan developed so rapidly during/after the Meiji Restoration—supposedly more rapid than any other country in the world at the time. As you know, the motto of Japan at the time was "Wealthy Nation and Strong Soldiers" [usually rendered in English as "rich country, strong army" (*fukoku kyōhei*)] and Japan was so determined to go out of Asia and enter Europe, culturally, socially, economically, and even militarily. And they (. . . . We??) did it. We so successfully adjusted many parts of society to mimic Western styles and even become so strong as to defeat Russia, which must have been the biggest astonishment for most of the Western countries as well as for Japanese themselves. Western countries must've thought, "Oh no, (yellow) monkeys defeated humans!"

Again, after we lost the war, we determined one more time to rebuild our economy. This time, we pursued only economic development since we learned a very harsh lesson after the war, and people were somehow traumatized. And again, we successfully rebuilt our economy and became almost no 1. in the world. At that time, as you know, Japanese were called "Economic Animals," but at the same time, they were respected. *Japan as No. 1* [Vogel (1979)] was the best seller at the time. Many Asian countries were also encouraged by Japan's success.

But again, we were only trying to pursue economic development, according to the Western Capitalist System, and we never came up with our own creative idea to control the world.

Tanaka's narrative is interspersed with sarcasm that he would claim was acquired over an extended period of study at a university in the US. His parodic use of phrases like "yellow monkeys" and a "creative idea to control the world" distances him from the narrative he offers, treating it as an official, stereotypical, and racialized reading of Japan's history from the point of view of its conservative male state administrators. Tanaka's uncertainty over the degree to which he identifies with the narrative he offers is further demonstrated in his statement "And they (. . . . We??) did it" [escaped from Asia]. He offers the statement parenthetically, as a graphic representation of a moment of reflective distancing from his narrative.

Although Tanaka is ambivalent about his relationship to the narrative he crafts, that it is the one to which he ultimately refers and that it is one regularly cited by other administrators reveals the degree to which thinking of one's relationship to the Japanese nation requires the administrator to sense the weight of a history of Japan as "No. 1." Tanaka refers here to the iconic work by Ezra Vogel, *Japan as Number One* (1979), which Tanaka refers to as the "best seller of the time." Like Joseph Nye's *Soft Power*, the book was written by a Harvard professor, was broadly complimentary of Japan, and was widely circulated among and cited by Japan's elites, including Prime Minister Nakasone Yasuhiro.[17] It is difficult to overstate the importance of Vogel's work and the framing it has provided for Japan's state administrators to this day. At a training session I attended for officials of Japan's International Cooperation Agency (JICA), equivalent to USAID or the UK Department for International Development, one official referred to the book in the rehearsal of a speech he would present to his counterparts in Bangladesh. "My reason for becoming a civil servant is because I want to help make Japan number one," he said. As for many state officials, fulfilling this administrator's duty in the present incorporates a sense of concern over the nation's declining status in the recent past.

A similar expression of insecurity over Japan's status in the world and a turn to soft power as a remedy is illustrated by academic Yonezawa Akiyoshi's research on Japan's higher education. In an article on soft power's role in universities, Yonezawa (2008) describes Japan's contemporary political position as one of "crisis":

> Overall, Japanese education as a source of soft power is in crisis. Reflection on history and current conditions is indispensable to the development of a future vision. The report "Japan's 21st Century Vision" (Council on Economic and Fiscal Policy 2005) clarified the danger that Japan will be left behind in the process of globalization, and specified human resource development and education as priority areas for policy action. (55)

Yonezawa exemplifies how an anxiety over Japan being left behind by processes of globalization motivates strategic thinking of soft power in national policy. He is equally forthright in naming exemplary countries that serve as the prime motivators for Japan's soft power investment:

Japanese academics and students are aware that they are not at the
global center, and they feel the necessity to further internationalize
Japanese higher education to improve linkages with the global community. In contrast to the US example, the soft power of Japanese
education in the domestic context and in the global context are
clearly distinguishable. (55)

In Yonezawa's explanation, we find the reproduction of a familiar geopolitical model of the world that posits the United States at the top and,
below that, Japan, struggling to maintain its status as a leading Asian country: "Japan is no longer the only Asian country that can be proud of high
academic achievement and technological advancement" (55). Resonating
uncomfortably with similar attitudes in Japan's imperial past, he presents
a perceived geopolitical order of Japan at the top of Asia's hierarchy but
increasingly threatened, evoking a sense of anxiety in the present.

Yonezawa, Tanaka, and their colleague in JICA share a similar sense of
history. Beginning with the Meiji period, Yonezawa (2008, 56), like Tanaka,
appeals to the idea of *fukoku kyōhei* ("rich country with a strong military")
as the primary policy guiding Japan's modernization project. He goes on to
narrate three distinct periods of the historical relationship "linking education
and the military, the economy, and soft power" (56). In the process, he writes
soft power backwards into Japanese history, showing how it transformed
from a resource that first relied on military power (1868–1950), then was
accumulated with economic development (1950–1980), and finally became
employed as a tool for transforming Japan into a postindustrial society
(1980–2007) (56). In this reimagination of history, we see how anxious affects crystalize into a sentimental longing for contemporary sources of soft
power to alleviate an insecurity imposed by perceived threats of globalization. Yonezawa concludes, "If the Japanese fail in their efforts to establish
such educational environments [ones that ensure the well-being of citizens
living both inside and outside Japan], the soft power of Japan's educational
institutions and therefore of Japanese society itself will face very challenging
international circumstances in the not-too-distant future" (72).

Rehearsing hierarchical histories of the nation engenders a sense of
geopolitical anxiety among officials when that hierarchy seems threatened;
in turn, those feelings of anxiety intensify the impact of historical narratives in a looping effect. In this way, history is experienced somatically and
recursively. This pairing of anxious affect with stories representing a power

imbalance between Japan and other nations in the past serves as a preformulated script that elicits anxious affect when Japan is further compared
to other states in the present. Geopolitical anxiety, then, emerges as both a
consequence and a trigger of cultural comparison. This coupling of anxious
affect and national decline is evoked regularly in historical literature, from
Maruyama's intellectual history (1974) to Dower's (1999) cultural history of
Japan's defeat in World War II, to often-cited references to Japan's "Overcoming Modernity" symposium in 1942.[18] In turn, a comparative historical
framing comes to trigger anxiety in the present as public diplomacy efforts
seeking to advance soft power are organized in conjunction with those countries after which Japan has modeled its own diplomatic agencies in the past.

Administration as an Infrastructure for Cultural Difference

Public and cultural diplomacy efforts newly focused on soft power in
Japan take place within a bureaucratic register that is organized in parallel
to a set of corresponding agencies, bureaus, and departments in other nation states. This makes for a geopolitical order of political communication
and contest that is structured and sustained organizationally (Sassen 2007).
Importing its bureaucratic structures from the West guaranteed that Japan's
national administrations would be linked structurally with those it interacted with most regularly. It would also, however, consequently establish
an asymmetric flow of affectivity, or of power. Modeling the Japan Foundation (the state's agency for cultural diplomacy and international education
on Japan) after the British Council, for example, which was done in 1972,
guaranteed that administrative structures, styles of operation, and forms of
evaluation and critique would resemble one another.

This organizational symmetry is both a signature characteristic and
facilitator of modern global governance. Although anthropologists like Arjun Appadurai and Anna Tsing have drawn attention to the imbalances that
generate global flows of influence by appealing to such metaphors as "can-
nibalization" (1996, 43) and "friction" (2005) respectively, it is also symmetry
and compatibility that allow for the transmission of affect. Organizational
symmetry is represented in the parallel relationship of national administrative bodies: Japan's Ministry of Foreign Affairs corresponding, for example,
to the US State Department and the British Foreign Commonwealth Of-

fice; or the Japan Foundation to France's Alliance Française and Germany's
Goethe Institut. Paying attention to this geopolitical symmetry reveals how
"culture" emerges conjointly with the administrative structures organized
to manage it. The international correspondence of bureaucratic offices,
then, allows for the entrenchment of significant "cultural" difference along
standardized lines of cultural administration. So, for example, although
the US and Japan are both nation-states, they are from the official point
of view of administrators, different versions of them. One important site
for constructing Japanese "cultural difference" along national lines, then,
and the affects such difference engenders, is located not in an organic and
uniform national community but rather in the practices and performances
of difference exercised through policy within these organizations.

Compare, for example, the British Council and Japan Foundation,
equivalent organizations in charge of sharing the nation's culture with foreign citizens via language courses and cultural education programs. In Tokyo
in January 2009, the organizations hosted a joint symposium for their officials, "The Significance of International Cultural Relations in the World
Today" (*Kyō no sekai ni okeru kokusai bunka kōryū no igi*). Participating in
the event were the presidents of the British Council and Japan Foundation,
the director of the British Council's Japan headquarters, a number of Japan
Foundation officials, two professors of cultural policy, and the director of
a private foundation for arts funding.

Events like these show how a standardized platform of diplomacy facilitates the communication of certain kinds of cultural difference. Through
the course of the symposium, for instance, both Japan Foundation and
British Council officials expressed similar opinions on matters of cultural
relations and in similar rhetorical styles: representatives from both sides
advocated for cultural relations as a tool for peace and solving international
problems; they both offered the idea of arts and cultural traditions as global
public goods rather than national properties; and they both made nuanced
critiques of the use of the phrase *soft power* in cultural relations. Officials
from both sides wore suits; they spoke from prepared drafts and took questions; and after the formal presentations, they mingled with one other with
ease and familiarity. Organizational homology in public diplomacy thus
establishes structures and forms of communication that, precisely because
international communication is a major function of these organizations,
homogenize. Difference between organizations emerges only in forms these
homologous organizational structures allow.

For example, both the director of the British Council, Martin David-son, and the director of its headquarters in Japan, Jason James, took positions on cultural relations that played down the role of the state. "Cultural relations is not about business, government, industry," Davidson at one point said. "It's about people, cooperation, trust, understanding, communities, peace. It's about engaging overseas publics." Davidson imagined the British Council's role in the administration of cultural relations through the metaphor of a bridge between individuals and both government and non-government groups; it was about forming relationships and connections. This metaphor was echoed in an interview I conducted with Jason James: "We're trying to build two-way mutual relationships . . . to build a bridge between Japan and the UK that people can walk across in two directions." Similarly, in his speech to the symposium audience, Council director Da-vison made a special effort to distinguish the role of the British Council from that of the Foreign Ministry: "The British Council is aiming for an honest view of culture and leaves the positive view up to the foreign service." Although the practice of cultural relations builds influence, he later said, the goal is mutual understanding between people, not the achievement of foreign policy objectives. James, following up in an interview I conducted, added to this point, "We're not comfortable with power. We're not trying to exert power on Japan. We build relationships that can potentially be used by the Foreign Office but we would never use them ourselves. We just build relationships. We don't much like the word 'power.'"

While from the perspective of British Council officials, power and culture were not mutually constructive, for Japanese officials who feel themselves in a deficit of power, it is hard to avoid connecting culture to national interest (*kokueki*). As Japan Foundation president Ogoura Kazuo explained in his speech, "The question is of how to tie *kokueki* to cultural diplomacy." Included in this question were issues of globalization, Ogoura continued, of how to meet the other's mode of understanding in order to shape messages for transmission (*hasshin*) and reception (*jushin*). Although here Ogoura poses the relationship between national interests and cultural exchange quite diplomatically, he has elsewhere cast cultural diplomacy in more assertive terms. In personal published essays on cultural diplomacy, for example, he has characterized the role of cultural diplomacy in Japan's past as "motivated by the desire to respond to and dispel specific misunder-standings and prejudices on Japan" (Ogoura 2009, 29). And he has called for a more proactive approach, drawing, like the ambassadors cited in the opening to this chapter, on the notion of Japan as an agent that must "voice" and "express" itself:

> It is therefore high time for Japan to voice its vision on the future of the world community rather than simply defend its position. If Japan cannot summon the nerve and ambition to express its opinions on the shape of the world of tomorrow, it risks becoming more and more invisible in the global policy-oriented intellectual discussion. (2009, 29)

Ogoura reflects a concern I often heard among administrators for the fading visibility of Japan on the world stage, a fear that feeds efforts to leverage cultural diplomacy to assuage administrate anxieties.

Ogoura has also regularly cited the value of applying culture for the purpose of "restoring a country's pride" where it is found damaged or lacking. He offered this in line with a number of other affective services he thought the Japan Foundation could provide through cultural relations, such as soothing or healing hearts (*kokoro iyashi*) and welfare (*fukushi*). It is difficult to imagine representatives from the British Council making a similar point, and in fact, in Davidson's speech to the Japan Foundation, he expressed an alternative view: "Culture should carry any amount of criticism. One should have enough confidence in one's culture to be willing to undertake such critique." Where Davidson connects pride in one's national culture to the ability to accept criticism of it, Ogoura emphasizes the necessity to build pride where it is found lacking. While Davidson embodies a pride that is open to critique, Ogoura seeks a form of critique that can build national pride. These distinctive "styles" of national imagining, to borrow Benedict Anderson's phrase ([1986] 2006, 6), materialize out of a set of affective capacities to feel differing degrees of confidence in a set of cultural traits, objects, or practices one officially deems one's own.

Perceptions of power imbalances emerge as a sense of urgency and anxiety in not just Ogoura but also among other Japan Foundation officials, connecting an insecurity over one's political status to a hope that culture, and increasingly *popular* culture, can play an explicit role in alleviating it. Such power imbalances, perceived sometimes more and sometimes less keenly, are heightened by the contemporary intensification of economic competition between regional partners in East Asia in the field of the culture industries (Otmazgin 2013), which renders China and South Korea into cultural "threats" (*kyōi*). Contemporary public and cultural diplomacy efforts within the Japan Foundation are inescapably structured in response to this sense of urgency, illustrating how a geopolitical "arrangement" (Slaby, Mühlhoff, and Wüschner 2017) of affect can strongly link cultural policy to a sense of national security.

While many of the male officials I interviewed, such as Tanaka above, expressed a form of administrative affect that posited national security as rooted in Japan's ability to reclaim prestige, if not its global position as "number one," several female officials I spoke with took a different view. One official whom I worked with in the Japan Foundation's Pop-Culture Team, newly created to leverage perceptions of Japan's pop-culture appeal abroad to public diplomacy, framed the link between culture and national security as a question of education and connection:

> Indeed, culture could be a scary thing should it become a mere tool. Where to draw the line between using culture for the purpose of fostering peace and for gaining power for your own country over others is difficult. The recent popularity of Japanese pop culture emerged, for better or worse, not out of a desire to gain attraction overseas; rather, culture produced in local Japanese settings simply happened to become popular overseas. The idea that some people have since expressed that if Japanese pop culture is this popular we should use it for diplomacy as well is not a very deep one, in my personal opinion. Pop culture is ultimately only a virtual [bācharu] thing. I think it's important from there to deepen an interest about the real [riaru] Japanese culture and people. It's less about nationalism and more about security [sekyuriti].

When I asked her to elaborate, this official whom I call Maeda offered the following:

> I haven't studied the academic meaning of the word "security" [sekyuriti] but for me [jibun no naka de wa] one part of security [anzen hoshō] is based on the people of other nations looking positively (or at least not having feelings of animosity) at the Japanese people and the nation called "Japan" [Nihon to iu kuni], which I think involves politics, economics, and the study of culture. So, the ultimate purpose of the Japan Foundation is to increase the number of people abroad who like Japan and the Japanese people. If we can use culture for the "utilization of peace" [heiwa riyō] then

> I think it's a good thing. I want to contribute to programs that use pop culture as an entryway [*iriguchi*] for people to take an interest in the real [*riaru*] Japan and Japanese people.

Concern for the national image is here expressed as something that can be addressed by cultivating an affinity for Japanese culture among foreign publics. Maeda's narrative serves to shape anxiety's complex affective origins and effects into something manageable in ways less activated by and less dependent on Japan reclaiming national prestige, expressed by her male colleagues. In this way, an affect of insecurity becomes an object accessible and amenable to the administrative work of building human security through culture. Here we can see both the politics of anxiety and the circuitry of affect and emotion at play: anxiety inspiring different stories of cultural security, and policies of cultural security operating on affective anxiety.

Maeda's description of soft power and popular culture as possible tools of security reflect a perspective of soft power from the point of view of administrators who feel the asymmetry of cultural power relations in ways their British counterparts did not. As the former Japan Foundation president Ogoura Kazuo has written:

> The concept of soft power is usually put forward by the party exercising the power and discussed from the perspective of that party. . . . While words like *attraction* and *influence* may appear "soft" to the party exercising the influence, those on the receiving end of the soft power often perceive elements of compulsion, threat or coercion. (2009, 43)

For certain Japan Foundation officials thinking about soft power, its "power" element is simultaneously that which inspires hope that Japan can achieve prestige in the way that the US or the UK commands it, as well as that which sustains the anxiety that Japan's future is indefinitely tied to nation-states perceived as historically and presently superior to it. Given the contested nature of this politics of anxiety even within Japan, the meaning and application of soft power in the context of bureaucratic administration is at times debated within government settings.

Soft Power in Advisory Councils

In these final sections of the chapter, I want to bring an anxious sense of history to bear even more closely on present administration. While many academic studies of soft power in Japan focus on references to it in policy papers, direct observation of administrative deliberation best demonstrates how soft power is practically integrated into administration and constitutive of an asymmetric politics of geopolitical anxiety. One important setting where formal discussions took place over how to best leverage the nation's popular culture to build soft power was in ministry working groups and advisory councils known as *shingikai*. Although the highly organized structure and the vast amount of preparatory paperwork that go into these meetings ensure that they proceed according to the plans of the bureaucrats who design them, the councils nonetheless offer a venue where one can witness the accommodation of soft power ideology to policymaking. One venue for these councils is the Agency for Cultural Affairs (ACA), an organization within the Ministry of Education that is in charge of Japan's domestic cultural policy, the administration of national museums and cultural and religious artifacts, arts education, and indirectly, although most importantly for Japan's content industries, copyright law. These shingikai are made up of government officials and rotating experts from the private sector. They are organized by all government ministries and are one of the many structural forms of Japanese bureaucracy that facilitate *kanmin yuchaku*, "the growing together of the public and private sectors" (McVeigh 1998, 91).[19] Although shingikai are often promoted as government listening to public concerns from a wide variety of social sectors, they often nevertheless produce a consensus adhering closely to Ministry policies.

For committee members from outside government, it is generally seen as a privilege to be invited to participate on such panels, and rarely are overly critical opinions voiced. Moreover, as members are selected and invited through informal networks of social capital established by ministry officials, opinions tend to be uniform. Reports drafted in these councils, usually by ministry officials themselves, serve as evidence that careful deliberation has taken place and that the enactment of the proposed policy is justified. As these meetings operate entirely outside parliamentary approval and expenditures do not appear in government budgets (McVeigh 1998, 91), they serve as a primary mechanism sustaining the often criticized but seldom reformed system through which bureaucrats rather than politicians are said to control Japan's government policy and administration (Soga 2016).

Over the course of fieldwork, I attended several meetings of different advisory councils within the Agency for Cultural Affairs. Key phrases like "soft power" and "cool Japan" could be heard throughout these meetings but the most common thread uniting the variety of these panels was the notion of Japan as a "cultural nation" (*bunka kokka*). The ideological framework in which Japan as a cultural nation is imagined in relation to contemporary popular culture is best illustrated in a 2005 book called *Imitating Japan* (*Mohō sareru Nihon*), by Hamano Yasuki, a professor in the graduate school of media studies at Japan's most prestigious academic institution, the University of Tokyo. Hamano was also a member (in one as the deputy chairman [*kaichō dairi*]) of other advisory councils I visited. In the introduction to his book, Hamano constructs a comparison between France and Japan, noting how in the past France was known as a cultural nation and Japan as an economic one. "However," he says, "in contrast to then, now in France it is common to hear one say, 'cultural Japan, economic France'" (2005, 8). While in the past, Japanese people embraced French fashion and brand name products, now patterns have changed:

> The value of Japanese animation has been rising among French people, shops focusing on Japanese manga and Japanese pop culture goods are growing in the Bastille area of Paris, and there are frequent events focusing on anime and manga. Moreover, there are many photographic journals focusing on Japanese youth street fashion being published. (2005, 8)

In repeated examples like that above, Hamano inverts the historical trope of Japan as imitator to Japan as imitated (*mohō sareru*).

Hamano refers, as do other articulators of Japan's pop power cited in the introduction, to Douglas McGray and his evaluation of "Japan's Gross National Cool." He combines this reference with another recognizable citation: Ezra Vogel's (1979) *Japan as Number One*. Hamano writes,

> Just like the time of Ezra Vogel's *Japan as Number One* that praised Japan's economy, Japanese people who are constantly having critique thrown at them from the outside have jumped at this essay by McGray. The axis of Japanese critique has all of a sudden changed from economy to culture, specifically to pop culture. (2005, 11)

Hamano's account is simultaneously a reflection on and an endorsement of those recognizable historical scripts crafted by foreign—often US—authors through which national cultural identity is framed through the figure of Pop-Culture Japan.

The US and the powerful feelings its image elicits often surfaced in administrative deliberation. In the ninth meeting of the cultural advisory panel on culture policy (*Bunka shingikai bunka seisaku*) within the ACA, at which Hamano was in attendance, the section meeting deputy chairman (*bukaichō dairi*), Fukuzawa, opened the meeting by asking members to look at the first reference document (*shiryō*) of the stack of papers customarily provided at each meeting. It was a two-page printout from Barack Obama's official website, titled "Barack Obama and Joe Biden: Champions for Arts and Culture," along with a two-page translation into Japanese. Fukuzawa introduced the policy summary as an encouraging example of the substantial energy and resources the United States was putting into improving arts education. He followed the point by stating that both China and South Korea were also making enormous investments in cultural policy.[20] Implicit in his comments was the view that if the US was investing heavily in culture, then so should Japan. Even more embarrassing was that both China and South Korea seemed to be investing more in culture than Japan was. It was this sentiment of embarrassment that had clearly pushed Fukuzawa to introduce Obama's policy statement into the council meeting.

Later in the meeting, in response to Fukuzawa, a member named Takahagi, who at the time was the vice president of the Tokyo Metropolitan Art Space (Tōkyō Geijutsu Gekijo), voiced a counter-perspective that highlighted how soft power anxieties are sustained by administrative apparatuses that do not necessarily hold sway outside state government. Takahagi highlighted a specific passage in the Obama policy summary: "The purpose of arts education is not to produce more artists, though that is a byproduct. The real purpose of arts education is to create complete human beings capable of leading successful and productive lives in a free society." Takahagi's comment is representative of someone not directly affiliated with bureaucracy but rather with arts promotion in the private and civil sector. Reflecting this, the passage to which he drew the committee's attention was not a statement by the author of Obama's policy position but a quote by the chairman of the US National Endowment for the Arts. Takahagi's statement was politely received but not discussed, and attention quickly turned to other members.

Takahagi's statement reveals the difference in motivation for Japan's investment in cultural policy between arts administrators and national administrators of the arts. While Takahagi understands art as having inherent value, on the government side, Fukuzawa's emphasis is focused first and foremost on the nation. Inextricably linked with perceptions of so-called advanced countries (*senshinkoku*), national agencies demand of their administrators attention to the nation's relational status with other states. The difference in perspectives helps distinguish Pop-Culture Japan as a figure produced primarily by state administrators and fueled by geopolitical anxieties.

The National Media Arts Center

In another council meeting hosted at the Agency for Cultural Affairs, a similar tension between arts administrators and state administrators of the arts played out in relation to hopes for building a National Media Arts Center (Kokuritsu Media Geijutsu Sōgō Sentā), at the estimated cost of 11.7 billion yen (US$120 million).[21] Because manga and anime dominate the imaginary of Cool Japan, there was substantial hope among officials at that moment in 2009 that a national arts center could serve as a powerful institution for featuring these forms of popular culture. The original plans received significant support from officials in the Ministry for Foreign Affairs and the Agency for Cultural Affairs, including endorsement from then Prime Minister Asō Tarō, who served from September 2008 to September 2009 and is known for his love of manga. Subsequently, plans for the center were entrusted to the Committee for the Preparation of Establishing the National Media Arts Center (Kokuritsu Media Geijutsu Sōgō Sentā Yakuritsu Junbi Iinkai). This comparatively large committee, made up of fourteen permanent members and an additional five to six temporary members and advisors that rotated with each meeting, included ACA officials, academics, arts administrators, business leaders, and a number of prominent figures in film, manga, anime, and video games.

The committee was led by the same Hamano Yasuki whose book *Imitating Japan* I cited earlier. As the chairman of the committee and as one who served as the mediator for the meetings, Hamano commanded significant influence on the direction of the proceedings. At the third meeting of the committee, held at the Ministry of Education's headquarters in Kasumigaseki (the site of Japan's government ministries), Hamano took a strong stance on the center, which had been receiving criticism from Democratic

Party of Japan (DPJ) lawmakers intent on capturing power from the Liberal Democratic Party (LDP), which was then in the majority.[22] Expressing urgency in the meeting, Hamano proclaimed, "The international competition is severe [*hageshii*], so we have to do something now! Why is there a manga museum in Korea and not in Japan?" The heightened emotional tenor of Hamano's plea was atypical for these generally mild-mannered proceedings. There was little dissent from the committee.

In a later meeting on the National Media Arts Center, however, I heard a comparatively critical opinion from a professor specializing in cinema at one of Japan's national universities. I call him Kobayashi. Although Kobayashi struck a detached and analytical tone with his comments, he offered a more cosmopolitan perspective on the center that contrasted with Hamano's nationalist tone. Speaking from an academic point of view in the council meeting, he offered ideas on how the center could be used to facilitate research. He suggested that the center could be used less for the "pursuit of profit" (*rijun tsuikyū*) and more for education and research, creating an "international public cultural asset" (*kokusaiteki na kōkyōteki bunkazai*). Although supportive of the center, the tone Kobayashi struck was implicitly counter-nationalist. Later, in a private discussion, Kobayashi explained to me that his position was rare in Japan, saying that such "ideas are almost completely absent on Japanese websites and blogs, perhaps all 704,000 sites I hit on Google [for the center]." From his point of view, the officials were locked into a nation-centered discourse that wasn't able to take his position seriously:

> For the committee members from industry, possibly the economic benefit is the most powerful driving force. For the rest of the members, nationalism is the rationale to accomplish their plan. . . . To some extent, I understand it is natural that they are all trying to appeal to nationalism because they have to convince the taxpayers to invest money in their project. But if they only consider their own benefits and the ones of the nation, I think the prospective center would not be useful for researchers, educators, and general users around the world. I would like the committee members and bureaucrats to elaborate on how they can practically serve the users well, rather than on how they will raise Japan's presence and economic effects. But in the hearing I attended, I got an impression that they spent most of the given time for confirming to themselves how excellent Japanese products were.

Ultimately, with the DPJ's ascension to power in 2009, plans for the National Media Arts Center were scrapped. But there is little indication that the national hopes among bureaucrats for building Japan's pop-cultural resources dissipated along with it. Like Takahagi, the vice president of the Tokyo Metropolitan Art Space mentioned above, Kobayashi's comments reveal a stark division between himself and fellow researchers on the one hand and the bureaucrats and administrators on the other.

This distinction between a nationalist and cosmopolitan ethos is easy enough to identify in rhetoric. But is it possible to identify how a concern for the nation operates affectively—in its *propensity* to manifest in discourse rather than in its ultimate emotional articulation? That affects are not easily and simply expressed in language has been well documented. Richard Handler's ethnography on Quebecois national identity features a number of frustrating moments where affect manifests as a force that is difficult to articulate. At one point in a conversation, after repeated attempts to capture the signifiers of Quebecois identity, Handler asks his informant directly what makes him Quebecois. Reaching an energetic peak in the conversation, his interlocutor finally responds that Quebecois identity is not a rational thing: "I don't know! It's just something you feel!" (1988, 32). This moment of impasse is significant, as it points to the vibrant force of affect that doesn't easily settle into an emotional script, even if it might be conditioned by it. Despite the challenge, Handler nonetheless proceeds in an interpretivist frame, suggesting that what explains his interlocutor's feeling is a "relationship to local territory and a style of living or code of conduct."

While such explanations provide some insight, "explanation" always falls short of communicating affect. Also important is evocation, as ethnographic experiments from Kathleen Stewart (2007), Anne Allison (2013), and Susan Lepselter (2016) illustrate and as Stephen Tyler famously argued in an essay in 1986. That said, attuning more carefully to affect need not require only one or the other of these approaches. Given that affect expresses itself as an unqualifiable force and yet, at the same time, is conditioned by the qualitative experiences of social exposure and habituation, it seems better to pay attention to the mutual relation of affect and its discursive expressions in emotion across a gap of intelligibility. The affect-emotion gap offers one way of formalizing this problem conceptually. In the next chapter, I apply this view to examine how strategies of nation branding function to transduce anxious affects across this somatic-semiotic gap into strategies of hope.

2

Nation Branding

The Hypernormalization of Cool Japan

Building on and integrating soft power ideologies, nation branding constitutes a second major component of Pop-Culture Japan. Like the adoption of soft power in Japanese administrations of national culture, state investments in nation branding strategies similarly draw motivation from stories repeatedly circulated about the nation's status and presence abroad. These stories stoke sentiments that stick to dominant representations, digital commodities, and material objects signifying Japan's global reputation.

In one of these well-known stories of the nation, remembered in Japan more than in the US, where the events took place, US senators in 1988 smashed a Toshiba radio on the steps of the Capitol. They were protesting the decision of Toshiba, a Japanese electronics and technology manufacturer, to join "a Norwegian consortium to illegally sell submarine technology to Moscow" (Tolchin 1988). Out of this incident the phrase *Japan bashing* (*Japan basshingu*) was invented, or so goes one version of the event.[1] A similar story, with parallel resonance both to the Toshiba incident and to President Nixon's decision to visit China without informing Japanese officials in 1971, comes from 1998, when President Bill Clinton spent nine days in China and returned home without stopping in Japan. In the wake of this incident and playing off the already popular phrase *Japan bashing*, the phrase *Japan passing* (*Japan passhingu*) was invented (Chang 2009). It was perhaps inevitable, then, that in the 2000s one would begin to hear a phrase circulating in the media that seemed to aptly characterize the previous three decades of US-Japan relations: "Japan bashing, Japan passing, Japan nothing" (*Japan basshingu, Japan passhingu, Japan nasshingu*).[2] A characteristically broad stroke for Japanese mass media, the phrase captured national sentiments first of the 1980s, when Americans were seen as fearful of Japan's rapid economic growth, then of the 1990s, when such growth—and associated political influence—seemed to be in decline, and finally of the 2000s, when it was anxiously perceived that Japan's influence in world affairs was disappearing altogether. Under such desperate circumstances, it should come as little surprise that Joseph Nye would rekindle hope with his claim that "Japan has more potential soft power resources than any other Asian country" (2004, 85).

While Nye has distinguished soft power from economic power in theory, many Japanese officials view them as interconnected in practice.[3] Given that the strong memory of Japan's postwar status as "number one" (Vogel 1979) was so inextricably tied to the nation's rapid economic recovery and consumer culture rising through the 1970s, and with the increasing conflation of high art and pop culture commodities represented in Japan's most globally recognized artists (e.g., Murakami Takashi) and authors (e.g., Murakami Haruki), officials turned to the nation's popular culture industries as the primary source for building cultural power.[4] As the example of US senators smashing the Toshiba radio indicates, however, what seems like an inevitable turn to the state promotion of popular culture was unthinkable just a couple decades prior to the emergence of Japan's pop-culture diplomacy. As Koichi Iwabuchi has demonstrated, in the wake of Japan's economic decline, global perceptions of Japan underwent a dramatic transformation that shifted Japanese marketing strategies from seeking in the 1980s to erase the national essence or odor (*mukokuseki*) of commodities to aiming in the 2000s to actively manufacture it (2002, 24–28). The goods that indexed Japanese presence in foreign markets in the 1980s, such as VCRs, computer games, video cameras, and Walkmans, evoked little sense of Japanese culture or lifestyles at the time. And given the virulent nature of economic competition between the US and Japan, it was perceived that Japanese advertisements for these goods appealed to images of Japan only to a company's detriment. As Japan entered economic recession in the 1990s, this sense of international competitiveness shifted. Conjointly, as consumption of anime, manga, and video games produced in Japan increased around the world and as the otaku fan culture that was associated with it in Japan went from the margins to the mainstream in the global imaginary (Galbraith 2019), branding commodities with a new fragrance of Japan became seen as profitable, both economically and politically.

This transformation in marketing strategies thus incorporated a shift in political consciousness. The notion that branding a country's goods with images of the nation could be economically profitable inspired the correlated reasoning that branding the nation with images of the country's goods could be *politically* profitable. "Nation branding," the application of brand management strategies to the nation (Dinnie 2008, 14–15), has since the mid-2000s in Japan come to occupy the center of soft power strategies. This is not only because of the potential that nation branding as a strategy promises for building economic and political prestige but also because the marketing logic of branding has become naturalized as a common strategy of public diplomacy on a global scale. Nation branding's proponents argue that each nation must market its image to compete in the global economy. One of the first textbooks on nation branding explains that nation branding is a "benign force at the disposal of all nations" (Dinnie 2007, 251). Given that nation branding has become a ubiquitous field of international competition, the text goes on to argue that nation branding can help "smaller, poorer or otherwise struggling nations . . . compete effectively on the world stage rather than being trampled upon by more powerful rivals" (251). Such a perspective fits well with the idea offered by Japan Foundation officials in the previous chapter that popular culture can serve as a means for building human security.

However, counter-perspectives to the enthusiastic endorsement of brand strategizing, such as Naomi Klein's (2000) critical account of the emergence of the "new branded world," challenge the neutrality that Dinnie ascribes to nation branding. Deregulation and privatization policies of the 1980s, Klein explains, not only opened public service sectors to private investment but rendered them dependent on it. With the logic of branding and the growing power of the logo already expanding since the late 1970s, privatization facilitated a brand competitiveness that finally engendered a metaphorical shift in which products carrying a brand name were eventually swallowed by the brand itself. Goods became "empty carriers for the brands they represent" (Klein 2000, 28). This freed the brand name from the product and enabled the branding of culture and of lifestyle itself. Far from a neutral exercise of corporate-consumer communication, branding became a pervasive new logic tying together global capital competition, public space, and personal identity. Adopted by state administrators, nation branding in Japan thus became a tool of geopolitical competition with domestic effects, as countercultural identities associated with practices of popular culture were transformed into political resources.[5]

In this aspect, nation branding strategies function as what Andrew Graan (2016, S70) describes as "interventions within and across public spheres." That nation branding initiatives implicate multiple and overlapping publics is key to understanding its various social effects. While Japan's nation branding projects primarily target overseas publics, the effects of those strategies reverberate among publics at home who are newly interpellated as producers of and participants in Pop-Culture Japan.[6] While I analyze the feedback effects on domestic publics of branding Cool Japan in more detail in subsequent chapters, here I want to analyze how a logic of nation branding operates self-reflexively on its managers, engendering an anxious style of administering affect while intensifying their efforts to newly brand commodities of Japan's popular culture as communicators of Cool Japan.

Nation Branding and the Affect-Emotion Gap

Before discussing the specific programs and projects through which nation branding took hold in Japan, however, I want to return briefly to what I've called the "circuitry of sentiment" and, in particular, the "affect-emotion gap" as a critical part of it. Doing so shows how the theoretical figuring of a productive friction between affect and emotion can shed light on administrative anxiety among Cool Japan's managers. As I discussed in the book's introduction, the epistemological gap between what one feels and what one makes known about what one feels opens up multiple sites for political and capital investment. Much like William Mazzarella (2003) has demonstrated in his analysis of the emergence of global advertising strategies in India, nation branding appeals to a particular technology of marketing in staking its claim in a productive region of affectivity between the felt and the figured expression of feeling—between affect and emotion. That this space of slippery and never quite satisfactory correspondence between affect and emotion is continually tapped for opportunity indicates most importantly not that it is an inexhaustible frontier for exploitation, but rather that the plasticity, mutability, and relative opacity of the gap makes it resistant to singular and authoritative accounts of it. In other words, the proliferation of discourses one often finds surrounding sentiments, such as of foreign desire for Japanese commodities, suggests that one can neither hold in place nor guarantee a compatible fit between an affective sensation and its formulation in a consciously recognized emotion or emotion-laden word, symbol, or narrative. This makes the affective field a richly productive source for political and economic investment and a highly contested site for the politics of political anxiety. As a discursive intervention not only into the "public" (Graan 2016) but also into the *affective* domain, nation branding depends on integrating economic, political, and cultural logics into a single project of brand management—or in other words, into a project of administering affect.

The logic of nation branding stakes a claim in the space between consumption and identity, between a desire for commodities that arises as affect and a narrative that names that desire. It recognizes that consumers affectively invest not only in the things they buy but also in the *way* they buy. As scholars of popular culture and the culture industries have illustrated, consumers both affect and are affected by their commodities. From Marx's (1867) discussion of the "commodity fetish" to classic anthropological studies of gifting (Malinowski 1922; Mauss 1925) and theoretical work on commodity exchange and consumption (Horkheimer and Adorno 1944; Baudrillard 1970; Fiske 1989; Featherstone 1991; Storey 2018), the commodity serves as a mechanism for cultivating and modulating affect through both the materiality and symbolism of goods. Nation branding strategies suggest to hopeful administrators that if consumers attach positive feelings to desired commodities, then they might equally attach positive feelings to the nation-state in which those commodities are produced. If Chinese youth show affection for manga and anime, for example, perhaps they might show affection for Japan at large and thus be more receptive to its policy decisions.

The responsibility of brainstorming and designing strategies based on this reasoning falls to politicians and bureaucrats in various government agencies charged with the task of thinking through nation branding's potential relative to their administrative domains: economy (the Ministry of Economy, Trade and Industry; the Japan External Trade Organization); foreign relations (the Ministry of Foreign Affairs); public diplomacy and cultural outreach (the Japan Foundation); domestic cultural assets (the Agency for Cultural Affairs); and communication (NHK). In their varied investments in nation branding, administrators confirm empirically what is theorized in the abstract by philosophers of affect: that there is a modal, logical difference between affect and emotion and that the dynamic transformation from the former to the latter is at once an epistemological and political project—a project of knowledge creation and legitimization that, because of affect's complexity, is open to contest.

The Emergence of Cool Japan

In the early 2000s, Japanese politicians set into motion plans and programs that would contribute to building the Japan brand and ultimately stoke the imagination for Pop-Culture Japan. Prime Minister Koizumi Junichirō's speech to the Diet in 2002 marks a watershed moment in this process, formally initiating what many politicians and bureaucrats hoped would jump-start Japan's transition to an "intellectual property-based nation" (*chizai rikkoku*) (Dinnie 2007, 211; also see Iwabuchi 2015). Although Japan has been trumpeted as a cultural nation (*bunka kokka*) repeatedly since the end of World War II, primarily emphasizing Japan's traditional culture, this time Koizumi's speech inaugurated administrative actions that committed government resources to contemporary popular culture.[7] The most significant of these was the enactment in 2002 of the Basic Law on Intellectual Property (Chiteki zaisan kihon hō) and the formation of the Strategic Council on Intellectual Property (Chiteki Zaisan Senryaku Honbu) within the cabinet of the prime minister (Kantei). Created to "pave the way for Japan to become an intellectual property-based nation" (Arai 2005, 5), the Strategic Council on Intellectual Property was composed of the prime minister, high-level politicians and ministers, and experts from industry. In 2003 the Strategic Council drafted the *Intellectual Property Strategic Program*, which outlined 270 measures for the "creation, protection and effective utilization of intellectual property" (Dinnie 2007, 211). This strategy report is renewed each year and has since its inception increased its scope to include not only technology but also design, brands, media content, music, movies, gaming software, and animation.

Since the creation of the Strategic Council on Intellectual Property in 2002, numerous state agencies and committees have been launched to help promote what became known as the Cool Japan campaign. These include the Committee for Tourism Nation, the Committee for Info-communication Software, and the J-Brand Initiative, all in 2003 (Iwabuchi 2015, 423). In 2004, the Public Diplomacy Department was created within the Ministry of Foreign Affairs, and it formally began its pop-culture diplomacy strategy in 2006. Other committees set up in this period include the Research Committee for Content Business, established in 2005, and the Council for the Promotion of International Exchange in 2006 (Iwabuchi 2015, 423). In 2010 the Ministry of Economy, Trade and Industry created the Cool Japan Room (Kūru Japan Shitsu) to promote "creative industries," which included not only digital content and IP but also food, fashion, regional goods, and tourism. In 2013, Cool Japan was inscribed into law with the Cool Japan Fund, which provided a 60 billion yen (US$580 million) investment fund split between government and private investors, for the first time enabling direct investment to companies promoting Cool Japan as determined by the fund's joint public-private managers.

While many programs and committees supporting Cool Japan have come and gone over the last two decades, the affective excitement feeding a commitment to Pop-Culture Japan remains. As recently as 2019 the managers of the Cool Japan Fund planned to increase their 2020 investment to 120 percent of their 2019 spending level. And this was despite the fund's loss of 17.9 billion yen (US$166 million) since its inception (Kodachi 2019). Such examples of Cool Japan's resilience in the face of empirical evidence for its demise demands researchers attend to the affective dimensions of Pop-Culture Japan. I suggest that the circulation of intense feelings feeding Cool Japan and the nation branding logic that channels those feelings into policy can be best demonstrated by two early projects I describe below: the neo-Japanesque project and the public broadcaster's (NHK) television program *Cool Japan*.

The Neo-Japanesque Brand Promotion Council

In 2003, the Strategic Council on Intellectual Property launched a new program, The "New Japan Style" project (*Shin Nihon yōshiki*). The project would be overseen by Japan's Intellectual Property Policy Headquarters (Chiteki Zaisan Senryaku Honbu) and administered by Japan's Ministry of Economy, Trade and Industry (METI). It was created to foster the production and global reach of a new Japan brand. Managing the details of the project would be the Neo-Japanesque Brand Promotion Council. The council's website offers a mission statement outlining the raison d'être for the project:

> With advancing globalization and its pressures to enhance international competitiveness, many in Japanese government and industry feel an urgent need to establish a distinctive brand for products and services originating in Japan to serve as a mark of excellence.
>
> In this context, and in light of recommendations of the *Neo-Japanesque* (Japanesque Modern) Brand Promotion Coun-

cil, a Ministry of Economy, Trade and Industry advisory panel, a Committee (Japanesque Modern) has been set up on the belief that enhancing the value of such a "Japan" brand—i.e., creating an integrated image encompassing Japan's culture, technology, and sensibilities and their strengths and benefits will serve to enhance the international competitiveness of products and content originating in Japan.

> The Committee's (Japanesque Modern) founding members envision a membership consisting of a broad range of industrial associations, enterprises from all industry sectors, and private individuals. The council's role will be to propel an extensive program of activities, including management of the (Japanesque Modern) brand, provide assistance in the development of products and content, and actively distribute information to the rest of the world. (Japanesque Modern 2006a)

Combining a haute French aesthetic with Japanese "sensibilities," the mission statement proposes the development of a nationwide brand as a key strategy that can generate not only economic but also cultural returns.

Given the distinction between soft cultural power and hard economic power in soft power theory (Nye 2004, 9), it is left to officials to reinterpret the connection of soft power to the national branding of goods. This is done less in theory than in practice, according to the demands of individual ministries and offices. Consider the following description of soft power offered by a chief official in METI's Content Industries section, Kitagawa. In response to a question I posed to him on the specific relation of economic and soft power, he offered the following:

> It's not easy to define the word *soft power*. It depends on the people who explain it. I'm in charge of content industry policy. The content industry is one of the main sources of soft power of a country. I mean, through the content industry we express our lifestyle, Japanese animation, TV broadcasting, etc. If we provide our content to markets abroad, it is one of the best ways to promote understanding of our lifestyle. . . . If people look at Japanese content, such as movies or animation, people may want to buy Japanese goods, such as Japanese cars, Japanese televisions—I mean, cool gadgets.

Kitagawa sees his views on soft power and "cool gadgets" as reflecting an American sensibility, which he expressed through a personal reflection:

> In the 1960s, when I was a child, many of my friends watched TV programs from the US. So we understood what life is like in the US, and what is a better life: people drive big cars, live in a big house, and that kind of thing. At that time, young people wanted to buy big cars and to go to some theater or somewhere with a girlfriend, in an American style. And people wanted to eat hamburgers. Okay, that kind of thing. That is soft power. We can promote our lifestyle to the world market. There is no logical linkage between soft power and hard industry. It's kind of an emotional linkage.

If emotion links commodity desire to a desire for a national lifestyle, how do administrators formulate desire as an object of administration amenable to management? Part of this answer is rendered through the administrator's personal experience with American popular culture. Kitagawa's story reveals the importance of US popular culture to youth growing up in the 1960s, the generation largely occupying senior-level management in Japan's bureaucracies in the mid-2000s. These references to American popular culture inundate his generation's reflections on this period, and I heard them often in fieldwork. The most memorable of these moments was during the standing ovation to an especially energetic jazz set by three African American musicians in a small club in the Aoyama district of Tokyo. A high-ranking official of Japan's Agency for Cultural Affairs, by whom I was invited, turned to me and yelled enthusiastically, "Now that's soft power!"

Responding to the urgency of Japan's slipping economic and political prestige, hopefulness in the soft power discourse propels the term into an everyday idiom of national administration and branding. Kitagawa saw the formation of the Content Industry section of METI as a consequence of soft power discussions in Japan. Given that the meaning of *soft power* originally conceived of by Nye does not bear a direct relationship to, in Kitagawa's words, "hard industry," which is the target of METI's projects, framing economic revitalization in terms of soft power takes some discursive remodeling. McGray's article connecting Japan's media commodities to soft power and the subsequent "hypernormalization" of Cool Japan, which I elaborate in the following sections, aids in this effort. Recent programs administered by METI and other related organizations have similarly institutionalized an understanding of soft power that frames affection for Japanese lifestyles and the new pop-cultural products of anime, manga, and film that represent them, as resources for economic development. For METI officials, then, soft content translates into hard economic power, and nation branding facilitates this process.

For officials in METI thinking about nation branding, a primary strategy is to attach images of Japan to as many profitable products as possible. Kitagawa explained this logic to me straightforwardly: "If people look at Japanese content, like movies or animation, people may want to buy Japanese goods." Simple enough. The question that follows is, then, How can goods made in Japan be turned into Japanese goods?

The New Japan Style 100 Selections campaign (*Shin Nihon yōshiki 100 sen*), launched in 2003, was the inaugural project of METI's Japanesque Modern Committee. The phrase "100 Selections" refers to one hundred specific items chosen by the group that "represent the link between cutting edge modern technologies and our country's most highly valued traditional culture, expressed in modern lifestyle trends" (Japanesque Modern 2006b). The elegantly designed website of the project, no longer in use, displayed each nominated item along with a description. From "silent violins" to cell phones, pencils, toilets, manga, video games, and a number of other items described by Kitagawa as "cool gadgets," the items were all products readily available for purchase (see figures 2.1–2.3).

In its project description, the committee also listed criteria for how it selected each product. With products that include both contemporary media, such as anime, and items representing traditional crafts, the criteria help construct a uniform "Japanese" aesthetic that unites traditional and contemporary popular culture:

1. Products should fuse Japanese traditional culture, materials, techniques and spirit with cutting edge global technologies (hard and soft), including those from Japan. Further, such products should fittingly express Japan's traditional culture, materials, techniques, spirit and forms of modern lifestyle.

2. Products should realize the integration of "traditional culture and cutting-edge technologies" or "traditional culture and modern lifestyles."

Additional criteria more specifically addressed product type:

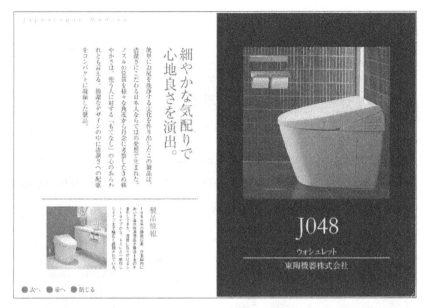

Figure 2.1 Item J048, Washlet toilet. Source: Japanesque Modern website in February 2010. Project archived at https://web.archive.org/web/20131206011755/http://www.tepia-infocompass.jp/japanesque-modern/about.html.

Figure 2.2 Item J100, Animation, *The Girl Who Leapt through Time*. Source: Japanesque Modern website in February 2010. Project archived at https://web.archive.org/web/20131206011755/http://www.tepia-infocompass.jp/japanesque-modern/about.html.

Figure 2.3 List of selected items from 2006–2007. Source: Japanesque Modern website in February 2010. Project archived at https://web.archive.org/web/20131206011755/http://www.tepia-infocompass.jp/japanesque-modern/about.html.

1. Made by Japanese industry (including individual and entrepreneurial Japanese bodies)
2. Products "Made in Japan" ["Made in Japan" is posted in
   English]
3. Objects are not limited to the genres of products, content,
   service, systems, and space. (Japanesque Modern 2006b)

The emphasis on the fusion of traditional culture and modern lifestyle
trends shows how an ideology of soft power posits an aesthetic guiding
Pop-Culture Japan as rooted deeply in the nation's cultural heritage. This
rhetorical exercise connecting Japan's contemporary popular culture with
traditional arts is performed repeatedly by senior administrators, as is seen
in a speech by Prime Minister Abe Shinzō in 2007, titled, "Establishing
Japan as a Peaceful Nation of Cultural Exchange":

> Japanese pop culture such as manga (comic), animation, games,
> music, movies, and TV dramas, as well as modern art, literature,
> theater arts, and others are referred to as "Japan cool." It is gain-
> ing popularity among the younger generation around the world.
> Japanese lifestyle represented in its cuisine and fashion has also
> widely spread in other countries. However, [it is not only] the at-
> tractiveness of [contemporary] Japanese culture transmitted and
> spread through cultural exchanges [that can] be classified as being
> "cool." As shown by the fact that Japan is the very country of the
> cradle of "Japanimation," Japanese contemporary culture's coolness
> is founded in and derived from its traditional culture. (Abe 2007)

Such discursive integrations of traditional and contemporary arts strength-
en the nation's cultural integrity from the point of view of politicians and
state administrators. Because Japanese traditional culture has served as a
source of pride throughout the course of Japan's modernization (Ivy 1995),
the strategy of connecting traditional with popular culture draws on readily
available habits of association in the minds of administrators. Speech acts
such as Abe's that connect traditional arts with contemporary culture are
easily modeled by other government officials and communicated to mass
media—a process readily facilitated by Japan's press club (kisha kurabu)
system in which journalists report on formally prepared announcements
from government ministries with little variation between news agencies
(Hall 1998).

In conjunction with the practice of selecting products that typify the new Japan brand, the Japanesque Modern Committee also sought to create a logo to secure its brand image. Aiming to capture both an aesthetic of Japanese artistry as well as the affection overseas consumers feel for such an aesthetic, the committee created the Japanesque Modern Design Mark (Figure 2.4).

The committee's website provides an explanation of the logo's design:

> Within Japanese calligraphy, this shape embodies the originality and meaning of *tome* [to fix], *harai* [to brush], *ore* [to weave], and *magari* [to curve]. In the first stroke of a character and in the stroke order of the character, it delivers beauty's energy to the tip of the brush.
>
> Not limited to a literal meaning, the character's shape and significance represents the Japanese identity [*aidenteti*] flowing from the bottom of the heart, which is also seen in Japanese craftsmanship.
>
> Imbued with the Japanese heart, and combining the wonderful culture of deep sensibilities and aesthetic beauty with cutting edge technologies, "Japanesque Modern" embodies the originality and strong international competitive power of content unique to Japan. These are the things represented in this mark. (Japanesque Modern 2006b)

The explanation of the logo integrates three themes: a traditional Japanese sensibility; a haute but generic, French-inspired aesthetic; and an economic competitiveness premised on popular content and advanced technologies. Such themes reflect the fields from which the committee members were selected: Japanese academia, design, art, and theater.[8]

While the committee's description of its logo focuses on aesthetics, METI officials also understand the challenges that Japanese companies face in publicizing and popularizing trends from the top down. Kitagawa explained one particular obstacle in the field of film:

> The problem of our industry is that they [popular films] cannot go abroad. Why? Because we don't have a distribution network. Hollywood has it. Disney has it. Some European countries have global distribution channels, but they are much smaller. We don't have such things. We have big movie companies, but they are only

Figure 2.4 The Japanesque Modern design mark. Source: Retrieved from Japanesque Modern website in February 2010. Project archived at https://web.archive.org/web/20131206011755/http://www.tepia-infocompass.jp/japanesque-modern/about.html.

domestic. They don't have a distribution network outside of Japan. This is the biggest problem. So if we make good animation movies, we need to sell it to other distributors and they take the money. We cannot make money from that. We need to have a kind of branded distribution network. Disney itself is a brand. If you attach the Disney mark, there will be many buyers from abroad. But we don't have that kind of thing. One solution is that we make our own distribution channel. And that channel should have kind of a brand power. An image.

For Kitagawa, creating a brand image like that of Disney would serve as a powerful means for distributing soft content to global markets. Such statements suggest a desire among administrators to invest more directly in Japan's image, but when I asked Kitagawa about whose job it was to create this brand, he suggested it was the private sector's. He added, "The Chinese government might want to make their own government-branded network, but we cannot do that. We operate differently from that kind of approach." Like officials in agencies such as the Japan Foundation that are more focused on diplomacy than on branding, Kitagawa distanced himself from a perspective on nation branding that was suggestive of propaganda efforts. However, he nonetheless saw his role as supporting industry. In this sense, *industry* serves as a signifier for an ethical exercise of nation branding removed from direct government supervision and thus also free from the stigma of propaganda. METI's subsequent establishment of the Cool Japan fund in 2013, based on equal contributions from the government and the private sector, represents an effort to balance an avoidance of propaganda with a growing concern that without making direct investments in industry Japan would fall behind major regional rivals like China and South Korea.

NHK's *Cool Japan*

Despite its role as a public rather than a national government-run broadcaster, the Japan Broadcasting Corporation (Nippon Hōsō Kyōkai, NHK) has also incorporated nation branding logics into its programming. With a budget and staff more than three times the size of any private television station in Japan, NHK commands significant influence. Although the broadcaster takes administrative measures to ensure and communicate its organizational independence from government, most notably by collecting revenue through door-to-door solicitations by NHK officials, as Kawasaki (1997) and Kawasaki and Shibata (2004) have argued, in practice NHK has often acquiesced to the influence of the ruling government party.

The marketing campaign for Cool Japan, as former MOFA Public Diplomacy Department chair Yamamoto Tadamichi explained to me, was directly inspired by UK's Cool Britannia campaign of the 1990s. With McGray's article making famous the concept "gross national cool," the label "Cool Japan" was quickly adopted in the early 2000s as an idiom of new branding and diplomacy efforts across government agencies. The phrase "Cool Japan" has subsequently been stamped on a variety of media forms across government, from posters and videos published by Japan's National Tourism Organization to MOFA and METI white papers.[9] As in the Japanesque Modern program described above, the term is applied to a variety of commodities potentially marketable as "cool."

In 2008, NHK produced a television program titled *Cool Japan* that aired on both the broadcaster's domestic channel as well as on its international service, NHK World. The program continues to this day in 2021. A description of the show from the program's official website reads:

> COOL JAPAN—Discovering what makes Japan cool! *Cool Japan* is a term that describes the growing international interest in Japan. From the worlds of fashion, anime, architecture to cuisine, the cultural aspects of Japanese society that have long been left undiscovered are starting to make a strong impact on global trends. *Cool*

Japan is a television show that illustrates the quickly changing Japanese culture and how it is perceived by the international community that have recently made Japan their home. (NHK World 2010a)

Embedded in the production logic of *Cool Japan* is an irony that underlies much of the soft power discourse in Japan at large and the nation branding and pop-culture diplomacy efforts applied to soft power's realization. Jean-Marie Bouissou (2008), a political scientist and manga specialist, argues that "grassroots" and subculture consumers both in and outside Japan largely deserve credit for the growth of interest in Japanese popular culture that attracted the attention of Japan's politicians in the early 2000s. These consumers were primarily interested in Japanese counterculture, forms of artistic production that were often either understood as distinct from traditional images of the nation or that, as illustrated in Ian Condry's (2006) study of "hip-hop Japan," took mainstream images of the nation as objects of critique, distinction, or even ridicule. Media commodities attracting the most attention were manga, anime, and video games, whose consumers were in their respective societies seen not as mainstream but rather as marginalized: nerdy, techie, and geeky (Condry 2013, 188). Zealous fans of these commodities in Japan are called "*otaku*" (literally meaning "one's home"), a word that until recently connoted fanatic, uncool collectors of anime and manga culture (Galbraith 2010; 2019). When McGray used the word *cool* to describe an array of popular subcultures in Japan, however, he provided a means for shifting the imagined status of these commodities and created the possibility for subcultural trends to become authentic symbols of a new Japanese mainstream in the eyes of foreign publics. To the degree that these subcultures were claimed by media and bureaucrats as products of a typically "Japanese culture," they set a precedent for how commodities could be transformed from things made in Japan into *Japanese things*—and subsequently into Japanese soft power. "Cool Japan" was the label used to facilitate this process of rebranding subculture—and eventually almost anything made in Japan at all—as new, modern, and cool signifiers of Pop-Culture Japan.

NHK's *Cool Japan* program continues this trend by normalizing the label "Cool Japan" through media and publicizing an imagined vision of Pop-Culture Japan on not only a national but also a global scale. The format of the program begins by introducing a theme of Japanese culture for each week's show, providing a description and history of the topic, and then soliciting opinions on the theme's coolness from foreign residents in Japan. While some shows feature predictable and widely popular themes of contemporary Japanese culture, like manga, idols, and robots, the continuation of the show in subsequent years has resulted in increasingly innovative extensions of the "cool" label. Consider the following list of Cool Japan themes from previous shows:

> Stationery, shopping, winter, examinations, childbirth, child-rearing, memorial services, Japanese men, Japanese herbivorous men [*sōshokukei danshi*, the name given to men characterized by a lack of traditional masculinity and interest in women], Japanese women, mothers, fathers, anniversary parties, sweets, discipline, hot pots, sightseeing, toys, health, luck, *konkatsu* [activities helping singles seeking marriage], lights, rain/the rainy season, privacy, the Japanese language, Japanese companies (parts 1 and 2), prayers, gifts, tears, containers, soy sauce, shame, sleeping, books [including the book *Cool Japan* published by NHK about the program *Cool Japan*], and disaster prevention. (NHK World 2010b)

The humorous nature of the list would not likely be lost on most Japanese viewers of the program. And the fact that the list includes themes traditionally understood as markers of Japan's negative cultural traits (company culture, privacy regulations, discipline) seems to push the rhetoric of Cool Japan into the realm of satire through what Boyer and Yurchak (2010, 181) call a "hypernormalization" of discourse.

American *Stiob* and Cool Japan

In a collaborative analysis of "American *stiob*," anthropologists Dominic Boyer and Alexei Yurchak (2010, 180) examine forms of political satire analogous to societies of both late socialism ("Soviet and Eastern European socialist public culture in the 1970s and 1980s") and late liberalism (US and Western capitalist public culture in the late 2000s: *The Colbert Report, The Onion, The Yes Men*). Referring to the Russian term *stiob* to describe a form of critique in which the critic performs an overidentification with the forms characteristic of hegemonic discourses, they analyze standardized modes of address in late socialist and liberal ideologies that appear to resemble one another. Their critique draws attention to the institutional conditions that allow for the "hypernormalization of discourse": "Specifically, we argue that the highly monopolized and normalized conditions of discourse production that characterized the political culture of Eastern European late socialism anticipated current trends in Western media, political discourse, and public culture" (181). Characteristic of these trends was a style of discourse in which "it was often more meaningful to participate in the performative reproduction of the precise forms of authoritative discourse (as either producer or audience) than to concern oneself with what they might 'mean' in a literal sense" (182).

While I do not argue that nation branding rhetorics in Japan resemble stiob in late twentieth century Eastern Europe and early twenty-first century North America, processes of hypernormalization characteristic of stiob nonetheless make it a productive "portable analytic" to explain how highly institutionalized media systems can normalize and sustain discourse even in the face of widespread criticism.[10] What creates an "uncanny family resemblance" between hypernormalized discourses in contexts as diverse as socialist East Europe, the late-liberal West, and contemporary Japan is a highly institutionalized and monopolized media system and processes of digitalization that routinize rhetorical styles through presence and repetition. The standardization of television program scripts, the high percentage of domestic programming, and the pervasiveness of access through mobile devices that characterize stiob elsewhere apply similarly to Japan.[11] What is distinctive about Japan's case, however, is the lack of a popularized form of formal satire that emerges alongside the hypernormalization of Cool Japan. Most illustrative of this comparison, which might otherwise represent a benign case of different cultural histories of humor, is how the potential for critique in these diverse contexts is similarly subverted through its enfolding into dominant rhetorical styles. In this sense, the parody-like quality of Cool Japan discourses engender a "jouissance" (Mazzarella 2019) that is immune to critique because it takes pleasure in its own playfulness rather than questioning it.[12]

A central narrative device used in NHK's *Cool Japan* is a story about an aspect of Japanese culture deemed "cool" by young foreigners, often from English-speaking or Western European countries. Although the guests on the show, who are selected from online submissions that describe an aspect of Japanese culture they find genuinely intriguing, are clearly coached and coaxed to offer favorable impressions, the show can also enfold self-deprecating moments. In an episode on Japanese homes aired in July 2017, the show opens with short segments from foreigners who affectionately criticize rather than celebrate Japanese homes. One guest expresses shock at the tiny size of a typical Japanese apartment; another questions the use of nameplates (*hyōsatsu*) that publicly display the name of the people living in the house, claiming it feels like a "breach of one's privacy"; and another chides residents for accumulating so many goods: "If you don't have the closet space, why do you keep buying things?" (NHK World 2017). This practice of humorously defamiliarizing stereotypical Japanese customs through the eyes of foreigners is typical of Japanese variety shows, a format that dominates Japanese television. Additionally, with guests offering opinions in English and hosts rephrasing and responding in Japanese, the program effectively deflects the serious critique embedded in such comical ribbing and creates an environment of commensurable enjoyment between the sometimes critical foreign guests and always good-natured Japanese hosts.

While the show's format can accommodate discussions of cool culture that sound critical, more often the earnestness of guests combined with the overt labeling of everyday practices and goods as "cool" creates a sense of playfulness bordering on parody. The standard "pattern," or *kata*, for each program involves introducing an item of everyday Japanese life, following foreigners through Japan as they interact with it, and then consecrating it as an aspect of cool Japanese culture.[13] In one program featuring *kanji*, Chinese characters used in Japanese script, the Japanese host asks each of the seven foreign guests what he or she thinks is the coolest part of kanji. The scene takes place after a segment featuring some of the foreigners participating in a kanji study class taken by Japanese adults. The host asks one of them, "Andrew-san, what did you think was the coolest [*kūru*] thing about kanji?" (*Andoryū-san, nani ga ichiban kūru deshita ka?*).[14] Andrew responds, "I liked that a lot of Japanese people of all ages still study kanji. It's really nice" (NHK World 2009). This practice of asking foreigners what they think is cool about particular elements of Japanese culture and then having the hosts respond in confirmation—"*naruhodo, kanji wa kūru desu ne*" (Ahh, I see—kanji are cool, aren't they)—renders aspects of everyday Japanese life into markers of a uniformly "Japanese" cool aesthetic. Incidentally, the style closely resembles that of another NHK show, *Kawaii International*, which features elements of Japan's "cute culture." This time, however, instead of confirming the coolness of Japanese culture by appealing to the foreign word *cool*, the reverse strategy is taken, attempting to export the Japanese word *kawaii* as a particular—and particularly marketable—trait of what Christine Yano calls "pink globalization" (2013b).[15]

Reflecting rhetorical strategies employed by nation branders connecting Japan's contemporary popular culture to its traditional culture, an additional pattern central to *Cool Japan* takes the inverse approach, transforming traditional culture into reflections of contemporary Japanese cool. Another segment on the show follows a student from Israel through a day with an American writer of haiku. The two visit a park in Tokyo and discuss the charm of haiku while composing poems along the way. Transitioning from the video footage of the two writing haiku in the park to the studio where hosts and foreigners engage in discussion, a female narrator's voice says in a high-pitched style representative of kawaii aesthetics, "Haiku, condensing the eternity of time into short passages: cool, isn't it!" (*mijikai bunshō ni eien no toki o gyoshuku suru haiku: kūru deshō!*, NHK World 2009). Even though many poets and scholars of "pure" Japanese literature (*junbungaku*) might consider this an offense to a carefully curated Japanese literary canon (see Miyoshi 1991), the show reads a sense of cool into Japanese literary history, appropriating what was traditionally the symbol of Japan's high traditional arts as a resource of soft power rooted in the spread and circulation of the Cool Japan brand.

In a similar segment on handmade pillows in an episode focusing on sleep (*suimin*), a young American, David, concludes his visit to a small artisan's pillow- and futon-making shop with an obviously well-coached narration: "I really respect the amount of effort and craftsmanship that went into their family business. And it made me realize that a pillow is not just a pillow; there's a lot that goes into it. And giving someone a goodnight's sleep is very important and very cool" (NHK World 2010c). David ends the scene, backed by a sentimental music track, with a thumbs up. A woman's voice narrating the segment concludes, "Stuffed with Japanese tradition and the spirit of craftsmanship, traditional pillows *are* cool." Curiously, the English translation voiced over the Japanese for the version produced for foreign viewers emphasizes "are" rather than "cool," as if defending the claim that pillows are cool to someone who believes otherwise. After a discussion with other foreign guests and the hosts in the studio, and following comments by a professor of Japanese culture from the University of Tokyo, a male narrator's voice says, "Blended with traditional materials and traditional skills, custom-made pillows *are* cool." Again, "are" is drawn out. Like a caricature of a director closing a scene with "Aaaannd cut!" the segment punctuates its point with a proclamation that traditional Japanese pillows are, like sleep culture in Japan in general, cool.

In no way is the jouissance of such embellished performances lost on the show's producers. Instead, these formats, or *kata*, represent a style of collaborative creativity that NHK has institutionalized through a highly standardized style of producer training and program design (see Krauss 2000; Condry 2013). As discussed elsewhere (White 2014), NHK producers understand this conventionalized style as a product of a long-established consensus between producer and audience. As Gabriella Lukács (2010) has argued in her study of "trendy dramas" in the 1990s, this aspect of conventionalized storytelling is typical of highly standardized production processes that are rooted in the organizational structure of TV production in Japan, whether in public or private broadcasting. This collaborative production process further facilitates the hypernormalization of discourse characteristic of institutionalized media apparatuses like NHK.

With the *Cool Japan* program launching in 2008 and still running in 2021, NHK has contributed substantially to the popularization of the Cool Japan discourse. And while shows like *Cool Japan* are not necessarily the product of explicit soft power policy strategies, they play a major role in circulating and standardizing Cool Japan as a common idiom of Pop-Culture Japan and illustrate the degree to which that idiom is internalized and normalized. This is important for at least two reasons. First, and as I illustrate further in the next chapter, the circulation of an image of Pop-Culture Japan is itself often viewed as one major goal of soft power strategies of cultural diplomacy. While government bureaucrats may not want (or be institutionally allowed) to directly influence the messages of private or public media circulated abroad, they can affect the *degree* to which media on popular culture are circulated by investing in and publicizing Cool Japan programs. Second, the circulation of "Cool Japan" normalizes the slogan as a legitimate characterization of Japanese culture at large. The term thus facilitates the normalization of Pop-Culture Japan through a hypernormalization of Cool Japan branding discourses. To the degree that this discourse attracts publicity and establishes presence in media spheres, it becomes a part of everyday language, increasingly calling on everyday citizens to account for their relationship to the nation in terms of its "cool" culture. These interpellations of cultural citizenship might be easily dismissed as momentary and isolated if it were not for the fact that the Cool Japan campaign has been operative for nearly two decades. The robustness of the discourse and the frequency and breadth of its application suggest that significant shifts are taking place in the way citizens in Japan are interpellated to feel when imagining their relationship with and sense of belonging to Japan.

Hypernormalization and the Affective Dimensions of Cool Japan

The hypernormalization of discourses, Boyer and Yurchak (2010) claim, is characterized by conditions of media integration, institutionalization, and digitalization. But these are not in their opinion sufficient conditions for it, at least in the case of their analysis of "late-liberal political discourse" (209). For them, a "final and crucial generative element" lies in geopolitical power shifts—namely, "the collapse of Eastern European and Soviet state socialisms in the years between 1989 and 1999" (209). While regional shifts of power in East Asia may not, in the eyes of Western historians, generate a sense of "history ending" (Fukuyama 1992) on par with transformations in Eastern Europe, events such as China surpassing Japan to claim status as the world's second largest economy in 2010 can nonetheless feel just as transformative to Japan's state administrators. The number of times this concern over China's ascension was cited to me by interlocutors suggests as much. It also suggests that attending to the affective consequences of such dramatically narrated shifts in geopolitics can allow for alternative analyses of Pop-Culture Japan that address not only policymaking but also "world making."[16]

The future that certain administrators imagine for Pop-Culture Japan has in some ways begun to materialize through Cool Japan branding strategies, if still largely contained within administrative worlds. A 2020 report from the Cool Japan Policy Division of METI's Commercial Affairs and Services Group (Shōmu Sābisu Gurūpu Kūru Japan Seisakuka) illustrates how Cool Japan as branding campaign has become transformed into a generalized description of foreign sentiment toward Japan. The document lists three motivating "aims for establishing a Cool Japan framework" (*kūru Japan kikō no nerai*): the need to connect foreign demand to economic growth in light of Japan's decreasing domestic consumption due to population decline; the task of meeting foreign demand with unique Japanese charm that other countries cannot imitate, given intensifying global competition; and the challenge of intensifying Japanese content industries, fashion, food, regional goods, and local and foreign tourism (METI 2020b, 1). To meet these aims, the group proposes strategies such as dispatching information, developing cool goods and services for foreign markets, and investing in inbound tourism. Critically, what links these strategies to the Cool Japan policy division's overall aims and what renders them viable from the perspective of administrators is the identification of an "evaluation" (*hyōka*) made by overseas consumers of Japanese goods. The document's authors write, "We aim to employ those goods and services that make use of the special Japanese lifestyle and culture and that no other countries can imitate: goods that convey Japan's unique charm and that are evaluated by foreigners as 'cool'" (*gaikokujin ga 'kūru' to hyōka*) (METI 2020b, 1). The hypernormalization of Cool Japan cultivated through nearly twenty years of discursive repetition has produced in the minds of administrators the very world they imagined through nation branding: a world where a variety of Japanese goods produced in Japan is perceived by foreigners as "Cool Japan."

In this sense, administrators of the state's culture confirm through bureaucratic practice a figure of Pop-Culture Japan coming into being, facilitated by their sensitivity to "intensified geopolitical competition" (*gurōbaru kyōsō ga gekika suru naka de*). While motivations for Japan's contemporary investment in soft power include many sources, the hypernormalization of the Cool Japan discourse reveals itself to be a powerful mechanism for transducing geopolitical anxieties into specific concerns amenable to administration. This channeling of anxiety through narrowly constructed narratives of coolness, cuteness, and international appeal concentrates affect into conscious emotions like hope, pride, and even love for a new national culture dominated by popular media commodities. Contributing to this process, the globalization of nation branding strategies has normalized the term *soft power* as an idiom of international relations and, as a consequence, legitimized new and more ambitious forms of government investment in the field of culture. The normalization of soft power, thus, fuses a national concern for popular cultural consumption with international political competition. For those bureaucrats in Japan invested in political strategies that attempt to nationalize cultural commodities that previously circulated independently of national imaginaries, such as Toshiba radios or Power Rangers, Cool Japan discourses of nation branding connect pride in one's culture to its economic success overseas. The value of "cultural citizenship" (Miller 2002, 2007; Clarke 2013) at home thus becomes increasingly indexed by the presence of the nation's highly symbolic cultural goods in the worlds of consumers abroad.

The description of soft power as a source of "security," offered by Japan Foundation officials I described in the previous chapter, attests to this reconfiguration of culture as resource and resonates with discourses of Cool Japan. In order to secure the economic, political, and cultural stability of the nation and a healthy personal identity that depends on it, officials must secure the nation's cultural commodities and presence in foreign markets. It is in this sense that nation branding functions not only as a political strategy among administrators but also as an intervention into both foreign and domestic public spheres (Graan 2016). Linking a sense of global competition felt in the body of the administrator to a sense of administrative duty to craft responses, nation branding emerges as a strategy for realizing security in ways that closely integrate economy, political prestige, and personal identity. While this geopolitical structuring of anxiety seems pervasive in Japan's offices of state, the ethnographic point I emphasize here and in subsequent chapters is that for the majority of Japan's national cultural administrators, what motivates nation branding campaigns and soft power strategizing is not most often an ultracompetitive and calculated assessment of national interest but rather a low-level sense of anxious urgency. It manifests not as an explicit call to arms but rather as a subtle excitement over Japan's possible and hopeful futures imagined through popular culture. Further, and to emphasize once again, such an affective energy does not constitute a uniform structure of feeling but rather an affectively contested *politics of anxiety*. Certain concerns about the state are publicized sometimes more and sometimes less than others in attempts to tie anxieties generated through national imagining to an ethically adequate narrative of that anxiety—or, in other words, to tie together the two sides of the affect-emotion gap. In the next two chapters I analyze this political negotiation of anxiety through prominent examples of Japan's pop-culture diplomacy: anime diplomats and the Ambassadors of Cute.

Anime Diplomacy

Characterizing Obligatory Nationalism

On March 19, 2008, Japan's Ministry of Foreign Affairs promoted one of the country's most famous animated characters, a robot cat from the future named Doraemon, to the post of Anime Ambassador. The press announcement for the event reads as follows:

> On March 19 (Wed.), the inauguration ceremony of the Anime Ambassador took place at the Ministry of Foreign Affairs, and Mr. Masahiko Koumura, Minister for Foreign Affairs, handed Doraemon a letter of assignment to inaugurate the character as Anime Ambassador.
>
> Then Mr. Koumura told Doraemon that he wished people around the world to know more about the positive side of Japan through Japanese anime that are universally popular, and he hoped Doraemon, as the Anime Ambassador, would travel around the world to introduce Japan.
>
> In response, Doraemon said, "I hope through my cartoons I will be able to convey to people overseas what ordinary Japanese people are thinking, what sort of life we are leading and what sort of future we are trying to create!" (MOFA 2008)

The inauguration of Doraemon as Anime Ambassador in 2008 centered the importance of *animated* characters in publicizing a new *national* character. In Fujiko Fujio's long-running manga series (1969–1996),[1] Doraemon is a character who travels from the future to help a young boy in the present named Nobi Nobita; in MOFA's press release, Doraemon is imagined as a character in the present who can help create Japan's new future. In this regard, Doraemon embodies the affection that cultural administrators hope foreign publics will hold not only for animated characters but also potentially for Japan itself.

MOFA's promotion of anime and its characters is part of the state's investment in pop-culture diplomacy, the third discursive pillar of Pop-Culture Japan after soft power and nation branding, outlined in the previous two chapters. Inaugurated by the Public Diplomacy Department of Japan's Ministry of Foreign Affairs in 2006, pop-culture diplomacy aims to "further the understanding and trust of Japan" and builds on MOFA's perception that "pop culture such as manga and anime" is capturing "young people's" attention in recent years (MOFA 2017; Iwabuchi 2015, 420). Transcribing this perception into policy, MOFA has established three components for its pop-culture diplomacy. The first is the Japan International MANGA award, which a MOFA announcement explains in English was "established in May 2007 upon the initiative of then-Minister for Foreign Affairs Mr. Taro Aso with the aim of awarding MANGA creators who contribute to the spread of MANGA culture overseas and international cultural exchange through MANGA" (MOFA 2017; capitalization in the original). The second component is cosplay. The same announcement explains, "Cosplay also enjoys strong international popularity in recent years," and the "Ministry of Foreign Affairs has conferred a Foreign Minister's Prize on the best costume-player at 'the World Cosplay Summit,' the biggest annual Cosplay event in Japan, since 2007" (MOFA 2017; capitalization in the original). Finally, inaugurating Doraemon in 2008, MOFA began its third component with the Anime Ambassador project, "with the aim of increasing the interest of people overseas in Japan through Anime" (MOFA 2017; capitalization in the original). Unimaginable just a decade prior to Doraemon's promotion, the enlistment of anime to advance Japan's global interests marks a productive commensurability between the affective power of Japanese animation and a hope among administrators that it might be effectively leveraged to public diplomacy.

As I have argued thus far, one motivating driver of Pop-Culture Japan is an administratively generated anxiety over Japan's geopolitical status in the world relative to Western nations such as the US and regional neighbors like China and South Korea. I have further argued that soft power and nation branding rhetorics render this anxiety manageable by channeling it into hopeful sentiments for a more promising future. In this chapter, I examine how the process of transforming anxious affect into hope through pop-culture diplomacy projects draws on and reproduces a style of administering affect. I call this embodied affective capacity *obligatory nationalism*. In short, obligatory nationalism refers to those practices by which expectations, commitments, and concerns demanded of an individual for one's organization are affectively transduced into concerns for the nation at large—and in the wake of soft power ideologies, for the emerging figure of Pop-Culture Japan.

Importantly, because I want to draw attention to the politics of anxiety in bureaucratic spaces—to the ways that anxious feelings are differently conditioned through obligatory ethics that shift from one government agency to the next—I compare obligatory nationalism in two different agencies: the Ministry of Foreign Affairs (MOFA) and the Japan Foundation. Because affective demands placed on administrators differ based on the varying remits and organizational ethics of each agency, I attempt to "characterize" the type of obligatory nationalism I find in each agency. To do so, I draw theoretical inspiration from scenes of administrators interacting with anime characters like Doraemon. While several sophisticated studies address the role of animation and its characters in Japanese popular culture (Allison 2006; Azuma 2009; Condry 2009; Manning 2009; Steinberg 2009; Occhi 2010, 2012; Nozawa 2013; Yano 2013b; and Galbraith 2019),[2] I want to focus more closely on how politicians, bureaucrats, and the government managers and mandarins of Pop-Culture Japan undergo processes of what Shunsuke Nozawa (2013, 1) calls "characterization." As I describe below, given pop-culture diplomacy's emphasis on anime and its characters, this practice of characterization—of "becoming-character" (Nozawa 2013, 8)—is not only a figurative process but also at times a literal one, such as when Prime Minister Abe Shinzō appeared at the closing ceremony of the 2016 summer Olympics in Rio de Janeiro dressed as Super Mario. The playfulness of scenes like this one demands serious attention, as increased state investments in anime diplomacy feed back into the practices, styles, and sentiments of administrative affect among national cultural administrators.

Before proceeding into this characterization of varying styles of administering affect among MOFA and Japan Foundation officials, or of what I call *administrative affect*, I want to clarify what I mean by this phrase and how it illustrates how sentiments of nationalism can be felt as obligatory. In general terms, *administrative affect* refers to a mode of feeling that is cultivated through activities of daily administrative labor and that becomes an embodied ethos of bureaucratic practice. Because as a conceptual term it comes with some ambiguity, however, I use the next section to explain it with an analogy to another kind of public feeling in Japan, called *meiwaku*. I reason that by starting with meiwaku, I can better explain how affect can operate as an automatic and often nonconscious capacity of the body that responds to triggers in the world that are, importantly, also culturally coded by social interaction. Understanding this process should, in turn, better illustrate what I mean by obligatory nationalism and how it develops among administrators.

Meiwaku in Public Culture

As anyone spending more than a few months in Japan's public spaces knows well, the notion of meiwaku plays a critical role in organizing interactions in public culture. Translated into English, *meiwaku* means something like "disturbance," "bother," or "trouble"—as in "to trouble someone." But providing English equivalents to *meiwaku* offers only limited assistance, as using the term correctly demands not so much an understanding of its meaning as a sensing of its presence. In Japanese public spaces, one is in constant danger of causing meiwaku. To avoid this, one should refrain from talking on a cell phone in the vicinity of others, especially on the train; one should minimize the volume of music playing through earphones, lest it be heard by adjacent passengers; students talking with friends should not walk through narrow residential passageways (and police officers sometimes stand at entryways to these shortcuts with signs saying so); and one should always, *always* separate and dispose of trash in the allotted areas and officially designated bags (of which there are several).

Understanding meiwaku takes time, as it operates less through the acquisition of knowledge and more through the accommodation of the body. One could certainly try committing to conscious memory all the behavioral codes that protect one against causing meiwaku, but there are far too many to learn very quickly, and one often forgets. It is better to trust one's feeling. This field of bodily intensities is what cultural theorists largely mean by the term *affect*. As discussed in the introduction, while important critiques (Ahmed 2004; Leys 2011; Martin 2013) have warned of the dangers of universalizing a model of affect that is rooted in the biology of human bodies rather than in the interaction between bodies and socially variegated environments, encounters with meiwaku illustrate how the social and biological are of an inextricable piece. Meiwaku operates through experiences that are at once social *and* somatic. A body moving through public space in Japan will record innumerable pairings of actions (talking on a cell phone on a train) and reactions (sideways glances from nearby passengers) that over a long period of time build associations of bodily action and social-environmental consequences.[3] Given the many conventional, if subtle, signals of public approval and disapproval in Japanese spaces, bodies accommodated to them eventually signal inappropriate behavior via somatic warnings, such as a subtle increase in heart rate or a slight uneasiness in the stomach. Bodies that develop these capacities learn to navigate social space with ease and reduce meiwaku; bodies that do not encounter increasing signs of resistance, friction, and eventual frustration. People say of the former group that they can "read the air" (*kūki o yomeru*) and of the latter group that they cannot (*kūki o yomenai*). This is how social space can, often nonconsciously and seemingly automatically, *feel*.[4]

Upon visiting Japan for the first time many years ago, I learned appropriate behaviors in public spaces quickly enough. I avoided the usual faux pas of loud speech around others, cell phones on trains, and so on. But it was only after living there for some time that I became somatically accommodated to it. The difference between those early days and now is, literally, palpable. I now *sense* meiwaku. It feels more or less equivalent to feelings of embarrassment, cousin to what Ruth Benedict (1946) identified classically, if far too characteristically, as shame. Of course, there is nothing particularly "Japanese" about meiwaku, but people accustomed to living in Japanese public spaces together with any amount of success know, feel, and experience it in similar ways.

Understanding meiwaku helps illustrate the mode of feeling I call "obligatory nationalism" that I identified among administrators at both the Japan Foundation, where I conducted an internship, and at the Ministry of Foreign Affairs, where I held several interviews and attended committee meetings. Consider a typical moment in the evening at the Japan Foundation, the state's administrative arm of cultural and public diplomacy. The Japan Foundation's offices are spread across nine floors of a modern but plain-looking office building in Yotsuya, Tokyo. For those who are not rushing off to a Japan Foundation–sponsored post-work event, of which there are several each month, work at the agency inevitably slows toward evening. There are no more meetings to prepare for, no more deadlines to meet, and very few tasks that cannot be put off until tomorrow. Employees are thus usually engaged in more mundane activities: researching on the internet, reading relevant journal or newspaper articles, or browsing materials from the stack of bottomless *ringisho* (documents required to be circulated to all employees). An employee can sense a tangible shift at this time from work that demands immediate attention to work that doesn't—a change that usually comes just before six in the evening, the official time until which employees are required to be at work and marked by an electronic chime. Employees take more relaxed positions in their chairs at this hour and more frequently steal glances at the clock on the wall.

Despite being officially allowed to leave the office at six o'clock, few people do, with officials more often leaving around nine, and usually only after their section or division chief has left. (Departures usually begin from the top of each section and work down the chain of command.) To breach this code of conduct takes significant courage as employees' bodies are conditioned to feel a substantial degree of self-conscious unease at being the first to depart. Before an employee can entertain the idea of leaving for the day, she or he would have to be sure that their daily contribution to work had sufficiently met the expectations of colleagues.[5] Upon finally feeling it acceptable to leave, employees start to gather their things to head home, already attracting the untelevised attention of colleagues. Finally, the official stands, and loud enough for all in the office to hear announces the departure with "*Osaki ni shitsurei shimasu*" (Excuse me for leaving before you). Colleagues look up and confirm the announcement with "*Otsukaresama deshita*" (Thank you for your efforts).

Practices of office culture like these are nearly ubiquitous throughout Japanese companies and are not uncommon to modern bureaucratic organizations more generally. Through these habits of labor and public displays of commitment, feelings of obligation to both one's colleagues and one's administrative duties are built into subjects. One cannot fulfill the latter without respecting the former. In agencies like the Japan Foundation and the Ministry of Foreign Affairs, duties demand that officials work toward the positive communication, representation, and cultivation of the nation's culture. Failing in these tasks is equivalent to failing one's colleagues and results in negative feelings unpleasant enough to motivate officials to avoid failing in the future. Thus, by fulfilling their obligations to colleagues, officials must at the same time fulfill their obligations to the nation-state through administration. This is how national administrators are made to cultivate sensitivity in their roles *as* bureaucrats and to feel obligated to and personally invested in the status of the nation's culture. That these feelings might be recognizable across state administrations around the world suggests that bureaucratic organization comes with structural components that make obligatory nationalism part of any state administration. However, by reference to the concept of meiwaku and with subsequent discussion below, I also hope to illustrate how affect takes on local variations and specific political dimensions and degrees of intensity.

Although such obligations pervade Japan's state administrations, a form of what Foucault in his analytical framework of ethics called "subjectivation," the content or specific demands of the obligation can differ.[6] In the rest of this chapter I examine how affects of obligatory nationalism within bureaucratic agencies similarly oblige officials to care for the nation as they would care for their immediate colleagues and occupational duties. However, I also analyze how the *content* and *force* of that obligation differs from one agency to the next. Because anime diplomacy projects are often jointly but uneasily administered by MOFA and the Japan Foundation, they highlight these differences well. Thus, by looking at ethical obligations of varyingly nationalist and more cosmopolitan content that became associated with each agency's approach to anime as a political tool, we can see how discourse, through habits of administration, can cultivate differing styles or "characterizations" of administrative affect.

Organizing Anime Diplomacy between MOFA and the Japan Foundation

Anime diplomacy has become one of several contested symbols of pop-culture diplomacy feeding a politics of anxiety in state administration. For many in the Ministry of Foreign Affairs, anime diplomacy represents a cutting-edge technology of foreign relations. For others in government administration, it is an example of Japan's misguided Cool Japan campaigns. While some of the many people outside administration I spoke with about anime diplomacy programs liked the idea, others objected to government budgets being spent on potentially embarrassing (*hazukashii*) activities. These tensions are characteristic of the feelings evoked by Pop-Culture Japan. They also reflect the different approaches to cultural diplomacy as expressed by MOFA and Japan Foundation officials.

Despite the Japan Foundation establishing semi-independent status from MOFA in 2003 as an "independent administrative body" (*dokuritsu gyōsei hōjin*), many administrative and personal connections still govern the relationship between the two organizations. As such, some projects and decisions in the Japan Foundation are still beholden to MOFA intervention and oversight. At the time of a research internship I conducted there in 2009, two-thirds of the Japan Foundation's budget came directly from the Ministry of Foreign Affairs, with the rest coming from a variety of donations and other private investments. Roughly two-thirds of the Japan Foundation's programs are conceived of internally or in conjunction with other arts organizations in Japan or with counterparts abroad. Of the remaining one-third of programs, many are created directly by MOFA or by officials in MOFA's consulates overseas. Anime diplomacy projects are examples of these, often having been brainstormed by a handful of people in and associated with MOFA's Public Diplomacy Department. Consequently, it is largely the Ministry of Foreign Affairs that carries out the planning for these projects and the Japan Foundation that offers administrative support.

During my time interning at the Japan Foundation, I worked closely with the newly created Pop Culture Team (Poppu Karuchā Chīmu). The team's main task at the time was to facilitate an event at the Japanese embassy in São Paulo, Brazil, that would feature presentations on both Japan's anime and the Ambassadors of Cute. (Although these presentations are often delivered and administered conjointly, contributing to a collective picture of Pop-Culture Japan, I address these two different aspects of pop-culture diplomacy separately in this and the following chapter in order to highlight different aspects of how the programs channel political anxieties into nationalist forms of hope.) The Pop Culture Team's main tasks for the São Paulo event were to assist with arrangements for travel, accommodation, and transportation; monitor the expenses of the trip to assure it stayed within the budget; and finalize the presenters' schedules based on input from the embassy. Officials within the Japan Foundation team thus offered only minor contributions in terms of the program's content, and the program's design and format were left in this case primarily to MOFA administrators and advisors.[7]

Anime diplomacy exemplifies how Cool Japan as an ideological construct is applied at the program and policy level. While concepts like soft power and nation branding are employed regularly by high-level officials who find them readily applicable to overarching strategizing, the terms do not accommodate so easily to middle-level bureaucrats who are charged with designing programs with specific measurable outputs that meet various ministry objectives. Strategizing within each ministry is guided by distinct aims that sometimes outright conflict with those of other ministries. In fact, Japan's state agencies can often take on the character of independent bodies that compete rather than collaborate with one another, as they are dedicated to separate ministerial remits.[8] The Ministry of Economy, Trade and Industry's primary objectives, for example, are to support, stabilize, and invigorate Japanese industry; the Ministry of Foreign Affairs' aims are to guarantee the security of the nation-state and realize national interests in the foreign sphere; accordingly, the remit of the Japan Foundation is to build understanding of and stimulate interest in Japanese culture abroad.

The variation of these responsibilities means that individual state agencies can share a vocabulary while disagreeing on what that vocabulary means and how it should be applied. For example, when terms like *soft power* and *pop culture* were first incorporated into major government-wide policy documents, such as in 2009 when they featured in the government's most important annual policy report from the prime minister's office (Kantei), the *Annual Policy Plan for the Japanese Economy* (*Keizai zaisaku kaikaku no kihon hōshin*), government agencies were obliged to notice. Although each government ministry took notice of the emphasis placed on soft power in such reports, the different interests of each office led to a fracturing of soft power ideology into programs that helped each agency meet its respective demands. This process transformed soft power from an ideological problematization into a problem of practical policy application. The result was the creation of programs that revealed differing perspectives on soft power and exposed some of the ambiguity and contradictions embedded in the figure of Pop-Culture Japan.

For example, splitting the administration of anime diplomacy between MOFA and the Japan Foundation, each with its own internal and highly rationalized criteria for what counts as legitimate policy, revealed how the political value of popular culture was sometimes interpreted differently even within a single program. Important to recognize in this process is how different affective dispositions cultivated within separate agencies can fracture ideas about how soft power should be appropriately understood and applied. In her analysis of political emotion, Sara Ahmed shows "how emotions operate to 'make' and 'shape' bodies as forms of action, which also involve orientations towards others" (2004b, 4). The distinct position one takes toward anime diplomacy—either enthusiastically favorable or reservedly critical—is characterized by a distinct tone of feeling: either excitedly hopeful or moderately embarrassed. In the following sections I offer a brief comparison of both the bureaucratic and broader sociological conditions that distinguish variously receptive and critical feelings surrounding anime diplomacy in MOFA and the Japan Foundation.

Characterizing Affective Types: The Ministry of Foreign Affairs

Like the character Doraemon, selected to represent not only Japanese animation to the world but also the national character of Japan, state ministries in Japan acquire reputations as having certain characters: a style, a set of embodied values, and a characteristic set of political positions and attitudes. Bureaucrats in one state agency can easily, if abstractly, describe what administrators in other agencies are generally like. This characterization of other agencies and their administrators illustrates how practices of social-theoretical typologizing are as common among administrators as they are among the social scientists who study them. The administrator and the anthropologist, thus, might apply typologies to different ends, but they are similarly strategic in doing so: while an administrator may characterize an administrator from a different agency as a way of calibrating expectations, the anthropologist characterizes administrators in order to illustrate a relational pattern of organizational infrastructure, ideological value, and administrative practices of policymaking. Both administrator and anthropologist have their generalized starting points from which each seeks to move to thicker and better descriptions.

Max Weber calls this figure of social theory the "ideal type," an abstracted "mental construct for the scrutiny and systematic characterization of individual concrete patterns" (1949, 100), and whose goal of "concept-construction is always to make clearly explicit not the class or average character but rather the unique individual character of cultural phenomena" (101). Importantly, Weber recognized that the ideal type was not only a tool of the social scientific interpreter of "value"—that "unfortunate child of misery of our science" (107)—but also a tool of those the scientists studied:

An ideal type of certain situations, which can be abstracted from certain characteristic social phenomena of an epoch, might—and this is indeed quite often the case—have also been present in the minds of the persons living in that epoch as an ideal to be striven for in practical life or as a maxim for the regulation of certain social relationships. (1949, 95)

That idealizing, typifying, or characterizing is a practice shared by researcher and interlocutor alike is neither an original sociological nor, even less so, a novel ethnographic observation. But by drawing attention to this fact, we can better observe how practices of what Shunsuke Nozawa (2013, 1) calls "characterization"—the "transformation of some thing into a character"—function not only as social-theoretical mechanisms for generating knowledge about what administrators, in general, are like but also as practical methods administrators employ to achieve what they feel organizationally obliged to become. Nozawa writes:

> Rather than, or in addition to, asking the question of what characters mean to people or even what people performatively accomplish through anthropomorphic characters, we might as well consider characterized people and inquire into the condition of this modification, that is, characterization as a semiotic modality. (2013, 1)

As administrators nominate characters like Doraemon to fulfill a political function, Doraemon as Anime Ambassador of Pop-Culture Japan in turn suggests to administrators the value of adopting some of the character's qualities, such as affection, playfulness, and helpfulness. In this act of "becoming-character" (Nozawa 2013, 8), fictional characters help mediate and materialize the imagined figure of Pop-Culture Japan.

In idealized terms, the MOFA official engaged in public diplomacy is held administratively responsible for, and thus primarily concerned with, the ability for a program to generate positive appeal for the nation-state. Grounded in a government ministry that is faced with the hard facts of global security, anime diplomacy is thus seen as a resource of soft power that can be leveraged through publicity measured both in the quantity of images circulated and in the perception of the affective qualities those images elicit and represent. These representations hold significance not only for consumers but also, and even more importantly, for administrators themselves. Monji Kenjirō was the head of MOFA's Public Diplomacy Department in 2009. During a conversation we had at his department office in Kasumigaseki, Tokyo, he laughed at the situation in which he now found himself. He explained to me that the previous year he had been mostly interacting with members of Japan's Self-Defense Forces in Iraq, where he served as ambassador. Having returned to Japan to head MOFA's public diplomacy, he was now mostly interacting with fans of anime and cosplay. Monji handed me a 9″ × 11″ sheet of paper with two pictures. The top picture showed him in Iraq during his appointment as ambassador, posing in front of a Humvee with members of Japan's defense forces and Iraqi translators.[9] The bottom picture showed him with the winners of the World Cosplay Summit championship, held annually in Nagoya, Japan, where young fans dress up as their favorite anime and manga characters.

Monji took pleasure in the juxtaposition of the two images. Aiming to maintain the friendly atmosphere, I laughed too. As I did so, however, my mind was drawn to other pictures I had encountered that evoked similarly disorienting effects. One was of former Foreign Minister of Foreign Affairs Kōmura Masahiko presenting the life-size figure of Doraemon with his assignment as Anime Ambassador of Japan, introduced at the beginning of this chapter and portrayed in figure 3.1. Another was of members of the Japanese Self-Defense Forces distributing water in Iraq; on the side of the Japanese water tanker truck was an image of Captain Tsubasa, a character from a famous 1980s soccer anime in Japan that was popular throughout the Middle East, where he was known as Captain Majid (figure 3.2). Yet another image that came to mind was of the Ambassadors of Cute (figure 3.3), three young women selected to communicate Japan's kawaii fashion around the world, which I discuss in more detail in the next chapter.

Whereas each of these images taken alone might elicit a casual smile at the ironic juxtaposition of playful cuteness and hard-line security operations, taken as a series, they illustrate how the integration of animation, characterization, and security combine to fortify not only the figure of Pop-Culture Japan but also the character of those administrators responsible for promoting it. Monji's approach to the relationship of soft power and popular culture is grounded in a perspective on security and foreign affairs that makes up the remit of his ministry. Monji worked specifically on security issues for twenty-seven years before moving to his post in the Public Diplomacy section. And as mentioned above, immediately before his move he served as the ambassador to Iraq, where he was admittedly far more focused on hard rather than soft power strategies of diplomacy. He explains:

For the first twenty-seven years of my career I was in charge of security, either in Japan or in Brussels, where the head of NATO security is, or in London. Iraq was the first time I was sent to the

Figure 3.1 Inauguration ceremony for Doraemon as MOFA's Anime Ambassador, March 19, 2009. Source: Website of the Ministry of Foreign Affairs of Japan (https://www.mofa.go.jp/mofaj/press/release/h20/3/rls_0319e.html).

Figure 3.2 Water tanks in Iraq provided by Japan's Grant Aid with the popular anime figure Captain Tsubasa (Captain Majid in Iraq), from Takahashi Yoichi's manga series. Source: Website of the Ministry of Foreign Affairs of Japan (https://www.mofa.go.jp/policy/other/bluebook/2007/html/h3/h3_11.html).

Figure 3.3 Ambassadors of Cute Fujioka Shizuka, Kimura Yū, and Aoki Misako at the Ministry of Foreign Affairs, March 12, 2009. Source: Michael Caronna, photographer. Reuters.

front lines. And I enjoyed it very much. Iraq is where hard security counts most. But at the same time I also discovered that soft power is a tremendous strength—that is, the image of a country. Japan is very popular in Iraq. Also, it is well respected and trusted by people. Of course, we have no difficult historical past in the Middle East. And we have an especially good reputation in Iraq, because in the 1970s Japan and Iraq established a special economic relationship. There were more than 10,000 Japanese living in Iraq at that time. Many Iraqi people worked in Japanese companies and have good memories of that experience working with Japanese people. And, of course, Japanese products have a good reputation there. But Iraqi people also look to Japan as a model for the reconstruction of a nation, for nation building. I was often told how Japan is admired for its miraculous construction after the war in such a short time and in its own way. Not like the European way. So, they wanted to build their nation learning from Japan's experiences because this is the first time Iraqi people have become able to build their nation. [Because] they looked to Japan, that helped my job enormously—my job of diplomacy as an ambassador. I really enjoyed it. Of course, economic assistance or reconstruction assistance by the Self-Defense Forces or by grant aid or by loans were much appreciated by Iraqis, but this good image, which is soft power, helped me quite a lot. So, with this understanding, I'm now in charge of soft power in a different ministry. So in this sense I'm very pleased.

Stories of Japan as a model nation, as an economic miracle, and as a global leader resonate with Monji. This kind of nationalism makes bodies particularly receptive to positive stories of Japan's leadership status, such that he heard in Iraq. Evidence for this can be seen in the reproducibility of the "Japan as number one" trope, flexibly applied to different periods of Japan's history: reconstruction in the postwar period, miraculous economic growth in the seventies and eighties, and now cultural resurgence through Pop-Culture Japan. Such stories create affective dispositions of politicized and bureaucratic bodies that are oriented to seeking confirmation of Japan as number one in new narratives of Japan's prominence.

This process of developing an administrative sensitivity to the nation's status is recursive: narratives sensitize bodies, and sensations feed emotional narratives of the nation. Soft power and Cool Japan narratives fueling Pop-Culture Japan thus propel the administrator through the circuitry of affect and emotion, as the habituated sensations of the affective side are rendered intelligible in the emotional side. As seen in chapter 1, a common way bodies are made capable of feeling moved by stories of the nation is through the discursive exercising of its histories in the present. Monji illustrates this in the context of responding to my question about current anxieties over Japan's economic status:

> We faced a major challenge in recent history. We say "Restoration" [referring to the modernization processes of the Meiji Restoration formally dated to 1868] but it looks more like a "revolution." We were afraid of colonization, so we worked really hard to prevent it. It was said that millions would have died of starvation [in the postwar period]. No one thought Japan would become such an economic power in such a short time, but because we strived for that, we worked so hard. When I was in elementary school, I was taught that Japan is small and has no resources, so we must work very hard. This was wrong. Actually, Japan is big. Its size and population is greater than most countries in Europe. We were told we would

have to work so hard and that's how we could survive. That's what made Japan today's Japan, so if we are concerned about the future, then we can overcome difficulty once again. . . . But now we look at our current status and if we realize our real strength—that's what I mentioned before about soft power in close collaboration with hard power—in that case Japan's future is bright. All this depends on people's attitudes, just like Japan did in the past.

In a common refrain that echoes historical perspectives from other male administrators with whom I spoke, Monji articulates the very narratives that in part shape his affective disposition toward the nation and that guide his obligation to his ministry today through public diplomacy.

National pride of this kind takes root in simple and sanguine narratives of history. As Michael Bell (2000) has shown, sentimentalism operates best through straightforward, well-structured story lines. Todd Hall (2015) and David Leheny (2018) have also illustrated how sentimental stories of the nation routinize sentimentalism itself as a common trope of political discourse. More than providing powerful story lines, however, I suggest that these stories actually condition sentimentalism as a capacity of bureaucratic bodies in Japanese administration. Monji's account portrays the nation as a singular, uniformly integrated body. The rhetorical abstraction of the nation from its people (*minshū*) reduces its multiple, complex parts into a single figure whose image can be neatly cultivated, protected, and strengthened. In turn, this simplified figure of the nation facilitates the channeling of affect in bureaucratic bodies, as administrators respond positively to praise and attention paid to the "national body" (*kokutai*), an illustrative metaphor.[10] Leveraging personally internalized histories to policy, the administrative culture of MOFA emphasizes security of the national body to help the nation flourish and conditions sensitivity in the administrator's body as an affective capacity that aids this process.

In closing this section, I offer one additional note on Monji's process of transitioning from an administrator of security forces in Iraq to one of co-splay actors in Japan. If this metaphor of "becoming-character" that I borrow from Nozawa sounds viable for the hyper-consumers of anime and manga known as "otaku," but too far-fetched for administrators, one might consider again Japan's administrator-in-chief, former Prime Minister Abe Shinzō. In the closing ceremony of the 2016 Olympics in Rio de Janeiro, when Japan was to make a major public debut as the host for the Olympics in Tokyo

2020, Japan's Olympic committee members chose to do so in character. In a film displayed during the ceremony on the jumbotron at Maracaná stadium, in the buildup to the host handover, Abe is shown rushing to the stadium in a government car. Checking his watch and discovering that he may not make the ceremony in time, Abe nods and is promptly transformed into an animated figure of Super Mario. With the help of Doraemon, who installs a warp pipe connecting Tokyo and Rio, Super Mario traverses through the center of the earth to arrive at the other end of the pipe in Rio. As the video ends, the audience's attention shifts from the animated warp pipe to a physical pipe at stadium center. Dropping his costume and removing his bright red hat, a live Super Mario transforms back into the prime minister, who waves to the crowd. I cannot think of a more powerful act of publicity for announcing to the world the new national character of Pop-Culture Japan.

Characterizing Affective Types: The Japan Foundation

The administrative ethos applied to national culture in the Japan Foundation differs from that of MOFA in two principal ways. First, although Japan Foundation officials certainly imagine the nation as led by a state apparatus of which they are a part, they are also taught that public diplomacy today is not about country-to-country relations but rather about public-to-public or people-to-people exchange. Second, because the Japan Foundation's charter obliges the organization to work to "deepen the mutual understanding of Japanese and other foreign cultures" (Japan Foundation 2010), simply circulating popular images of Japan through anime ambassadors is insufficient for administering culture. The job of its officials is rather to provide multiple and more in-depth portraits of Japanese culture as a matter of education. These two facets of cultural administration in the Japan Foundation—people-to-people exchange and cultural education—require officials to reflect on the potential for programs to deepen the understanding and relationship between people of different national cultures. Anime and manga may evoke images of Japan as a pop-culture powerhouse, but in the eyes of many cultural administrators, if not connected to other aspects of culture that deepen an understanding of Japan, their merit as components of cultural diplomacy is less clear—a principle that has led to fewer endorsements and advertisements of anime characters in Japan Foundation campaigns where they are not managed conjointly with MOFA.

Figure 3.4 Prime Minister Abe Shinzō as Super Mario at the closing ceremony of the 2016 Olympics in Rio de Janeiro, August 21, 2016. Source: Stoyan Nenov, photographer. Reuters.

An articulation of this ethos of deepening cross-cultural understanding through national culture—the ideological counterpart to Monji's more explicit nationalism—is best articulated by the Japan Foundation's former chairman, Ogoura Kazuo, in an essay on Japan's cultural diplomacy:

> Many players engaged in contemporary Japanese cultural diplomacy, including the Japan Foundation, have adopted the policy of viewing "Japanese" cultural traditions not as Japan's property but as the precious heritage of all humankind. This implies that Japanese cultural diplomacy should not only propagate Japanese thought and traditions to the world but also aim at introducing non-Japanese culture to Japan to enrich the cultural heritage of the world. This helps to preserve cultural diversity, thereby contributing to the maintenance of a rich cultural environment for all humankind. (2009, 18)

Ogoura's comments express a view of culture that is only recently being adopted by administrations of public and cultural diplomacy in Japan:

that of culture as "international public good" (*kokusai kōkyōzai*):

> If we look upon culture not as the property of one nation or ethnic-
> ity but as international common property that belongs to all hu-
> man beings, then efforts must be made in the field of diplomacy to
> preserve not only the culture of one's own country but the cultures
> of other countries as well. Policies to preserve the cultural diversity
> of all humanity should be developed. (Ogoura 2009, 30)

This ideological understanding of culture is formulated specifically with
practices of cultural exchange (*bunka kōryū*) in mind, the primary activity
of the Japan Foundation:

> If we regard culture as the common property of all human beings,
> we will clearly understand the importance of "cultural exchange for
> the sake of cultural exchange itself." In other words, it is important
> to implement cultural exchange in a true sense, rather than out of a
> narrow sense of national interest or for mere diplomatic purposes.
> (Ogoura 2009, 31)

Despite Ogoura's critique of using culture to meet narrow national interests, it is difficult to escape the kind of national thinking that soft power
rhetoric makes central to Pop-Culture Japan, illustrated in Monji's comments above. Grounded in a framework that views cultural resources as
the propriety of distinct national cultures, adapting soft power thinking to
cultural administration tempts one to conflate culture with the state. This
intimate coupling of national interests and soft power makes discussions
of soft power within an organization seeking "exchange for the sake of
exchange" difficult. And even where the Japan Foundation might seek to
deemphasize the status of culture in Japan as *national* culture, that a state
organization administratively represents the culture of Japan makes its activities seem in the eyes of outsiders as effectively consecrating culture as
"Japanese." Simply put, there is an obvious tension in the act of a national
organization named for the state itself (the Japan Foundation) administering culture that is argued as not necessarily belonging to or originating in
Japan.[11]

For this reason, the Japan Foundation's chairman, Ogoura, has strug-
gled with the term *soft power* and even made explicit criticisms of it. For
example, despite his agency administering projects seen by politicians and
members of MOFA as building soft power, he has also warned that misin-

terpretations of soft power could lead to a kind of hypocrisy (*gizen*) (Ogoura 2006, 60). The point is based on his reasoning, rejected by Nye, that soft power cannot exist exclusive from hard power. While Nye (2004, 9) argues that "soft power does not depend on hard power," Ogoura points out that this possibility depends on the viewpoint of the party exercising influence and the one being influenced: "Within a velvet glove one can view an iron fist" (*koromo no shita kara yoroi ga mieru*) (2009, 44). For those administrators sensitive to geopolitical power imbalances, soft power may very often look like hard power in disguise.

Rather than doing away with the concept altogether, however, Ogoura attempts to redirect the concept toward the benefit of an international community rather than to nation-states exclusively. His explanation of this is worth citing at length:

> Insofar as Japan has little or no leeway to exert coercive force through the use of hard or economic power, which is a precondition for the exercise of soft power, it is doubtful whether using soft power in tandem with public diplomacy can be truly effective. There is the popular argument, based on the "Japanese cool" concept, that Japanese culture should be thought of as a form of national power, but to remove from the equation the issue of who will use this power and to what ends renders this argument meaningless.
>
> It may well be desirable for the sort of cultural content embodied in "Japanese cool" to spread naturally around the world through market forces or people's efforts, but this will not necessarily lead to an increase in understanding of Japan. Those on the receiving end of contemporary cultural activities either from or related to Japan, such as anime or fashion, are not necessarily aware of any Japanese connection. Indeed, we should bear in mind that linking culture to the state carries a high risk of impeding, rather than promoting, the spread of cultural activities around the world.
>
> The view that culture is a form of power is connected to the belief that there is a self-evident link between culture and the state, but this belief is itself fatally flawed. The worldwide spread of Japanese culture is a manifestation not of Japanese power but of how the notion of state-based power is gradually losing its meaning in an increasingly globalized world. If the concept of soft power has

any benefit, therefore, this benefit comes not from its use by the state but from the power of people engaged in cultural, religious, or educational activities to cultivate a common global awareness, increase creativity, and enrich the international community as a whole. The term "soft power" should be used only in this sense. (2006, 65)

Ogoura's recontextualization of soft power to a global rather than national community represents a liberal interpretation of Nye's original concept, which explicitly defined soft power as a tool of realizing a nation's interests. In his most concise articulation of his point, Ogoura (2006, 61) argues that "soft power should be discussed in connection with the exercise of power in the international community rather than in the context of domestic politics." One could easily imagine this advice as directed to Monji and the Public Diplomacy Department in the Ministry of Foreign Affairs, highlighting the contested politics of anxiety within Pop-Culture Japan. For Ogoura and the Japan Foundation, however, the specific application of soft power for national political interest challenges the institutional ethos of the Japan Foundation's cultural education programs.[12]

Despite the differing views of MOFA and Japan Foundation officials on soft power, which characterize their varying approaches to cultural diplomacy, embedded in both perspectives is an anxiety over the status of Japan's representation in the world. For Monji of MOFA, circulating publicity about Japan's pop culture can boost its national reputation in the world. For Ogoura of the Japan Foundation, cultural programs can protect the diversity of culture in a world where certain cultural traditions, such as Japan's, are seen as under threat. That these two organizations that differ in administrative ethos nonetheless share the responsibility for several pop-culture diplomacy programs casts ideological differences as a practical problem of administration.

Managing National Affect through Anime Diplomacy

Managing the representations of Pop-Culture Japan within the micro spaces of cultural administration means negotiating the meaning of terms like *Cool Japan*, *soft power*, and even *anime* in order to maintain harmonious relationships between oneself and one's colleagues. It requires meeting obligations imposed upon an official by superiors and fostering the conditions for the smooth operation of the bureaucracy as a whole. In this way, the process of managing nationalist sentiment attached to images of the nation becomes entangled with managing interpersonal relations within administration. Consider the different approaches to anime diplomacy within MOFA and the Japan Foundation.

To facilitate pop-culture diplomacy, MOFA employed the services of a Special Advisor to MOFA on Matters of Anime Diplomacy (Gaimushō Anime Bunka Gaikō ni kan suru Yūshikisha Kaigi Iin).[13] This advisor is frequently sent abroad as an informal ambassador of Japanese anime through programs organized jointly between MOFA and the Japan Foundation. At cultural expos and Japanese embassies overseas, the special advisor often presents a PowerPoint presentation titled "The Secret of Japanese Anime's Power" (*Nihon anime no pawā no himitsu*). This title draws on a familiar trope of Japan as a pop-culture power circulated among advocates of Cool Japan since the early 2000s, and most explicitly represented in the title of popular animation history writer Tsugata Nobuyuki's 2004 work, *The Power of Japan's Animation* (*Nihon animēshon no chikara*). Similar themes of anime's political power also feature in several other works celebrating the potential of Japan's new pop culture industries (Koyama 2004; Hamano 2005; Nakamura and Onouchi 2006; Sugiyama 2006; Shima 2009; Sakurai 2009a, 2009b, 2010a, 2010b).

I reviewed this presentation as part of an internship assignment with the Japan Foundation's Pop Culture Team. The presentation the advisor had prepared for in Brazil was scheduled to take place at the Japanese consulate in São Paulo and was advertised in advance, attracting mostly young students and fans of Japanese manga and anime. The presentation, this time retitled (for reasons I return to below) from "The Secret of Japanese Anime's Power" to "The Secret of Anime's Power" (*O Segredo do Poder do Animê*), began with a discussion on Cool Japan. The heading on one slide in the presentation proclaimed in English "Japan is Cool!" and stated in Portuguese "Japanese anime is being warmly embraced by young people all over the world" (*O animê japonês é calorosamente apoiado pelos jovens do mundo todo*). Subsequent slides presented statistics representing anime's global popularity, measured in the number of people attending major anime and Japanese pop culture expos in Italy, France, Spain, and the US. The presentation showed pictures of these events featuring young attendees who, often dressed in cosplay, clearly seemed to be fans of manga and anime. The presentation went on to list the most popular anime across the world and explained processes of anime production. It then listed some notable characteristics of Japanese anime, such as its "diversification," "the portrayal of actual Japanese fashion, culture, and society," and its "ability to spread via the internet."

Rather than introduce anime culture, which would reflect the Japan Foundation's mission, from my perspective the presentation read more like a celebration of anime's popularity around the world, reflecting sentiments more characteristic of MOFA administrators. At the heart of these sentiments is not only a desire among MOFA administrators to introduce Japanese popular culture to foreign publics, but more immediately, a desire to communicate the popularity of Japan's culture to publics at home. In a particularly illustrative example, in a conversation between journalist Nagata Kazuaki and Special Advisor to MOFA on Matters of Anime Diplomacy Sakurai Takamasa, Sakurai demonstrated his disappointment at how little Japanese people understand of anime's global appeal:

> Most Japanese people do not know about the popularity of Japanese pop culture overseas. Many young people in other countries grow up with Japan's anime. For instance, there is a bookstore near Lac Leman in Geneva that has about 11,000 Japanese comic books. You don't see a lot of bookstores with 11,000 comics, even in Japan! (Nagata 2010)

Reflecting a sentiment I often encountered among MOFA administrators, anime diplomacy here seems as much a practice to confirm Japan's cultural appeal overseas as a program to cultivate it. In one segment of the anime presentation in Brazil, a slide titled the "Evolution of the Reception of Japanese Pop Culture" started with anime and progressed through manga, the Japanese language, fashion, and finally "interest in Japan in general" (*interesse sobre o Japão em geral*). Through the logic of soft power and nation branding, the slide transforms fans of anime into fans of Japan, implicitly marking the audience of anime fans as soft power resources.

Administering Affect, Accommodating Tension

I have introduced this micro example of anime diplomacy in order to highlight the perspective taken toward anime diplomacy by MOFA officials. I also draw on this example to indicate where that perspective contrasts with that of Japan Foundation officials and how the tension elicited by that contrast is reconciled administratively. Given my role as intern tasked with supporting the Japan Foundation's Pop Culture Team, I was able not only to observe where tensions arose but also—even if only minimally—to feel them myself to the degree that I modeled the ethos that the Japan Foundation expected of its employees. Using examples of my own experience not only saves me from risking the confidentiality of my colleagues but also supports my suggestion that affects of what I call obligatory nationalism are not rooted inflexibly in "culture," "nation," or that classic object of fieldwork that anthropologists call "ethnos" ("Greek for 'a people'" [Rees 2018, 1]) but can be cultivated through administrative practice, even among anthropological interlopers. Additionally, and speaking more pragmatically, because often my task was to offer assistance with translations of project materials, it also became evident that I could not demonstrate my "usefulness" to my colleagues—at least one half of my justification for being among them—independently of expressing my own position and opinions on content that appeared to me as falling outside the Japan Foundation's charter.

Consider two examples. In the first, I was asked to look over the MOFA presentation materials on anime diplomacy described above. As I mentioned, the PowerPoint presentation prepared for this occasion in Brazil by the Special Advisor to MOFA was titled "The Secret of Anime's Power" (*O Segredo do Poder do Anime*) and documented evidence of the popularity of Japanese animation around the world to a Brazilian audience. The original title to the presentation, however, was listed as "Japanese Anime Past, Present, and Future: Investigating the Secrets of International Competitiveness" (*Nihon anime no kako, genzai, mirai-sono kokusai kyōsōryoku no himitsu o meguru*). From my perspective, the title did not communicate a desire for cross-cultural understanding from the perspective of the Japan Foundation so much as a desire among MOFA officials for increasing Japanese competitiveness in global markets. While the title might have clearly expressed the soft power hopes of MOFA officials, it was less clear how the same title would capture the hearts of young anime fans in Brazil.

In fact, there was little in the presentation that, from my perspective, met the standards of the Japan Foundation expressed by Ogoura for how soft power should be employed in cultural diplomacy. And yet, the Japan Foundation's Pop Culture Team was tasked with supporting the project in Brazil. I raised some of these points to a team member I call Takada, who politely agreed with my assessment. However, the content of the presentation, he indicated, was at this point largely up to MOFA's special advisor.

Takada's job was largely to ensure the smooth implementation of the event in São Paulo. In response to my concern that the program might discourage interest in Japanese culture on account of its somewhat self-aggrandizing tone, Takada responded optimistically that it might also stimulate interest in Japanese culture. Takada is a sharp and inventive thinker. He is discerning in the way he thinks about the merits of Japan Foundation programs, and he thinks about them a lot. However, in programs jointly administered by MOFA and the Japan Foundation and already well underway, there is little administrative space or reason to communicate the additional critique I had raised, or even more challenging, to suggest a change. As a rather elegantly engineered concession, Takada suggested an edit in the Portuguese version of the title, which would ultimately read, "The Secret of Anime's Power" (*O Segredo do Poder do Anime*). The Japanese title, however, retained a concession to MOFA: "The Secret of the Power of Japanese Anime" (*Nihon anime no pawā no himitsu*). The edit represented a minor but nevertheless characteristic exercise of the Japan Foundation's perspective in contrast to that of MOFA's.

A second example highlighting a tension between the national-inflected approaches of MOFA and the more cosmopolitan perspective of the Japan Foundation comes from another translation task. This time I was asked to help translate into English a general announcement for the Japanese pop-culture event in Brazil, including the profiles of the three Ambassadors of Cute who were also scheduled to appear. Given my understanding of Ogoura's advocacy for approaching culture as an "international public good" (*kokusai kōkyōzai*), a few passages in the Japanese version of the announcement elicited some concern. One example of a passage I brought to Takada's attention read, "As seen in the bustling excitement of the World Cosplay Summit held in São Paulo and the establishment of the Brazil J-Pop society in May 2009, now in Brazil, the opportunity to stimulate interest in Japanese pop culture is growing at the hand of Brazilian people" (*Ima, Burajiru de wa, Burajiru hito no te ni yotte Nihon no poppu karuchā o moriagete ikō to suru kiun ga takamatte imasu*). Why an announcement for Brazilians to learn about Japanese pop culture trends should also advertise the present moment as "opportune" (*kiun*) for growing those trends was unclear to me. From my point of view, the passage did little more than to reaffirm a self-serving satisfaction at the global proliferation of Japanese pop culture, a sentiment that did not, I feel, capture the Japan Foundation's ethos very well. Takada was again receptive to my point, although he did not think it critical enough to revise. I offered him an alternative translation that with some negotiation resulted in a compromise: "With the widely attended premier of the 'World Cosplay Summit' in São Paulo and the establishment of the Brazil J-Pop society in May 2009, Brazilians are stimulating a rapidly growing interest in Japanese pop culture" (Japan Foundation 2009).

In the broader debate over the meaning of soft power and the role of MOFA and the Japan Foundation in contributing to it via anime diplomacy, discussions like the one between Takada and me can seem trivial and inconsequential. But I suggest it is in these seemingly mundane, minute details where soft power is accommodated to the usual practices of administration within the Japan Foundation and where the character of Pop-Culture Japan crystalizes. It is very unlikely that a program featuring anime or the Ambassadors of Cute alone would have originated from within the Japan Foundation. It simply does not satisfy enough criteria for what counts as a program worthy of Japan Foundation investment—namely, one that significantly deepens an understanding of Japanese culture. However, with pressure from MOFA, the Japan Foundation ultimately carried out the project and in doing so, nudged a collective image of Japanese culture further in the direction of one representing Pop-Culture Japan. The advertisement for the São Paulo event was left unchanged in Japanese. Reflecting a similar strategy adopted for the title of the anime diplomacy presentation, my version negotiated with Takada was adopted in English. Takada thus effectively managed the minor disruption I had introduced to the system of administration. Believing no Japanese colleagues would likely contest the Japanese language version, he chose to leave it unedited, not wanting to occupy his colleagues' time with what was perceived as a minor issue. He allowed the change in the English version to appease my own concerns. By balancing concerns from multiple colleagues, Takada facilitated a resolution in interpersonal administrative ethics that simultaneously shaped the national character of program content.

From Banal to Obligatory Nationalism

Although the particular tension I highlight here between the interests of MOFA and of the Japan Foundation was engendered largely through my own intervention and illustrates accordingly the typical complicity of fieldwork among experts (Marcus 1998b), tensions like it arise elsewhere in administration in the minutiae of translation choices, policy announcement edits, and budget adjustments. The politics of anxiety in Japan and the degree to which that politics is channeled through more national or cosmopolitan language thus play out in part through seemingly mundane accommodations in administration. As illustrated above, tensions are resolved according to the needs of managing interpersonal and interoffice relationships, and ideological battles over pop-culture policy are often sidelined or sacrificed toward this end. In this sense, resolutions of ideological tension in administration, and indeed in bureaucratic administration at large, can appear as rather banal if also deeply interpersonal affairs.

Michael Billig (1995) has claimed that one understudied aspect of nationalism's power is found in its embeddedness in everyday life. He uses the phrase "banal nationalism" (1995, 6) to describe a broad category of mundane but nonetheless important ways that national sentiments are conditioned distinct from the forms of extreme nationalism academics often pay more attention to, such as in xenophobic or violent language, racist immigration policies, territorial disputes, or military exercises. Banal nationalism, by contrast, emerges in less obvious practices, such as in the privileging of national affairs in newspapers, in the singing of national anthems before sporting events, or simply in speaking officially designated languages which are held to be the property of the nation, even though doing so may marginalize others. While Billig's argument importantly draws attention to less-studied sites where national imagining is embodied at the level of routine habits, it might also readily lead one to imagine national sentiment as a structure of feeling uniformly distributed within a nation's geographic borders. Consequently, I think Billig's observations might in Japan's case be better applied not to national communities as a whole but rather to sites of state administration in particular, where seemingly small habits of managing the nation's cultural images can disproportionately affect how people feel about the nation.

One particularly powerful component of this process is the naturalization of national images produced in powerful sites of government. While the anime diplomacy program originated as a creative idea of a handful of mostly male bureaucrats in the Ministry of Foreign Affairs, this group nonetheless has the capacity to publicize its policies widely through a number of methods: the institutionalization of Japan's media organizations (see Hall 1998; Kraus 2000); a hierarchy of bureaucracy in which MOFA sits near the top; and the large coffers and extensive administrative infrastructure of the state. As Billig (1995, 37) notes, drawing from Roland Barthes, "ideology speaks with 'the Voice of Nature.'" The sociologist Pierre Bourdieu made a similar assessment when he said that "matters of culture, and in particular the social divisions and hierarchies associated with them, are constituted as such by the actions of the state which, by instituting them both in things and in minds, confers upon the cultural arbitrary all the appearances of the natural" (1993, 55). Once soft power aims are inserted into state bureaucracy, such as by MOFA requesting certain pop-culture diplomacy initiatives of the Japan Foundation, administrative logics can naturalize what seem to be at first unorthodox policies. Consequently, administration can facilitate the naturalization of Pop-Culture Japan relatively quickly as officials build its presence through the circulation of anime images.

While the state sanctioning of Cool Japan leads to the wide-ranging publicity of its imagery, evaluating whether the new figure of Pop-Culture Japan is ultimately embraced outside administration requires further consideration, which I offer in chapter 5. However, observations of pop-culture diplomacy in practice reveal how easily a commitment to one's organization embedded in the everyday demands of administrative labor can oblige an administrator to care for the nation itself—the phenomenon I call obligatory nationalism. The sensitivity that an administrator exercises in relation to colleagues, finely tuned to reduce the degree of disturbance—meiwaku—to the system, also makes the administrator sensitive to threats, however banal, to an image of Japan for which she or he feels occupationally responsible. While a particular sensitivity to meiwaku in Japan's public spaces or its corporate and organizational sites (Roberts 1994; Ogasawara 1998; Sedgwick 2007) may heighten this capacity for state administrators of culture to tie feelings of collegial obligation to national "duty" (giri), it does not necessarily dictate or codify its content. To be sure, bureaucratic practices within MOFA and the Japan Foundation—structures of decision making, styles of communication, habits of consensus building, formats for budgetary preparation—reveal similar patterns of labor. But the ideological ends to which those practices are leveraged differ substantially along lines of characterization. Despite private confessions of discomfort over anime diplomacy from some Japan Foundation officials, an administrative sense of commitment to the organization locks one into a form of obligatory nationalism. In this way Pop-Culture Japan emerges as a product of anxiety over the status of the nation from the viewpoint of certain highly invested and keenly sensitive administrators, such as those in MOFA, and a negotiated politics of that anxiety with other officials, such as those in the Japan Foundation, who are administratively obliged to accommodate that sensitivity. Such an ethnographic view shows how dominant discourses can take shape not only through the organization of consensus but also through an affectively managed politics of contest and accommodation.

In this chapter I aimed to show how administrative affect—a sense of obligation to both one's organization and the view of the nation it publicizes—is cultivated through practices by which employees adopt certain character types that are, in turn, characteristic of that organization's members. In the next chapter, I ask how the politics of Pop-Culture Japan that is ideologically split among different government ministries and their character types can also fracture along lines of gender.

4

Kawaii Diplomacy

Ambassadors of Cute and the Gendering of Anxiety

While Pop-Culture Japan is imagined in the eyes of administrators as a neutral and inclusive figure in which Japanese citizens can equally participate, the asymmetry between Pop-Culture Japan's mostly male managers and its predominantly girl-centered imagery warrants inspection of its selective representations. How do such dominant images leverage gender to secure the state's interests in geopolitical terrain? And how might those images variously standardize or stigmatize a sense of national belonging among those who are interpellated by Cool Japan campaigns?

On February 26, 2009, at the modestly sized and minimally decorated pressroom at Japan's Ministry of Foreign Affairs, Public Diplomacy Department Director Monji Kenjirō presented Kimura Yū (age 27), Aoki Misako (age 27), and Fujioka Shizuka (age 21) with their official appointments: New Trend Communicators of Japanese Pop Culture (Poppu Karuchā Hasshin-shi—Fasshon Bunya), commonly referred to as the Ambassadors of Cute (*kawaii taishi*) (figure 4.1). "The main mission of the three ambassadors," Monji explained, "is to transmit the new trends of Japanese pop culture in the field of fashion to the rest of the world and to promote understanding of Japan through their respective cultural projects carried out by the Japanese embassies and the Japan Foundation" (MOFA 2009). As the three young women lined up in front of flashing cameras, Monji elaborated:

> Pop culture, including fashion, is an integral part of today's Japanese culture. It enjoys worldwide popularity and we witness that its fans are ever-increasing. Pop culture is expected to help the people of

the world have more chances to know about contemporary Japan, hand in hand with other parts of traditional and contemporary Japanese culture. (MOFA 2009)

The introduction, part two of a daily announcement MOFA holds for the ministry's press clubs (*kisha kurabu*), followed a briefing on a symposium held a day earlier, a follow-up to the Tokyo International Conference on African Development IV, titled "Japan's Efforts to Promote Peace and Security in Africa: The Case of Sudan and Beyond." Foreign Ministry Deputy Press Secretary Kawamura Yasuhisa summarized Foreign Minister Nakasone's four major points concerning Japan's role in building sustainable peace in Africa:

> One, Japan's active involvement in ending conflicts and achieving peace by citing the cases of Sudan and Somalia. Two, Japan's active involvement in implementing peace agreements. Three, the importance of enhancing Africa's capacity for peace building. And, four, the necessity of strengthening Japan's personnel contribution to peace-building efforts in Africa. (MOFA 2009)

While these announcements took place a day apart, the ministry published them conjointly in a press release (MOFA 2009). Taken together, they illustrate how the logic of soft power links conflict in Africa with representations of kawaii fashion trends in Pop-Culture Japan.

In this chapter, I explore how pop-culture diplomacy imagined through the lens of soft power renders young Japanese women into commodified icons of Pop-Culture Japan and tools of foreign policy, while also transforming cultural consumers into resources for national security. After introducing the Ambassadors of Cute program in detail, I examine how a politics of anxiety over Japan's geopolitical status connects with a host of problematized affects surrounding fictional depictions of young women and girls (*shōjo*) in Japanese subcultures. I aim to analyze how certain government administrators invest in the ambiguous but powerful affects surrounding shōjo images and ultimately reproduce highly specific, politicized, and asymmetric frames for viewing gender through processes of manufacturing Pop-Culture Japan.

ポップカルチャー発信使（ファッション分野）

平 成 2 1 年 2 月
外 務 省 文 化 交 流 課

ファッション分野：通称「カワイイ♥大使」
（"カワイイ♥" Ambassador）

藤岡静香（ふじおか しずか）

世界各国女子に急速に浸透して
いる日本の女子高生制服風
ファッション界の代表的存在であ
り、「制服コーディネイトの魔術
師」と呼ばれる。ブランド制服
ショップ「CONOMi」のコーディ
ネーションのアドバイザーも務め
る。ドラマ「Around40」などにも出
演の新進気鋭の女優。

青木美沙子（あおき みさこ）

原宿で、雑誌「KERA」にスカウ
トされて、「KERA」「KERAマニ
アックス」「ゴシック＆ロリータバ
イブル」等の人気ファッション雑
誌で専属モデルを務めるほか、
世界各国でもヒットした映画「下
妻物語」でも注目されたブラン
ド「BABY, THE STARS SHINE
BRIGHT」のカタログモデルもつ
とめる。世界の女子が憧れる"
ロリータファッション"界のカリス
マあり、08仏Japan Expoの際に
も圧倒的な声援を得た。

木村優（きむら ゆう）

バンド「PEEP★4U」のボーカリスト。世界の女子が
憧れる"原宿系ファッション"の代表的な存在であり、
原宿を歩くだけで、外国人観光客からも写真撮影の
リクエストがかかるほど。ファッション誌の世界でも
活躍中。本職のミュージシャンとして、年間約100ス
テージをこなすかたわら、自らのファッションセンス
を活かし、ステージ衣装も自前で製作するファッショ
ンリーダー。

Figure 4.1 The Ambassadors of Cute as featured on the website of the Ministry of Foreign Affairs of Japan. Source: Website of the Ministry of Foreign Affairs of Japan (https://www.mofa.go.jp/ICSFiles/afieldfile/2009/02/26/G0242.pdf).

The Ambassadors of Cute

The Ambassadors of Cute, according to MOFA's Public Diplomacy Department director Monji Kenjirō, represent the cutting edge in the field of cute (*kawaii*) fashion trends in Japan. Running from 2009 through 2010, the program reflects a broader girl-centered approach to representing Pop-Culture Japan that continues to this day. While each of the adult female ambassadors were in their twenties at the time of the program's launch, they typify a style associated with the "girl culture" of urban Japan (Miller 2011a, 2011b; Freedman, Miller, and Yano 2013), which is why I at times refer to the ambassadors as "girls" in my description.[1] As introduced in the opening to the book, each ambassador represents a fashion style associated with trends in Japanese girl culture. While each style draws on urban Japanese subcultures, the depictions by MOFA are arguably simplified and standardized versions of the more diverse styles one would typically see on Tokyo streets (Miller 2011b).

Kimura Yū represents Harajuku-style fashion (*Harajuku-kei fasshon*), named after a popular shopping area near Tokyo's Shibuya district and its iconic bustling crosswalk, locally known as the "Shibuya *sukuranburu*." When MOFA officials were beginning to search for potential candidates to become Ambassadors of Cute, Kimura, originally an amateur pop singer and fashion model, had recently appeared in the youth fashion magazine KERA, then known as a Harajuku Lolita fashion magazine (Minami 2019). Although her style draws from several sources, Kimura was ultimately presented by MOFA as a general representative of Harajuku's kawaii fashion. The style is eclectic, mixing and matching items and accessories from kawaii clothing stores on Harajuku's main shopping street, Takeshita-dōri. Her arrangements are bright, colorful, and somewhat garish (*hade*), an aesthetic accentuated by her bright blond hair with pink highlights. As many of her fashion items are second-hand and comparatively affordable, her style evokes the social practices and pleasures of shopping with friends, discovering bargains, and creating eclectic ensembles.

Aoki Misako represents Lolita fashion (*Rorīta fasshon*), drawing its name from Nabokov's 1955 novel featuring a middle-aged professor's infatuation with a twelve-year-old girl. In contrast to the lascivious tones evoked by the novel, however, the style appears much more conservatively Victorian in taste, characterized by frills, lace, long skirts, and high collars. Aoki, in an unpublished interview with *Veja* magazine archived by Japan Foundation program administrators, claims to be nothing like the sexualized object portrayed in Nabokov's novel. And Lolita fashion fans in general deny there is anything sexual about the style, despite knowing the origin and allusions of the name. Instead, they emphasize an affinity for the refined cuteness of the aesthetic, which invokes for them images of nineteenth-century England and rococo fashions of eighteenth-century France. Although there are several evolving genres of Lolita fashion, including those of gothic and punk that can at times push the playfulness of Lolita fashion into parody, Aoki's style is the most conservatively and generically sweet, drawing from such brands as Baby, the Stars Shine Bright and Angelic Pretty. Compared to Kimura's Harajuku style, Lolita items are significantly higher in price, with dresses usually listed at between 20,000 and 30,000 yen (US$185 to $280), but sometimes going as high as 50,000 or 60,000 yen ($460 to $560), and accessories like hairpieces, shoes, and bags selling for between 10,000 and 20,000 yen ($92 to $185).

The actor and fashion coordinator Fujioka Shizuka represents high school girls' fashion (*joshi kōsei fasshon*), characterized by plaid skirts, blazers, white blouses, and scarves. Although similar to the mandatory uniforms worn by girls at most of Japan's secondary schools, the style has also emerged as a fashion genre of its own, sometimes called *nanchatte joshi kōsei* (kinda high school girl), with its own magazines, shops, and website (www.conomi.jp/). It is important to note that the high school girl uniform is a highly polysemic symbol in Japan, sometimes representing youth and purity, sometimes cute culture, and very often made into a fetishized sexual object (Leheny 2006b; Ashcraft and Ueda 2010; Kinsella 2014). Its polysemic power has not been lost on overseas audiences, where the uniform is popularized through manga and anime, many stories of which focus on young female protagonists and cater to girls (*shōjo manga*).

The fashion "styles" (*kei*) of each of the ambassadors draw from diverse practices of consumption characteristic of girl culture in Japan. A *kei* is a suffix that in Japanese subcultures refers as much to a style as a person who embodies it, and it carries its own identity and ethos. Given the number of subcategories within each fashion genre, the various sites and forms of leisure associated with those who adopt it, and the difference in product prices from one style to the next, each genre reflects a rich and complex set of cultural practices full of subtle distinctions and nuances. This social richness, creativity, and subtlety of kawaii culture is nonetheless often lost in presentations of the ambassadors at overseas events. In the following section I analyze recorded scenes featuring the Ambassadors of Cute at cultural expos outside Japan, which I reviewed as part of my role as intern with the Japan Foundation's Pop-Culture Team. In doing so I suggest that despite the diversity of kawaii cultural forms and fashions, such expressions are typically flattened out and given new meanings when curated by MOFA administrators and advisors.

Presenting and Publicizing Kawaii

Presentations of the Ambassadors of Cute at overseas consulates and cultural fairs illustrate how in practices of crafting and managing an image of Pop-Culture Japan, administrators stamp a uniform national brand upon otherwise diverse displays of kawaii culture. A typical presentation of the Ambassadors of Cute begins with an hour-long lecture on the popularity of anime that I discussed in the previous chapter: "The Secret of Japanese Anime's Power" (*Nihon anime no pawā no himitsu*). After the lecture, an administrator introduces one, two, or all three of the Cute Ambassadors, depending on their individual schedules and the funding available for each trip as administered through MOFA and the Japan Foundation.

At the 2009 Japan Expo in Paris, for example, a male special advisor to MOFA working on the Ambassadors of Cute program took the primary role in the presentation.[2] Playfully dressed in breeches, cloak, and ruff resembling those of the Elizabethan period and speaking through a French interpreter, the advisor began his introduction of Kimura Yū by asking his audience of about one hundred, "How many people know the word *kawaii*?" (The French interpreter left the word *kawaii* in the original Japanese.) The advisor pointed his microphone to the audience and raised his hand, eliciting a moderate response. After inviting Kimura to the stage and asking her to "turn around for the audience" (*chotto guru guru shite*), he asked again, "Who thinks she is cute?" Next, the advisor interviewed Kimura about what she was wearing and how she selected clothes for her ensembles. Following this segment, in which Kimura was featured only briefly and offered only short answers, he showed a slideshow of other kawaii fashion trends in Harajuku. Afterward, he asked Kimura to sing sections from two pop songs a cappella. The advisor closed the presentation by inviting audience members to bring their cameras to the front of the stage to take pictures of Kimura, a practice typical of marketing events that feature intimate settings between idols and fans and that began to change with otaku-oriented idol practices in the mid 2000s (see Galbraith 2012; Galbraith and Karlin 2012).

The presentation of Kimura emphasizes a version of kawaii culture that forestalls deep analysis and critique. This aspect of kawaii aesthetics, though dependent on the particular subculture in question, is commensurate with a number of critics' readings of kawaii culture (Ōtsuka 1989, 1991; Shimamura 1991; Yamane 1991; Miyadai, Ishihara, and Ōtsuka 1993; Kinsella 1995; McVeigh 1996). In his book *Cute Revolution* (*Kawaii kakumei*), for example, former pop-culture advisor to MOFA Sakurai Takamasa in fact advocated against defining or critiquing the meaning of *kawaii*, preferring to leave this up to the "value judgment" (*kachi handan*) of fans (Sakurai 2009b, 185–86). Similarly, asking young Tokyo women to define cuteness, McVeigh notes he was often met with a common answer: "Cuteness is something one can't talk about. It's something one can only feel, in one's heart" (1996, 294). Daniel Harris (2000) similarly argues that cuteness, at least in American versions of it, resists interpretation and functions primarily as an affective aesthetic. That said, for Harris cuteness can also be affectively troubling, as it evokes sentiments of the malformed, grotesque, and pitiable, triggering, "with Pavlovian predictability, maternal feelings for a maternal condition of endearing naiveté" (2000, 2). Cuteness is not something we find in subjects, he says, but something we do to them, effectively rendering them helpless and dependent upon our care.

Scholars of Japan's popular culture have offered rich accounts of kawaii expressions in Japan that challenge Harris's interpretation of cute aesthetics as merely disarming and disempowering (see Kotani 2007; Miller 2011b; Yano 2013b; Condry 2013; Lukács 2015, 2020). These critics argue that the semiotic politics of kawaii fashion, which are often "misread by elders and foreigners as a sincere effort to be charming or adorable," are often meant as "parodic swipe[s] at femininity norms" (Miller 2011a, 25). Despite this critical and versatile capacity of kawaii, however, MOFA's presentations of the ambassadors are often far more generic. In the case of the presentation described above, while projecting images of cute fashion from Harajuku on screen, the commentary of the MOFA advisor is limited to "Isn't it cute?" (*kawaii desu ne*). Little of the cultural context of Kimura's fashion is communicated, or of the social practices, interests, labor, or leisure activities typical of its subcultural trends. As Laura Miller (2011a, 23) says of the Ambassadors of Cute, they do not represent practices "grounded in any particular street culture or girl's subculture, of which there are several, but rather are wildly mashed-up aesthetics from the worlds of fashion, mass market product design, and popular media." During the presentation, seldom are questions solicited from the audience members who might be interested in the cultural context of Kimura's fashion, nor does Kimura have the chance to elaborate on this herself. What results is the smoothing out of a kawaii aesthetic sometimes associated with Japan's globally branded pop art movement known as "superflat" (Murakami 2000; Steinberg 2004; Looser 2006; Favell 2011; Shamoon 2015).[3] While design strategists aiming to create iconic characters (*kyara*) and brands recognize that simple designs invite diverse projections from consumers that can be leveraged to profit (Yano 2013b, 10), presentations of the Ambassadors of Cute nonetheless trade an opportunity to deepen understandings of kawaii subcultures for the opportunity to broaden publicity for Pop-Culture Japan.

News stories of the Ambassadors of Cute in the foreign press generally portray them as yet another example of quirky Japanese culture that is disproportionately featured in media on Japan, similar to stories on Japan's love hotels, high-tech vending machines, and unconventional gadgets and subcultural trends.[4] Many of these stories on the Ambassadors of Cute are tracked by Japan Foundation officials and filed in large plastic binders. Thus, officials are aware of some of the less flattering views on the Ambassadors of Cute in foreign as well as in Japanese media. However, they also have just as many articles highlighting the ambassadors' "appeal," which note their appearance at well-attended cultural expos featuring displays on Japanese anime, manga, and other aspects of Japanese subcultures. As such, the Ambassadors of Cute are a contested symbol, cited sometimes as evidence for Cool Japan's success abroad and sometimes for its embarrassing failures, depending on who is speaking.

For MOFA's Public Diplomacy Department, however, even negative press of the Ambassadors of Cute can serve the soft power interests of pop-culture diplomacy. In response to my question about criticism of the program, one former department director offered the following comments, which I offered in abbreviated form in the opening to the book:

> There are criticisms of course. I received a question from a woman member of the parliament whom I've known for a very long time. And she herself is a very attractive lady. And she said there may be some misunderstanding in a recipient country if a young girl walks around with a very short miniskirt. But, first of all, it is only one girl who shows her legs and . . . [laughing]. But my response was very formal, and I thought it was appropriate to answer in order for the culture or art of soft power: when we send or deliver this soft power culture, the most important thing is that it is well-received by the recipient country. So in order for that we have to make a thorough groundwork or survey in advance about local conditions, situations, and so-on, so certainly we're not sending her to Saudi Arabia [more laughing]. So it was my simple answer but see, there are so many articles, programs on TV, media, and it is a good thing. See, one of the objectives is already achieved, to attract people's attention to those activities by the Foreign Ministry.

This former director reasons that inasmuch as the Cool Japan brand can attract attention, it serves as a useful resource of soft power. And even despite criticism, he suggests that attracting attention alone, whether positive or negative, is useful—a version of public diplomacy that endorses the mantra of public relations famously attributed to P.T. Barnum that "there's no such thing as bad publicity." With soft power turning both commodities and consumers into producers of social and economic capital, the concept becomes in processes of administration enfolded into the logical production and branding of Pop-Culture Japan. Critically, this production of Pop-Culture Japan is enacted through a gendered lens, as illustrated by the director's conflation of the Diet member's attractiveness with that of the Ambassadors of Cute. His act of feminizing his critic also silences her, privileging a male-centered version of national popular culture. This commodification of national cultural symbols along gendered lines renders Japanese female attractiveness into a silent but salient resource of soft power managed by mostly male administrators.

As seen in the presentation of the Ambassador of Cute in Paris described above, while Kimura embodies the charms of kawaii, it is the advisor's task to explain it. From the perspective of soft power, Kimura is a resource of soft power while the male administrator cares for and cultivates it, ultimately rendering Kimura politically productive within a long history of government investment in women as primary reproducers of the nation as well as its anxieties, in both biological and social terms.[5] Through the introduction of Kimura and the solicitation of particular responses from the audience—"Isn't she cute?!" Audience: "Yeeeahh!"—a kawaii aesthetic is abstracted from Kimura as person and objectified as a cultural commodity that has its origins in a locally produced Japanese culture that domestic publics can take pride in precisely because of kawaii's national distinctiveness.

The Labor of Kawaii

It is worth pausing here to reflect on the broader economic contexts contributing to the emergence of the Ambassadors of Cute. It is no coincidence that young women overwhelmingly perform the labor of producing Pop-Culture Japan. Their disproportionate role can be understood in part as an effect of two structural dimensions. The first is the increasing liberalization of the global economy, whose variable and wide-ranging consequences have come to be glossed as "neoliberal" (Harvey 2005). The second is the highly gendered disparities between permanent and casual employment opportunities in Japan that have only increased since its economic stagnation in the early 1990s.

The first of the two dimensions, especially in its gendered dynamics, is expertly summarized by Nancy Fraser in her historicization of capitalism through its regime of liberal competition in the nineteenth century, of state-management and social welfare in the twentieth century, and the "globalizing financialized capitalism of the present era" (2016, 104). For Fraser, the latter regime "has relocated manufacturing to low-wage regions, recruited women into the paid workforce, and promoted state and corporate disinvestment from social welfare. Externalizing carework onto families and communities, it has simultaneously diminished their capacity to perform it" (104). The effects of Fraser's "regime of globalizing financialized capitalism" are easily recognizable in Japan considering how the first dimension of economic pressures abroad intersects with a second dimension of gendered stratification at home. As a result, contradictory pressures have manifested in a number of forms: in policies like Prime Minister Abe Shinzō's aggressive push to better integrate women into the workforce, known informally as "womenomics" (*ūmanomikusu*);[6] working mothers who would be supported by remedying the persistent insufficiency of childcare services; and in the consequential double burden of poorly paid part-time employment and unpaid care labor that inevitably falls on women. With the majority of female employees working in irregular jobs (70 percent) and the majority of the temporary workforce being female (80 percent) (Allison 2013, 9, cited in Gottfried 2009), the highly stratified structures of employment in Japan offer little encouragement for women to pursue the kinds of careers that the government's liberalization rhetoric seems to promise.

As a consequence, the liberalization of the global economy and the consequential burdens of labor it has disproportionately leveraged on women in Japan has, in conjunction with an emerging digital economy since the 1990s, facilitated the emergence of precisely the kinds of experiments in self-branding, promotion, fashion, and idol culture that the government has tapped in building Pop-Culture Japan. As argued most convincingly by Gabriella Lukács in her ethnography of women entrepreneurs, beginning in Japan in the 1990s, "the digital economy evolved in parallel with the deregulation of the labor market" (2020, 2). Because women had been traditionally excluded from salaried employment and many refused to accept unfulfilling work, many "turned to digital technologies in search of opportunities to develop fulfilling do-it-yourself (DIY) careers." However, Lukács argues, "while digital technologies have seduced women by promising them meaningful careers," those same technologies and the corporate platforms running them "only expanded the practice of extracting profits from women's unpaid labor," thus absorbing their labor and "making it invisible" in the process (2020, 1–2).

If the structure of the digital economy made the DIY labor of entrepreneurial women invisible, the structure of the internet and the branding strategies brought to it by the publishing industry also rendered invisible the realistically poor chances of entrepreneurial success. Of the numerous photographers, net idols, bloggers, cell phone novelists, and independent financial traders that Lukács studied, very few succeeded. As she explains (2020, 26), "The percentage of female traders among professional traders remain perplexingly small, and to gain visibility in the crowd of twenty-eight million bloggers (on Ameba, which is Japan's largest blogging platform) is a formidable task, if not impossible." However, despite the odds, entrepreneurs were also able to "keep a powerful ideology alive—the ideology of the possible, which has inspired millions to try to develop DIY careers" and, ironically, facilitated "the devaluation of salaried employment and the crumbling of job security" (27).

This coupling of the global and Japanese economies, evolving through a highly gendered stratification of labor, creates an uncomfortable commensurability between young women's "ideology of the possible" and older men's hope for Pop-Culture Japan. Facilitated through transformations in the economy from manufacturing to what theorists like Hardt and Negri (2004) call "affective labor,"[7] which focuses on the production of feeling and emotional connection rather than goods, a key product of this commensurability between personal and political hope is the Ambassadors of Cute. In identifying young women generating economic and affective capital with fans through their fashion, blogs, and art, government officials applied the emerging logics of nation branding and soft power to translate the invisible labor of women, long marginalized from the mainstream economy, into highly public representations of kawaii culture capable of producing Pop-Culture Japan.

Gendering and Regionalizing Anxiety

The selectively male and state-oriented perspective enacted by MOFA in policies such as the Ambassadors of Cute inverts kawaii fashion by turning fashion-savvy agents and producers of subculture, expressed in opposition to mainstream Japanese fashion trends, into reflections of a new national

culture of pervasive cute. I have argued that motivations for programs serving Pop-Culture Japan are driven in part from anxiety over Japan's geopolitical status in East Asia vis-à-vis its relationship with the West. But to what
degree might we read this anxiety as particularly "masculine" in character?

The literary critic Sianne Ngai has argued that when connected to
perceptions of power, anxiety appears as a particularly male-dominated
affect. In her literary readings of "spatialized representations of anxiety" in
works by Herman Melville, Alfred Hitchcock, and Martin Heidegger, she
sees anxiety as acquiring a "certain epistemological cachet" for the present
(2005, 212–213). She finds parallels to this male expression of anxiety in
the "primary model of gender differentiation" of Freud's psychoanalysis
as well as in the Continental tradition of existentialist philosophy, where
the "privileging of anxiety as a key for interpreting the human condition
is accompanied by its being secured as the distinctive—if not exclusive—
emotional province of male intellectuals" (213). In contrast, women are
attributed with less traumatic and "less profound" affects like nostalgia
and envy. Through these literary readings of Euro-American culture, Ngai
examines how anxiety comes to acquire a special status as the distinctive
"feeling-tone" of self-inquiry and self-management, slowly replacing its
precursor of a melancholia that was the intellectual's signature sensibility
prior to the modern period.

While Japanese administrators may not have directly imported this
form of anxiety from the West as a signature affective style of intellectual
inquiry or state management, Ngai's critique helps illustrate how gendered
"feeling-tones" can be reproduced socially and selectively through styles of
cultural production, whether of art and literature or of policy and governance. Given the male-domination of the political administration of Japan's
modernization processes, it is reasonable to ask how the anxiety experienced
through a historical relationship with a threatening "West" in the past is
rehearsed, reproduced, and recirculated in the present through mostly male
agents of management. As indicated by bureaucrats' references to Japan's en-
tanglement with the West discussed in chapter 1, this historical consciousness
is never far from the minds of administrators today. And given the anxiety
historically reproduced through styles of political and cultural soul-searching
among elites through subsequent periods of Japan's modernity—in the new
Japanese state post-Meiji Restoration, in its pre–Pacific War military escala-
tion, in its post–Pacific War depression, in its economic "miracle" expansion
particularly though the 1970s and 80s, and now in the malaise perceived to

hang over Japan through two if not three "lost decades"—it is easy to read
the contemporary administrative anxiety displayed through Pop-Culture
Japan programs as a distinctively male affect.

Such a reading is consistent with the genealogy of the Ambassadors
of Cute program, which emerged out of discussions by a handful of men
in the Ministry of Foreign Affairs. Its critiques, such as that voiced by the
female member of parliament cited above, reflect a concern not only with
the reduction of women to commodities and political resources but also
with a style of nationalism that seems narrowly centered on stories of Japan
as unique, number one, and, perhaps consequentially, alone in the world.
Laura Miller has argued that the "Cool Japan ideology" (2011b, 101) expresses
not only an implicitly gendered view on the nation's culture but also an
explicit "anxiety about actual adult women" (2011a, 22). She suggests that the
"obsessive molding of cute female types can be seen as a method for displac-
ing anxiety" (2011a, 27).[8] This reading of Pop-Culture Japan as a product
of a particularly male anxious affect also finds support in a comment from
the director of a prominent graduate program in cultural policy in Japan.
When I solicited her thoughts on policy examples like the Ambassadors of
Cute project as administered through MOFA and the Japan Foundation,
she fell back in her chair and let out an unrestrained laugh. In a dismissive
and skeptical tone, she explained, "The Japan Foundation is just a money
bag for MOFA; I never know what those bureaucrats are thinking!" Despite
substantial investment in Pop-Culture Japan, for this critic well connected
to policymakers, it represented little more than one hopeful but desperate
stopgap against an impending national crisis. In our exchange, and indeed
in her writings on cultural policy (which, to protect her anonymity, I do
not cite), I could identify little of the anxious urgency I had elsewhere encountered among other, mostly male, officials. Such examples point to how
a gendered anxiety consequently genders depictions of Pop-Culture Japan.

The History of Kawaii: Critical and Revisionist

While it is fair to suggest that state administrators have historically
viewed the nation through the frame of gender, it is also important to note
how these gendered frames have shifted. Tomiko Yoda has traced what she
sees as a series of metaphorical shifts in the way political elites have imagined Japanese society. For example, Yoda argues that a concept of maternal
society (*bosei shakai*) came to characterize ideologies of social management

in the late 1960s. These were later reconfigured into what was called the "enterprise society" (*kigyō shakai*) during the 1970s and 1980s (2006b, 240). More recently, she has seen yet another shift, with this maternal "metaphor of power and order" giving way to a "vogue of paternalism" (241). Yoda's critique is useful in showing how rhetorical abstractions of the national body rely on shifting models of gender in their articulation. Building on Yoda's analysis, I want to zoom in even more closely into those sites of central national administration where such metaphors are disproportionately produced and distributed in Japanese society. Considering the structure of Japan's historically male-dominated "bureaucratic system" (*kanri seido*), it makes sense to view policymaking as a fundamentally gendered activity, with the Ambassadors of Cute serving as an especially potent example of it. However, to be clear, I think this gendering of society can be read not only historically but also organizationally.

The very organizational structure of bureaucratic agencies can split services into differently gendered categories. For example, in Japan welfare and health services are often gendered as female, ascribing symbols of maternity to the notion of "society" (*shakai*); on the other hand, and in binary terms, agencies addressing foreign affairs and military are gendered as male, ascribing symbols of paternity to the "nation" (*kokka*) which is imagined in terms of its prestige and status.[9] In turn, the personified language of international relations that I described in chapter 1, such as in the example of Japan appearing in the eyes of officials as occupying the role of a wife in relation to a husband (figured in the United States), demonstrates how this gendered framework also engenders fears of emasculation among male officials. That conservative calls for Japan's restoration have also taken highly gendered tones is also suggestive of this framework, seen in literary works written by male politicians, such as Hayashi Yoshimichi's *The Restoration of Fatherhood* (*Fusei no Fukken*) (1996) and Ishihara Shintarō's *No Father, No Nation* (*Chichi nakushite kuni tatazu*) (1997). As Yoda (2006b, 240) demonstrates, these works exhibit a clear sense of male anxiety tied to Japan's political status, and call for Japan to become a stronger, more assertive, and thus more masculine nation.

Such accusations of the emasculation of Japanese society have become a common trope in Japanese literature on national character (*bunkaron*). They are often made in reference to Article 9 of Japan's postwar constitution, which renounces war as a sovereign right of the nation (Dower 1999, 394–98). Japan Studies scholar Dennitza Gabrakova (2018, 57) writes, "Ar-

ticle 9, connoting a conspicuous 'lack' in the political body, the renounce-
ment of military capacity . . . has been discussed often in gendered terms as
shameful castration." This trope of emasculation also features prominently
in Japanese popular culture. Christine Yano (2013b, 256) notes a particularly
stark example, identifying the legacy of a gendered imagination around
Article 9 in the contemporary popular art of Murakami Takashi:

> Calling Japan a "castrated nation-state" (Murakami 2005, 141),
> Murakami believes that Japan has anesthetized itself through two
> contradictory but intertwined aspects of popular culture: (1) hy-
> perviolence, such as monsters, explosions, Armageddon-like scenes
> of ultimate destruction; and (2) hypercuteness, in kawaii products
> and figures, such as Hello Kitty.[10] Murakami finds the conjoining
> of these twinned tendencies in the figure of the *otaku*, a much-
> maligned, nihilistic misfit-geek who fetishizes schoolgirls.

This "Cute-Cool" aesthetic that Yano sees in Murakami, so much a part
of Pop-Culture Japan, represents for Murakami the "revenge of the otaku
nation of Japan" (Yano 2013b, 256).

Where this male gendering of the national body intersects with Japanese cool and kawaii culture, it also lends itself to the refiguring of kawaii
aesthetics in Japanese history. Seeking to leverage cute aesthetics to political
expediency, some administrators have sought to naturalize kawaii culture as
an enduring legacy of the nation's traditional art history. Yamane Kazuma's
(1986) and Sharon Kinsella's (1995) historical accounts of the emergence of
kawaii aesthetics challenge recent efforts of certain politicians to ground the
aesthetics of Pop-Culture Japan in traditional culture. In a widely cited study
of Japanese subculture in recent history, Kinsella, drawing from Yamane,
traces the origin of Japanese cute to the practice of junior high and high
school students in the 1970s who started writing in a creative and feminized
script: "rounded characters with English, katakana and little cartoon pictures
such as hearts, stars and faces inserted randomly into the text" (Kinsella
1995, 2). The handwriting went by a number of names according to Kinsella,
such as "*marui ji* (round writing), *koneko ji* (kitten writing), *manga ji* (comic
writing) and *burikko ji* (fake-child writing)" (1995, 2). Associated with the
popularization of cute speech and baby talk in the 1970s and combined
with transformations in mass consumption habits, companies like Sanrio
began to capitalize on these new youth trends by offering so-called fancy
goods, the essential ingredients of which, says Kinsella, "are that [they are]

small, pastel, round, soft, loveable, not [a] traditional Japanese style but a foreign, . . . European or American style" (1995, 4). Consumers today recognize these qualities in Sanrio's most iconic commodity, Hello Kitty, the small white cartoon cat created in Japan but who, as her biography indicates, is originally from England and whose face now covers everything from toasters to assault rifles (Yano 2013b).[11]

Although these histories of kawaii aesthetics suggest that kawaii is a recent and globally interconnected phenomenon, administrators operating within the framework of Pop-Culture Japan have sought to locate its origins in the nation's traditional heritage. Two of Japan's recent prime ministers have made allusions to the continuum between Japan's traditional and contemporary popular culture. Asō Tarō, speaking at an event at Japan's Digital Hollywood University in 2006, before becoming prime minister in 2008, identified both traditional and contemporary pop culture as equally a part of a single national heritage:

> We continue to get the word out on Japan's truly splendid traditional culture, and we are very fortunate that in addition to the items of Noh drama and Bunraku, tea ceremony and flower arranging, Japan also boasts many newer forms of culture that have a high degree of appeal. This would be pop culture, including anime, music, and fashion among others, and the Ministry of Foreign Affairs is really going all out to "market" this, so to speak. (Asō 2006)

Former Prime Minister Abe Shinzō's address to the National Diet in 2007 even more directly integrated contemporary and traditional culture: "Japanese contemporary culture's coolness is founded in and derived from its traditional culture" (Abe 2007).[12] Similar statements were repeated to me numerous times in interviews with officials and administrators from multiple government agencies. This rhetoric linking Japan's contemporary popular arts to its traditional culture, contradicting narratives of popular culture provided by Kinsella (1995, 2000) and Yamane (1991), only grows more conventional with the plethora of publications trumpeting the "pop power" of Japan's "cool culture" (Koyama 2004; Hamano 2005; Nakamura and Onouchi 2006; Sugiyama 2006; Shima 2009; Sakurai 2009a, 2009b).

The Ambassadors of Cute program illustrates how projects that leverage the reimagining of history to political expedience can further embed gendered views into national cultural administration. Insofar as the future of the nation is seen as securable through the creation of Pop-Culture Japan, cute symbols of newly nationalized culture reinforce a link—in another manifestation of the affect-emotion gap's looping properties—between administrative anxiety and cultural uniqueness. Soft power policies thus promise to alleviate the former by reconfirming the latter. But what do such promises risk in the process? To what degree do soft power policy endeavors, fueled in part by male affects of geopolitical anxiety, wager cultural security on the commodification of young Japanese women? How much room is there in Pop-Culture Japan for the diverse subcultural expressions of girl culture, anime and manga fandom, and otaku identification? And what do administrators sacrifice by selling, or, in Laura Miller's (2011a) provocative articulation, "pimping" Japan through simplified and sexualized versions of these subcultures?

The Politics of Affect in Two- and Three-Dimensional Worlds

At the center of Pop-Culture Japan's gendered politics is a conflict over an overlapping set of representations of "young women/girls" (*shōjo*), "cute girls" (*bishōjo*), high school girls (*joshi kōsei*), and girl culture at large. In academic literature, this conflict manifests as a tension between, on one hand, studies that emphasize the creative imagination and sociological background of often—but not always—male creators and fans of anime and manga and, on the other hand, studies that consider the potential negative effects of shōjo representations on the stratification of gender in Japanese society. Given the enormous and ever-growing amount of academic literature on Japan's popular culture, any attempt to summarize these viewpoints risks simplifying what is multifaceted and nuanced work. As such, I do not offer a synopsis of prominent debates but rather look at how viewing them through the lens of affect sheds new light on the gendered politics of anxiety as it relates to the making of Pop-Culture Japan.

Guiding my inquiry is a curiosity about what kind of affective power administrators like those designing the Ambassadors of Cute project seek to tap into to advance Japan's cultural capital and what consequences such strategies bring about once their particular versions of kawaii culture are consecrated as tools of political diplomacy. As outlined by Yamane (1986); Ueno (1989); Kinsella (1985); Miller (2011a); Yano (2013b); Berndt, Nagaike, and Ogi (2019); Lukács (2020); and others, consumption practices surrounding kawaii fashion and goods in Japan incorporate a vast array of practices developed among and *for* young women. However, the Ambassadors of Cute program, designed and presented by men, invokes more specifically male-oriented practices of consuming images *of* young women. This raises concerns both inside and outside Japan on gender inequality, misogyny, pornography, censorship, and the freedom of expression and imagination. Cutting across these debates and inspiring much of their contention is a question posed in terms of dangerous affect—or in other words, of what somatic and nonconscious effects certain images of young women have on both men and women. As focusing on images alone is not, I think, ideal for framing an anthropological analysis of affect, I look briefly at how affect has been problematized in the recent history of anime and manga to provide context for better understanding the defense, critique, and affective consequences of the Cute Ambassadors program at large.

While there are contested timelines for tracing the story of how male fans began to take interest in manga written for young girls (*shōjo manga*), as well as in girl characters featured in these manga, also called *shōjo*, scholars like Ōtsuka (1991); Lamarre (2009); Condry (2013); Galbraith (2019); and others agree on some important landmarks. The most important of these begins with the shōjo manga boom in the 1970s. As Galbraith (2019, 23–24) explains, while mostly written by and for young women, men who felt marginalized by mainstream standards of masculinity at the time also found comfort in the alternative gender expressions of shōjo manga, as well as in related genres of Boys Love (BL) manga and fanzines.[13] As a growing consciousness of male fandom around these manga emerged, mostly through interactions at comic markets, artists began producing manga and anime with this new audience of both young and adult males in mind. During this period, key publications would later be recognized as critical to this transformation. Galbraith cites the female artist Takahashi Rumiko's manga *Urusei Yatsura* (Those Obnoxious Aliens, 1978–79), as well as the manga magazine *Manga Burikko* (Manga Girl, 1982–86), as important sources of a bishōjo aesthetic that catered to male fans, mixing elements of the cute (*kawaii*) and erotic (*eroi*) into a style of "cute eroticism" (*kawaii ero*). Importantly, it is also in the magazine *Manga Burikko* that the word *otaku* emerged for the first time to describe these male fans of anime and manga that felt affection for shōjo characters. Thus, while the word *otaku* today is used to refer to a wide variety of anime, manga, and character fans, it emerges at this time in the early 1980s specifically in the context of desires characterized as marginal, abnormal, problematic, and generally stigmatized.[14]

At the heart of the bishōjo aesthetic was a sensation described by male fans as *moe*, which comes from the verb *moeru* ("to bud," or, with alternative characters, "to burn").[15] The term describes not a quality found in girls but rather "the yearning desire to care for, or nurture, them" (Condry 2013, 191). Galbraith calls moe an "affective response to fictional characters" (2019, 82). Reflected in the term's homonymic versatility, moe is a polysemic and playful category, mixing sensations in response to bishōjo of affection, admiration, vitality, care, protection, and a desire that sometimes does and sometimes does not include erotic and sexual elements. Galbraith sees the crystalization of the bishōjo aesthetic in relation to moe illustrated best in *Manga Burikko*'s artistic transition under the editorial guidance of manga critic and scholar Ōtsuka Eiji in a critical period in 1983. Definitive of the magazine's shift, writes Galbraith, were three components: "the orientation toward fiction"; the decrease in "depictions of explicit sex"; and gender fluidity (2019, 43–44). Galbraith identifies in this third point an emphasis on experimentation with alternative gender identities that arguably overlap with queer identities as discussed by scholars like Eve Sedgwick and Jack Halberstam. He writes, "The bishōjo characters in *Manga Burikko* were not fetish objects drawn solely by and for men, but rather were the culmination of movement across gender/genre lines—of men consuming and then producing shōjo manga, women drawing for men, and the emergence of a space of fluid and hybrid expression" (2019, 43–44). Fiction and fantasy worlds thus offered spaces for experimenting with nontraditional gender roles and escaping from mainstream expectations.

Most importantly for Galbraith, this experimentation with alternative worlds and gender play depends on a critical distinction between the fictional world of anime and manga, sometimes also referred to by fans as "two-dimensional" (*nijigen*) worlds, and the less preferable "real," "human," or "three-dimensional" (*sanjigen*) worlds.[16] Galbraith takes enormous care in arguing that the power of fictional, two-dimensional characters in and on the nonvirtual, three-dimensional world is that "they are real and part of everyday life *as fictional characters*" (2019, 83). Such a finely drawn point is matched by Galbraith's expert demonstration of the "hazy" and "vague" (96) affects of moe and in the overlapping sensations of cute and erotic (*kawaii ero*), whose depictions can be seen in several of Japan's most famous male animators, such as Tezuka Osamu and Miyazaki Hayao. Many of these depictions predate the period in which the term *moe* became common. For example, Galbraith cites discussion of the "sexy poses" (*iroppoi pōzu*) and "erotic theory" (*iroppoi setsu*) surrounding Tezuka's *Astro Boy* (*Tetsuan Atomu*, 1952–1968) as early as the 1980s (86). He cites Miyazaki's infatuation with the young animated heroine of the first feature-length anime in color in Japan, *The Tale of the White Serpent* (*Hakujaden*, 1958): "And here I have to make a somewhat embarrassing confession. I fell in love with the heroine of this animated film" (Miyazaki 2009, 70, cited in Galbraith 2019, 95). Galbraith also discusses how erotic pleasure was folded into Miyazaki's adolescent heroines; for example, in an interview with the director in the *Nausicaä of the Valley of the Wind* (1984) companion book, when an interviewer states, "Nausicaä, the girl, is so attractive," Miyazaki responds, "Nasuicaä's breasts are rather large, aren't they?" (Miyazaki 2009, 338, cited in Galbraith 2019, 103). And in a critical passage from an essay from Miyazaki's collaborator Takahata Isao, which Miyazaki reportedly lauded, Galbraith captures particularly well the lively transmission, transmutability, and blending of erotic and cute, or "eroticute," as affect:

> [Miyazaki] wants to save beautiful young females from trouble . . . and he wants a young woman character to be so beautiful, sensible, action-oriented, and noble that he would like to suddenly embrace her. . . . And his feelings about his characters grow stronger and stronger, to the point where he finally becomes possessed by this or that young woman or monster that doesn't resemble him in the least. . . . He remains possessed by, and fuses with, his characters—to the point where the heightened fireworks of Eros that result actually transform his ideals into flesh and blood. (Takahata 2009, 456, cited in Galbraith 2019, 106)

As Galbraith demonstrates, cute aesthetics combine affects of erotica with a host of other feelings of cuteness, care, and affection, mixing and morphing, augmenting and amplifying each other across depictions that are both fictional, and, importantly, *as fiction*, real.

Granting this point on the reality of fiction *as* fiction, I suggest that an emphasis on moe and kawaii as affect also challenges the boundaries between characters as "real" and "real-as-fiction." As Ian Condry has argued, "The *moe* feeling should be seen not as a confusion of the virtual worlds and real worlds but . . . perhaps, as a question of whether there really is a distinction between virtual and real" (2013, 191). Building on Condry's point, I advocate for a granular approach, considering distinctions between the virtual and the real where they are contextually important, as Galbraith has carefully done in regard to the concept of fiction, and also considering where these distinctions break down, as I suggest they do in terms of affect. That is, what seems to me most powerful about the kind of affect theory discussed in this book's introduction is its ability to articulate how affect functions in a plane that is both virtual *and* real, conditioned through habits of exposure, consumption, and embodiment that do not so easily disambiguate between fictional and real worlds.[17]

As Galbraith concedes, the fantasy world that animators create and that fans consume condition lived experiences in the world. And this conditioning is in fact one source of Miyazaki Hayao's concern when in response to reports of otaku longing for his underage anime heroines, he says that it is "all 'pretend'—not 'real'—and should not be taken too seriously" (Galbraith 2019, 101).[18] The cultural grounding of this conditioning is keenly observed by another of Galbraith's interlocutors, the otaku scholar and popular writer Honda Tōru, who noted, "For kids of all backgrounds, manga and anime are part of growing up. You get used to seeing cute characters. Many people learn to draw them. The presence of these characters and attention paid to them is unique. Nowhere in the world are there cuter characters in greater numbers than in Japan" (Galbraith 2019, 94). Later, Galbraith (2019, 125) also cites Honda as stating that "*moe* has led to 'a new shared fantasy' (*atarashii kyōdō gensō*), which at least has the potential to affect reality" (Honda 2005, 173). This point highlights the critical cultural link between affect and shōjo representation in Pop-Culture Japan. If the potential real-world power of cute comes from the effects of exposure to its aesthetics over time, and if erotic and cute aesthetics are creatively combined through both industry conventions and fan practices of consumption and self-production, then perhaps questions on the politics of pop-culture consumption engendered by the Ambassadors of Cute program also need to address the real-world affective consequences of habitually reifying shōjo representations in spaces of public diplomacy.

This question on the broader social ramifications of shōjo representation generates an important point of concern for evaluating the gendered effects of Pop-Culture Japan. The concern has been articulated by feminist critiques of what Laura Miller (2011a, 27) calls "global otaku" culture, which is not without "violent and pornographic" components (2011b, 101), or what Azuma Hiroki (2001) calls "otaku nationalism" (cited in Miller 2011b, 102). Even if we grant that the world of imagination and fiction embeds its own rules of "as-if" experimentation, and even if we can compliment Galbraith and others for such rich and nuanced depictions of those worlds, we might add to this discussion further consideration of how affects generated through depictions of shōjo *transcend* two-dimensional worlds. Given that certain administrators and advisors promoting the Ambassadors of Cute see an affective power in the fantasy of shōjo that can be leveraged to improving the efficacy of public diplomacy, it is worth exploring how the gap between the feelings and meanings surrounding shōjo imagery can be operationalized for political gain.

The Unwieldly Affects and Effects of Administering Kawaii

While the genuinely diverse forms of kawaii aesthetics, shōjo and Boys Love manga, fanzines, and otaku and girl culture in Japan may afford affective experimentation in fantasy worlds rich with the potential for creative play and social critique, this is not the world of Pop-Culture Japan promoted by administrators in MOFA. As Miller (2011a, 23) states in her critique of the Ambassadors of Cute, "MOFA is . . . promoting fantasy-capital in which women and girls might be consumed as the objects of desire." Most problematically, its representations of girls are not "grounded in any particular street culture or girl's subculture." This leads to a "trivialization of girl culture, while also allowing us to deny that it could possibly contain forms of agency or power" (26). The presentation format of the Ambassador of Cute Kimura Yū described above supports Miller's critical analysis, but how do the administrators themselves perceive the affective power of kawaii in girl culture?

In the comments outlined at the start of this chapter from one of MOFA's former directors of its Public Diplomacy Department, it is clear that he is focused not on the affects of moe specifically but rather on the affective dimensions of publicity, good or bad, that the Ambassadors of Cute generate. His view is commensurate with theoretical critiques that note how affects carry their own power of intensity and amplification, creating "feedback" (Massumi 2002, 34) and cascading effects that amplify a general level of excitement. Given the mercurial and volatile qualities of such excitement, this is not affect that MOFA officials can manage and control, but it is nonetheless affect they can tap into and, in their own way, administer.

Giving an account in 2009 of how MOFA decided to start investing in kawaii culture, the special advisor to MOFA on matters of popular culture writes about visiting the locally produced Japan Expo in Paris in 2008:

> Until this time [of the Expo], the government had basically taken a hands-off approach to events like this, but this time I had come appointed [to the Expo] with the task of exploring how the government might get involved. At that time, ministry officials began to doubt how much longer they could ignore an event related to Japan at which 10,000 people were gathering. In various places around the world, events focused on Japanese anime and manga are taking place. Now it's not at all rare to find events with over 10,000 people taking place in every conceivable place on earth as if it were totally natural. Most Japanese people have until now known nothing about this fact. (Sakurai 2009b, 15–16)

Arriving at the Japan Expo in Paris as a representative of MOFA, special advisor Sakurai Takamasa was shocked at the level of attention Japanese culture was generating among visitors. Committed to fulfilling his assignment, he naturally viewed the variety of subcultural trends on display through the eyes of someone sensitive to their relevance not as objects of counterculture from Japan, a status that resonated with counterculture consumers in France, but rather as indicators of the attractiveness and hope-fulfilling potential of Pop-Culture Japan.

Officials have been increasingly attracted to events like the Japan Expo in Paris, which has occurred annually since 1999. It is organized by Specialists for Public Oriented Events (SEFA), a private public relations company in France that organizes conventions showcasing Japanese entertainment. The event hosts numerous booths displaying manga, anime, food, film, martial arts, and Japanese arts and entertainment. It features a cosplay contest, fashion show, music concerts, and several interactive displays. Attracting only 21,000 attendees in 1999, this number had grown to 164,000 in 2009, when the Ambassadors of Cute were dispatched. Although late to attract the attention of government officials, both the Ministry of Foreign Affairs and the Ministry of Economy, Trade and Industry now send representatives to the Expo.

Sensing an energy growing around Japanese popular culture, officials in MOFA and the Japan Foundation have since 2008 displayed increased interest in what happens at the event and made their own inquiries and reports. During my fieldwork, officials shared with me a video record of the event that was made by the Japanese media outlet MX TV, along with representatives from MOFA and METI. Over the course of the event, an anchor for MX TV wanders the Expo interviewing French attendees and seeking confirmation of their affection for Japanese popular culture. Although the interviewer seeks to connect fans of Japanese subculture to mainstream Japanese soft power, he is met with resistance. In an illustrative segment of the video, the interviewer speaks with Jean-Marie Bouissou, a political scientist and manga specialist at the Centre d'Études et de Recherches Internationales. Curious about the political implications of the event, the anchor asks what Bouissou thinks about the relationship between soft power and Japanese pop culture. Bouissou provides a somewhat pessimistic response:

> In 2007 and 2008 the EU Manga Network (administered by me) conducted a survey of 1,600 people focusing on their image toward Japan. Of these manga lovers, the majority still had an image of Japan as a very traditional culture, meaning manga had not become soft power. And within that group, there were also negative images of Japan (violence, a stressful society, a grueling work environment). Of course there were also views of Japan as being a very technologically advanced society, but this in no way seems to represent this Cool Japan.
>
> We also conducted a study among people who do not read manga. The result was that this group had a slightly more positive image of Japan. However, as this favorable impression has not seemed to change from before, it does not seem to be producing soft power, meaning that it doesn't justify Japan supporting soft power at the United Nations or on the international stage.
>
> The number of visitors to the Japan Expo is increasing every year . . . but I don't think one can say this is producing soft power. (Unpublished interview, Tokyo MX 2009; also see Bouissou 2008; and Bouissou et al. 2010)

Bouissou's response seemed to deflate the Japanese interviewer, despite no shortage of similar critiques of soft power that had already been circulating in academic circles (see Leheny 2006a; Otmazgin 2008; Watanabe and McConnell 2008; Daliot-Bul 2009). This kind of exchange between Japanese administrators, who are hopeful for positive reports on Japan's soft power, and foreign attendees at Japan-related cultural events, who are more interested in the details of Japanese subculture, is not uncommon. The gap in interests between the two parties represents a gap in the perceptions of what kinds of affective pleasure might be derived from the power of kawaii culture.

While anime and manga fans who find pleasure in the moe of bishōjo and kawaii express a broad spectrum of affections and articulate diverse reflections on those affections, and while female fans who take interest in bishōjo characters may do so out of interest in fashion, anime, manga, or the pleasures of countercultural parody and identity play, the Ambassadors of Cute represent the conflation of these interests into a publicizable brand name: "kawaii." That hopes for kawaii to generate soft power persist among MOFA administrators despite ample criticism of the ability to practically wield soft power reveals the anxious energy underlying pop-culture diplomacy efforts. While this anxiety may be tied to general male concerns "about actual adult women," as Miller (2011a, 22) argues, I suggest it more specifically connects to styles of caring administratively for the nation that are shared primarily among male bureaucrats. Despite explanations of the fictional basis for shōjo pleasure, there are also practical consequences for the linking of geopolitical anxiety to particularly male-oriented representations of shōjo. Most importantly, practices of representing and reproducing cute girls in Japan do not take place in gender-equitable space, materially or semiotically—a fact that suggests a number of unaddressed points on the gendering of Cool Japan via selective images of otaku and girl culture. First, while practices associated with otaku and girl culture may be equally diverse, they do not receive equal treatment in government representations of Cool Japan, with male-generated images of bishōjo such as the Ambassadors of Cute taking center stage. Second, although male, female, and gender-fluid styles of representing and consuming young women may incorporate challenges to mainstream gender expectations in Japan, the particularly "violent and pornographic" (Miller 2011b, 101) forms of those challenges may be disproportionately publicized and subsequently perceived as threatening by consumers identifying as female or gender fluid. Finally, while the male consumption of bishōjo imagery might in some forms afford experimentation and resistance to dominant gender norms, those experiments may also appear as much or more homogenous, as much or more pernicious, and as much or more stratified as mainstream gender conventions, such as those Galbraith (2009) and Miles (2019) ascribe to self-identifying "unpopular men" (*himote*).[19] While the creative imagination is celebrated in both main and minor streams of popular culture in Japan, government efforts to publicize certain versions of the otaku imagination over others largely favor male-centric views and values.[20]

Theorizing Affect with the Ambassadors of Cute

As a program targeting the anxious affect of mostly male administrators as much as the affect of overseas consumers of anime, manga, and girls' fashion, the Ambassadors of Cute project incorporates a therapeutic element into habits of administering affect. While the program may have lowered administrative anxiety and generated excitement around images of Pop-Culture Japan, the program also proved conducive to consecrating male fantasies of shōjo that leak into the real world and that underrepresent the diversity of girl culture as practiced in Japan. From the point of view of affect theory, the moe attached to fictional representations of Lolita or high school-uniform fashion, for example, do not stay semiotically confined to two-dimensional worlds. For the philosopher of affect Brian Massumi, and even for many of the affect theorists that disagree with aspects of his analysis, the body's response to images of Pop-Culture Japan, such as that of Ambassador of Cute Fujioka Shizuka who is depicted as a high school student (*joshi kōsei*), is automatic. While culturally conditioned and mutable based on patterns of exposure, ethical discourses, individual practices of attention and reflection, and social consensus, the response is nonetheless instant and intimate. Furthermore, the affective responses generated by varying depictions of bishōjo in, for example, shōjo manga, fanzines, weekly news magazines, pornographic magazines, mainstream anime, dating games, or VR simulations; an image of the Ambassador of Cute; the live Ambassador of Cute; or a young woman dressed in kawaii fashion are differently nuanced and context-dependent, but they are not neatly packaged into tight, affectively bound semiotic containers. They variously leak, blend, augment, temper, amplify, reverberate, and ripple out into a slippery social space that confronts a great many people exposed to the predominantly shōjo-styled symbols of Pop-Culture Japan.

This affective fact makes the politics and ethics of regulating representation a notoriously difficult endeavor, as no academic discipline or field of expertise can credibly claim to speak authoritatively for how images ultimately affect. Such an assessment is impossible not because scientific methods of critique are still being refined, but rather because the social world is always changing, with personal microhistories of experience always modulating what is possible in the relationship between an image's immediate impact and its subsequent effects—or in other words, within the affect-emotion gap. This means that the consumption of gendered media will always require a feminist critique of politics to evaluate what effects certain dominant representations engender as they reverberate throughout society.

In the Ambassadors of Cute, we see how a dominant form of representation is secured within shared but unequally contestable social spaces, as largely male authorities backed by the coffers of the state exercise the power to circulate and consecrate selective images of the nation. The affects of kawaii images in the shape of the shōjo and its associated affective histories of moe become an ambiguous but powerful site of political investment. While advisors and administrators in MOFA may not be interested in or able to identify what, precisely, it is about kawaii aesthetics that generates so much appeal, the appeal itself is of political importance. In fact, it is the very ambiguity and multiplicity of cute affect—the fact that there is no one-to-one relationship between a single item of kawaii fashion and its effect, but rather many of each—that makes the politics of kawaii so amenable to political expediency. Thus, it is the gap between *affect* (e.g., ambiguous feelings elicited by mixtures of erotic and cute aesthetics) and emotion-based *labels* of affect ("moe" or "kawaii") that engenders cute power as political resource. Affects surrounding kawaii culture are targeted for administration while official depictions of kawaii culture also operate on the anxious affect of administrators themselves, transducing anxiety into hope for Pop-Culture Japan. By investing discursively and materially in the affect-emotion gap through the creation of the Ambassadors of Cute program, administrators aim to turn the affective power of kawaii into the political power of Japan. Cute, in kawaii, becomes an asset of the nation; in turn, fans abroad who are attracted to kawaii aesthetics become in the eyes of administrators fans as well as resources of Japan.

At the same time, it is also the ambiguity of affect that enables not only the political appropriation of cute aesthetics but also the exercising of cute aesthetics as a form of counterpolitics. As scholars applying feminist perspectives to images of the shōjo in literature (Aoyama 2005), anime and manga (Choo 2008; Saitō 2014), art (Wakeling 2011), and popular media in general (Kotani 2007; Miller and Bardsley 2005) have illustrated, shōjo play serves up serious countercultural statements on patriarchy in Japanese society. In producing spaces by and for young women, as well as for nontraditional men, and in emphasizing a youthful, alternative femininity unaffected by the pressures of social roles in the obedient daughter (*musume*) or the doting wife/wise mother (*ryōsai kenbo*), shōjo culture resists male-scripted roles of adult femininity by challenging adulthood itself (see Wakeling 2011, 131). As former Ambassador of Cute Aoki Misako has recently made clear, she intends "never to quit Lolita fashion" (*isshō Rorīta yamenai*), crediting its power as "combative clothing" (*sentōfuku*) that can save one from images of a "negative self" (*negatibu no jibun*) (Minami 2019). Aoki's statement suggests that shōjo fashion can not only afford women spaces for self-determination but also empower women against those forces of social patriarchy that manifest as affectively harmful.

The political creativity and potency of shōjo culture that is made for and by young women, as well as for non-gender-conforming consumers, makes its appropriation by male administrators of MOFA in the late 2000s all the more important to investigate. While shōjo play has inspired and expanded the expression of nontraditional and nonbinary forms of gender, it has also been flattened out into generic packages of political appeal for Pop-Culture Japan. That shōjo play is flexible enough to serve the interests of subjects who are both resistant to and representative of the state's patriarchy attests to its potential as soft power resource. It also accounts for the willingness of the young women who took on the role of Ambassadors of Cute from 2008 to 2010.

To be sure, the playfulness and diversity of shōjo and kawaii culture allows those who express its forms to coexist with political and male-dominated appropriations of that culture in innovative ways. Aoki Misako's Lolita fashions, for example, have both invited and resisted sexualization in multiple ways and through various evolutions of a kawaii culture that is constantly changing (see Monden 2013). The other Ambassadors of Cute have similarly leveraged the playful adaptability of kawaii culture to their own benefit since the end of their term in 2010. Kimura Yū has created several new fashion labels, including KawaiiHolic and KOKOkim. Fujioka Shizuka has appeared in photo books featuring the evolving forms of her *nanchatte seifuku* style. She continues to model kawaii fashion in social media spaces and has appeared in commercials, TV variety shows, and on stage.[21] Looking at the trajectory of their public lives, the former Ambassadors of Cute appear consistently innovative and politically playful and parodic in their roles representing kawaii fashion both in and outside of government.

In comparing various actors' investments in kawaii culture and finding that kawaii culture affords commensurability with soft power politics in the process, it is also important to remember the diversity of those actors' interests. Just as otaku and kawaii culture fans make up a heterogenous collective, so too do those officials invested in Pop-Culture Japan. While some administrators see soft power programs like that of the Ambassadors of Cute as a natural remedy to national malaise, such perspectives are not reflective of Japan's cultural diplomacy at large. Given the power hierarchy of Japanese state agencies, however, in which MOFA holds substantial influence, the anxious nationalism characteristic of its administrative style of affect produces the top-down architecture of Pop-Culture Japan. But if the "public" that the Ministry of Foreign Affairs' Public Diplomacy Department represents is not only that of the "public official," and if it includes other and multiple non-governmental publics and "counterpublics" (Warner 2002), then one must also extend a view of the politics of kawaii representation beyond MOFA's perspective. In the next chapter I explore how MOFA's administrative style of caring for the nation impacts others outside government who feel affectively compelled to care otherwise and even challenge what Pop-Culture Japan represents.

5

Administering Affect

Anxiety and the Everyday

In previous chapters I argued that Pop-Culture Japan emerges as a recent national figure produced primarily within administrative structures of national cultural policy and that it is motivated by a geopolitical anxiety keenly felt among mostly male bureaucrats. I also argued that while many projects feeding Pop-Culture Japan seek to target the affects of overseas publics, in fact, these projects operate more centrally on the anxious affects of administrators at home that arise through geopolitical contests for recognition and soft power. In this chapter, I explore the effects of producing Pop-Culture Japan on subjects within Japan but outside its bureaucracy, and whose feelings, because they are not daily cultivated through obligations of national administration (see chapter 3), do not manifest neatly as hope as they do for many administrators. Instead, for these subjects, the gap between the images of Pop-Culture Japan and subjects' own sense of belonging in relation to those images produces feelings of indifference, confusion, alienation, and anxiety akin to the economic and social desperation that Anne Allison (2013) calls "precarity." In this sense, I analyze how the administration of anxiety in state agencies of culture ends up *administering*—or, in other words, distributing and circulating—anxiety on a broader scale.

This argument depends on the premise that state administration affects people outside it on an intimate level. To justify this premise, I illustrate how Japan's state bureaucratic structures permeate everyday life, albeit in a variety of uneven ways, by following affect along the lines of different state structures. This integration of the state and society in Japan has been observed by other scholars as well. In his study of the rationality and rituality of state administration, Brian McVeigh says the following about the relationship between central bureaucracies and the publics they affect:

> What is significant for my present argument is that the ministries have set the pace, tone, and standards not just for the more obvious aspects of modernization, but also for the rationalized, bureaucratized, and ritualized resonance of daily life in present-day Japan. I also contend that Japan's bureaucracies have taken advantage of and sustained sociopolitical arrangements that do not always distinguish clearly between public (state) and private (society) interests. Thus, much of Japan's bureaucratic power rests on its ability to segment, fragment, and categorize society (gender, interests, regional, national, etc.) as it sees fit, thereby weakening state-society distinctions. (1998, 72)

McVeigh's evaluation of how administrative bodies in Japan blur the boundaries between the state and the publics it serves is consistent with Hanada's (1997) and Hayashi's (1999) reading of the "public sphere" (kōkyōken) in Japan as a space that conflates the interests and thus the independence of the state and civil society. Such an arrangement facilitates administrative mechanisms that not only deliver national policy, as well as the narratives and imaginaries that come embedded within it, but also magnify the affective impact of policy's effects in everyday life.

Drawing this conceptual link between the state and the everyday requires an explanation of how I came to view this relationship through the course of fieldwork, as well as how cultural critics have recently theorized this connection. To reiterate, Pop-Culture Japan emerges out of a sense of political crisis perceived most poignantly by the state's politicians and bureaucrats. As a consequence, to the degree that the state is able to, as McVeigh frames it, "bureaucratize" and create a "ritualized resonance of daily life in present-day Japan," it is also able to make its own concerns those of broader publics. When state administration entered the anxious post-bubble era of the recessionary 1990s, this cast the experience of everyday life in Japan less as an effect of processes of modernization, urbanization, and shared experiences of city life and labor, much as the "everyday" was conceptualized in both European critical theory and Japanese historiography,[1] and more as a government-manufactured effect of what Tomiko Yoda calls "Japan in crisis" (2006a, 33). Building on the trends of the financialization of capital and the increase of both precarious and affective forms of labor discussed in the previous chapter, this crisis entangled global with local dimensions. As Lauren Berlant has argued in the context of the contemporary United States, which resonates with Anne Allison's (2013) description of "precarious" Japan, "The Euro-modernist concern with the shock of urban anomie and mass society" that characterized early theories of the everyday has given way to a recognition that things have changed. Today, the everyday for many in global cities is characterized by shared exposures to mass information and an affective "mass sensorium" (also see Mazzarella 2013) that accompanies it, "engendered by problems of survival that are public and that induce a variety of collective affective responses to the shapelessness of the present" (2011, 8). Ordinary life emerges here as "an impasse shaped by crisis in which people find themselves developing skills for adjusting to newly proliferating pressures to scramble for modes of living on" (2011, 8). As the economic pressures that cook the geopolitical concerns of Japan's political administrators mix with the economic pressures that pervade the everyday concerns of Japan's multiple publics, Pop-Culture Japan imagined as a tool of geopolitics manifests as a series of questions for those struggling to just get by: What is Cool Japan, exactly? What is the government's intentions with it? How is it relevant to me?

According to many of Japan's cultural critics, such as Miyadai Shinji, Azuma Hiroki, and Genda Yūji, after three decades of what has felt like a state of ongoing crisis, a sense of skepticism has emerged for many over the possibility that things in everyday life—especially if facilitated by government intervention—can actually change. While some government agencies seek to regenerate a hope lost to economic recession through popular culture, many of those working in mass media, art, and education that I take up in this chapter have begun reflecting on and theorizing a sense of unchanging hopelessness that the sociologist Miyadai Shinji (1995) has called the "endless everyday" (*owarinaki nichijō*). Miyadai describes a state of daily life that persists without an expectation for fulfilling one's dreams or an alternative future, which was more typical of Japan in the 1960s and '70s (Miyadai, Kono, and Lamarre 2011, 233). Rather than lament this condition, however, Miyadai advises his readers to embrace it, cultivating skills (*sukiru*) and wisdom (*chie*) to live within the everyday as a safeguard against overly hopeful ideologies and alternative futures and fictions that can through processes of imagination turn dangerously real, such as with the 1995 sarin gas attacks on the Tokyo subway.[2] Miyadai and other critics theorizing the everyday point to the difficulty of conceptualizing such a nebulous object while at the same time illustrating what is at stake in nonetheless failing to grasp its lived experience and effects.

One way to evaluate the efforts of the state to administer healthy affect in order to address the negative consequences of everyday crisis—even if this crisis was to some extent a product of the government's own "discursive manufacturing" (Yoda 2006a, 16)—is to think about policy's impact on a sense of citizenship and belonging (Stolcke 1995; Ong et al. 1996). McVeigh's observation on bureaucracy's ability to extend its structures of control into the intimate spaces of private lives suggests that the state plays a critical role for the way people think through their relationship to a national identity in a process that some scholars refer to as "cultural citizenship" (Miller 2002, 2007; Rosaldo 2003; Clarke 2013). Cultural citizenship refers to a sense of belonging or "cultural lineage" (Miller 2002, 231) cultivated through mediated representations, discourses, practices, and socialities both "outside of and in relation to . . . statecraft" (Clarke 2013, 464). Although the concept has received less attention under processes of increasing global interconnection, it can nonetheless help us conceptualize how state administration plays a role in securing links between government policy and its effects in everyday life through highly publicized and mediated forms of communication. In Dewey's terms, we might call these mediated forms through which people cultivate a sense of belonging "art," and its producers, in the most general terms, "artists."[3] Thus, it is largely through artistic means of representation and the forms of belonging associated with them that cultural citizenship emerges as an operative link that connects the practice of state administration, forms of cultural consumption, and everyday experience.

To understand how art, in Dewey's sense, helps bring publics or cultural citizens into being around certain problems, or what Latour (2005) calls "matters of concern," we need to consider how financial and political structures of administration contribute to the consecration of certain dominant representations over others.[4] Doing so reveals how forms of anxiety and hope generated by state discourses impact other subjects whose affects are also invested in representations of national culture. In other words, while state strategies of representation can cultivate a sense of national cultural belonging for some, for others it can equally draw lines of exclusion that mark some consumer practices as outside of or opposed to an evolving figure of the nation. Considering McVeigh's claim that much of public culture in Japan flows from the top down through government administrations to those sites of the everyday that administration impacts, I trace a path by which the rhetoric of Pop-Culture Japan exercised in practices of administration affects life outside it, inviting, interpellating, and at times irritating subjects. However, convinced by fieldwork that this process does not unfold in a uniform manner, I consider Pop-Culture Japan's varying effects through three different sectors of society: mass media, artists and content producers, and higher education.

Mass Media

Japan's press club (*kisha kurabu*) system has long been regarded as a major institution through which government establishes influence and standardizes discourse. In Japan, news organizations do not compete equally for information but are granted or denied formal access to government briefings through passes allotted by each ministry. The Ministry of Foreign Affairs, for example, must grant an organization like the *Asahi Shimbun* (Asahi Newspaper) access for its journalists to attend briefings where information is disseminated according to a fixed schedule. While evaluating and conferring press credentials is a common component of organizing relations between states and media in liberal democracies, Japan's system has been characterized as notoriously rigid, producing a culture of self-monitoring and restraint (*jishuku*) that results in dramatically uniform reporting across news organizations (Hall 1998). Such a system limits access to government press officials to a small number of long-standing news agencies whose staff have cultivated a congenial rapport with ministry personnel. Investigative journalism and opinion pieces highly critical of government are rare in Japan's major newspapers. Government and press in Japan, thus, have established a cooperative and reciprocal relationship that is criticized equally by scholars of media both in and outside Japan (Kawasaki 1997; Hall 1998; Krauss 2000; Kawasaki and Shibata 2004).

NHK, Japan's public broadcaster and producer of the show *Cool Japan*, which I discussed at length in chapter 2, has been similarly criticized for its close relationship to government (Kawasaki 1997; Kawasaki and Shibata 2004). A story told to me and then later published by a prominent cultural studies scholar of Japan, Koichi Iwabuchi, illustrates how such proximity can facilitate the imposition of nation-centered discourses on otherwise cosmopolitan, transnational, and politically progressive perspectives on popular media. Iwabuchi begins his story by explaining how encouraged he was at reading a 2006 newspaper article stating that the Koizumi cabinet was looking to create new television channels within Japan that went beyond the usual programming in Japanese and English, providing broadcasts in Korean, Chinese, Portuguese, Spanish, Tagalog, and Thai. Iwabuchi writes, "I remember thinking after reading that article, wow, finally, even Japan can construct a media environment that respects the diversity of its multiple peoples" (2007, 114). The prime minister's office seemed to be finally getting the message of the need for more culturally diverse broadcasting, which Iwabuchi and other prominent academics had long been advocating. However, Iwabuchi's optimism deflated at reports of subsequent meetings:

> What I was shocked at was that the point of view emphasizing the importance of providing broadcasts in languages other than Japanese for foreign residents of Japan was at later cabinet meetings suddenly supplanted by the view emphasizing the importance of transmitting media from Japan to the world. . . . The Ministry of Foreign Affairs then quickly set up a foreign ministry advisory committee with the theme "strengthening Japan's transmission power" [*Nihon no hasshinryoku kyōka*] in order to discuss such things as policies to enhance NHK's international broadcasts. The committee was called the "Council on Foreign Relations" [Kaigai Kōryū Shingikai] and it invited the vice chairman of Toyota, Fujio Chō, to serve as the council's chairman. As former Foreign Minister Asō Tarō's words made perfectly clear—"It is important for the common people of foreign countries to have an understanding and a positive image of Japan. Shouldn't it be appropriate to have this done through foreign broadcasts of NHK like the BBC and CNN?"—what was being aimed for was to deepen an understanding of Japan through information and image transmission, and to build Japan's image in the world by tying this to Japan's interests on the political and economic front. However, the provision of a public broadcasting service for the various people living in the country and the transmission of information to the world for the aim of procuring "Japanese understanding" fundamentally differ. In this way the development of this debate suddenly twisted. (2007, 114–15)

Iwabuchi's story demonstrates how easily certain aims, projects, and discourses of administration can be transposed into different ideological registers. Early cabinet meeting discussions seemed to have taken place in a register of transnationalism and multiculturalism that aimed to transcend (*kokkyo o koeru*) the narrow framework of thinking in terms of a nation's interests (*kokueki*). From Iwabuchi's perspective, increasing the amount of coverage on foreign issues could help generate an international outlook that would open spaces for the emergence of a transnational consciousness in East Asia—a step that would go a long way in finally overcoming Chinese and Korean resentment rooted in memories of the Pacific War. Upon formation of the Council on Foreign Relations, however, the suggestion to increase international coverage was transformed into a plan to broadcast Japanese issues to an international audience. "Taking in" (*ukeire*) news from abroad was transposed into "transmission" (*hasshin*) as a coveted concept for public diplomacy framed in terms of soft power, one principle of which advocates that leaders target audiences with content and messaging from the broadcasting country in order to transform overseas publics imagined as soft power resources into political power.[5]

Following up on the council's recommendations, NHK began in 2009 refitting its sister corporation, NHK World, to increase coverage of Japan to foreign markets. Two of its five new mission points were "to present broadcasts with great accuracy and speed on many aspects of Japanese culture and lifestyles, recent developments in society and politics, the latest scientific and industrial trends, and Japan's role and opinions regarding important global issues" and "to foster mutual understanding between Japan and other countries and promote friendship and cultural exchange" (NHK World 2011). NHK World's flagship news program, *Newsline*, began broadcasting thirty minutes in English every hour on the hour to an increasing number of foreign locations, mostly within the Asia-Pacific region, aiming to compete not only with the BBC and CNN but also with agencies in China, South Korea, Singapore, and Australia.

As seen in Iwabuchi's account, discussions over what constitutes the ethical responsibility of a public broadcaster can be coopted for national interests. Through top-down deliberation, debates on what kinds of programming serves the needs of an increasingly diverse public are taken over by soft power thinking that legitimizes strategies that optimize the nation's interests, as defined by its most senior administrators. As Hanada (1997) and Hayashi (1999) argue, the nation (*kokka*) and the notion of an idealized public space (*kōkyōsei*) have long been conflated through the idea of the *kokumin* (literally, a "country's people") in Japan's modernity.[6] The reorganization of NHK World toward the purpose of increasing the presence of Japanese content in foreign media markets reveals how much the framework of soft power has been accommodated to fit existing bureaucratic structures. In reality, measuring the degree to which shows like *Newsline* and *Cool Japan* actually impact foreign viewers and thus build soft power is, as Jean-Marie Bouissou (2008) and other scholars of nation branding have illustrated, nearly impossible (also see Anholt 2007, 2013; Dinnie 2008; Watanabe and McConnell 2008; Aronczyk 2013; Snow 2016). However, although it is difficult to trace the actual impacts of soft power, one can nonetheless trace the influences that soft power and nation branding discourses have on local publics by focusing on the themes, concerns, and feelings that arise in conversation on "Cool Japan" endeavors—a topic I return to in the following section.

As Iwabuchi writes on this incident a few years later, "Cultural diplomacy maneuvered in conjunction with nation branding is not only directed externally, but also internally, as a tool for inculcating a narrative of the nation and a sense of national belonging" (2015, 427). His point illustrates an important connection between public diplomacy efforts and their effects on cultural belonging and citizenship. I opened this book with a press release about NHK's documentary series "Overcoming the 'Japan Syndrome.'" Shortly after the press release, the executive director-general of Broadcasting at NHK, Imai Tamaki, elaborated on the show:

> "Japan Syndrome" is the name that has been given by the Tomorrow's Japan project team at the News Department to describe the malaise that afflicts the nation. It refers to the loss of confidence and anxiety among large numbers of people in Japan. The nation is experiencing a falling birth rate, a greying population, a shrinking workforce, and the pressures of global competition. The ensuing economic and social malaise has shaken long-held values, and seen youngsters withdraw into themselves, and diluted family and community ties, which in turn has manifested itself in various ways, such as the atomizing of society and the numerous elderly people who have seemingly vanished without anybody knowing or caring about their whereabouts. Starting from the New Year, the News Department will focus on the Japan Syndrome and offer prescriptions and ways of overcoming it. (NHK 2011b)

As scholars of Japan have been arguing for years (Genda 2005; Leheny 2006b; Miyazaki 2006; Allison 2013), a sense of vague insecurity has been circulating in Japan during and after Japan's two lost decades (1990–2010) of economic stagnation. And despite former Prime Minister Abe Shinzō's highly touted "three arrows" of economic reform that was designed to finally lift Japan out of economic depression, media organizations are nonetheless speculating on whether Japan has just witnessed its third lost decade and whether it is headed for a fourth.[7]

Although a sense of economic precarity is widely discussed in Japan, it is important to distinguish it from the kind of geopolitical anxiety administrators experience over national culture and that is ultimately transformed into hope for Pop-Culture Japan, even if these two feelings of anxiety feed into and intensify each other. While economic precarity pervades Japanese labor sectors on a mass scale, geopolitical anxiety fueling Pop-Culture Japan is more directly circulated among state administrators, produced through a sense of geopolitical threat, and fostered through administrative obligations to care for the state. While economic precarity and geopolitical anxiety may feel similarly unsettling in bodies and thus make disambiguation through conceptual distinctions difficult, the reification of anxiety by labelling it in emotional language—in other words, by moving across the affect-emotion gap—renders each discourse perceptible through distinct symbols, narratives, and emotional lexicons (Frevert et al. 2014). I suggest we need to pay as much attention as possible to these granular shifts of affect if we are to understand how a politics of anxiety ultimately distills into uniform national narratives. That certain national narratives such as Cool Japan can be produced in agencies of government, circulated freely in media, and then widely taken up by academics as given objects of sociological analysis—not exempting my own—makes affect's gradations even more critically important to discern.

Despite these two different assemblages of anxiety in Japan—one of economic precarity and one of geopolitical cultural anxiety—soft power shows the potential to conflate the two, appropriating economic precarity to warrant the claims of an administratively produced Pop-Culture Japan. Under this logic, one's personal financial concerns are increasingly imagined and experienced in national and at times even nationalist terms. With series like the "Japan Syndrome," NHK operates as the storyteller of the nation, narrating people's personal concerns through the eyes of administrators connected closely with government. Such programs serve as a mechanism for moving from the affective to the emotional end of the affect-emotion gap, translating Dewey's ([1927] 1954, 131) "indirect" and "felt" consequences into publicly "perceived" sentiments. Although documenting the numerous responses to such programs would demand a separate research project of its own, the repetition of anxiety-themed programming in public broadcasting reveals the degree to which anxiety (*fuan*) and insecurity (*fuantei*) have become naturalized as common components of Japan's modern national character. In the next section, I consider creators, designers, and content producers whose work has not been specifically consecrated by Cool Japan discourses but who nonetheless feel obliged to reconsider their work in relation to it and to the increasingly dominant representations of Pop-Culture Japan.

Artists and Content Producers

In chapter 1, I discussed how despite the government's hopes that the nation's content industries might jump-start Japan's stagnating economy, economic reports from as early as 2005 show a plateau and in some cases even a decline in markets for popular media commodities (Kawamata 2005; Kawashima 2018; Oyama 2019; METI 2020a). However, statistics communicate little about the perceptions and effects surrounding soft power. In this section I explore how government-sponsored hopes for Pop-Culture Japan are received among minor and aspiring content producers.

In October 2009, the Ministry of Economy, Trade and Industry (METI), in conjunction with the Japan Licensing Association, organized a trade show called Tokyo Contents Market and Licensing Asia, which has since developed into a larger convention called Content Tokyo. The event assembled creators and licensors in a single venue in hopes of stimulating partnerships between industry and the arts. The program was created within METI's Creative Contents Division, whose director I discussed in chapter 1. The METI event took place at the iconic convention center called Big Site, in Tokyo's Odaiba, where some of the nation's biggest conferences, trade shows, and other events are held throughout the year—including Japan's iconic Comic Market, colloquially known as *Komike*. I paid the equivalent of US$12 for a pass to the two-day event and entered a spacious hall only moderately filled with small booths and stations. The hall was split down the middle with creators on one side and licensors and advertisers on the other, including major companies like Dentsū and Hakuhodo.[8] Participants in the show apply to METI for the chance to feature their artwork, with the ministry selecting those evaluated to have the most market potential. The atmosphere was easygoing and fun, with "soft characters" (*yuru kyara*), animated mascots that accompany a majority of Japanese products, companies, and events in Japan, populating the space in bright colors and multiple shapes.

I moved through the convention space from booth to booth, speaking with many of the participants about their hopes for the event and their thoughts about Japan's content industries. Many of the creators expressed gratitude to the ministry for sponsoring the event, as they have few opportunities in general for exposure to licensors. The creators I spoke with primarily saw themselves as artists who simply wanted to find an economically viable way to pursue their art. As a consequence, although few showed explicit interest in the government's investments in popular culture, most all of them had heard of its recent nation branding endeavors and generally welcomed them.

A typical participant in the event was a creator I call Ishikawa, who works for a company that produces animated graphics for movies and anime.[9] The company, like many of those in attendance, also does character design. Early in the conversation Ishikawa used the phrase "soft power" (*sofuto pawā*) in describing his work. He explained that he had heard the phrase used by a government official on the news about three or four years ago and, at that point, realized that Japan actually had a significant amount of charm (*miryoku*) abroad. Ishikawa was happy (*ureshii*) to learn recently that Japanese pop culture is popular overseas. This description, "*ureshii*," was by far the most common answer to the questions I asked about the circulation of Japanese popular culture abroad. Ishikawa compared Japan's case to South Korea, saying he hoped the Japanese government would support creators like Korea does: "*Yatto, mitai na kanji*" (It's a feeling like, it's about time!).

Another participant, whom I call Sasaki, works for a company that produces "ultra low-resolution painting." His work received one of the awards distributed by METI that recognizes particularly creative projects. Sasaki expressed a recognizably cosmopolitan outlook on government support for the arts. "I have no interest or pride as a Japanese or in the status of Japan in the world," he said. "I would use *Japan* in my work only if the name happened to sell, if it had the power to sell as some kind of representative or evocative image of Japan. But I don't care if I'm Japanese, Chinese, or American, whatever." Simplifying his point, Sasaki offered the example of how a hundred-yen bag ($1.10 at the time) can sell for 1,500 yen ($17.00) due to the brand name. "For Japan, this is the *only* way to compete in the world as China can always win on selling cheap items. Japan only has its contents [*kontentsu*]." Sasaki seemed far less focused on Japan surviving in the world than on surviving as an entrepreneur, a point that highlights the fractures between an administratively imagined Cool Japan and the meaning it has for creators. Although he considered that some of his colleagues might hold more enthusiastic feelings for the status of Japan in the world, he did not hear them expressed very often. "Perhaps we really need a crisis like a sinking Japan," he said, alluding to Komatsu Sakyō's famous 1973 science fiction novel *Japan Sinks* (*Nihon chinbotsu*), "in order to be able to evoke what national sentiments exist on nonconscious levels." Sasaki was familiar with the phrase *soft power* and interpreted it as an economic strategy, Japan's "only choice" to compete economically.

Another company participating in the fair was a computer graphics technology firm specializing in virtual reality technology for the medical education industry. They also work in open source software, 3D printing, computer vision, robotics, and motion capture. The company's founder, Hayashi, is in his early forties and, as he enthusiastically explained, a high school dropout. He is fond of Arthur C. Clarke and offered a favorite quote: "Any sufficiently advanced technology is indistinguishable from magic." The phrase is printed at the top of all the company's information pamphlets. His booth was significantly more decorated than the others, in an eclectic and tacky (*hade*) style that could equally have been a genuine attempt at playful product design or a lighthearted parody of it. Wine and plastic-wrapped cheeses were served, and an inflatable moose head adorned one of the booth's walls.

Reflecting on the relationship of his business to the nation, Hayashi compared his marketing strategy to war, where one can sell weapons to both sides. He quickly reformulated the statement, however, somewhat embarrassed at the analogy. He admitted he was disappointed in Japan's system of supporting creators because "there is no copyright protection and no [government] budget, so we can't compete with the United States." Hayashi has given up on going to a yearly licensing conference in the US that he had attended for the last fourteen years and now focuses just on technology. He said Japanese companies have creative computer graphics technologies but no budget. He added that the event's sponsorship by the Ministry of Economy was helpful because he had few chances to meet other clients on his own.

Yet another company at the event specialized in illustrations, character design, flash media, and web design. It is run by a young man, Miyazaki, who was inspired by Hanna-Barbera's characters. Miyazaki had not paid much attention to the government's Cool Japan campaigns but said quite brightly, "If we can spread our content through it, why not?" Indeed, he hoped that people abroad would take an interest in Japanese popular culture. Miyazaki, like Sasaki, showed little interest in economic competition on a national level. He did not feel threatened by US dominance in media markets like Hayashi did. He had no problem with Hollywood and Disney, saying that animation was a common medium for creation, which is a good thing. "If Japan can participate in that field, then great!" He also showed little concern for how anime was perceived overseas. "Animation is just one form of artwork [*sakuhin*], like Pixar. We should just enjoy it as such."

On average, creators and licensors alike showed little concern for Japan's economic status relative to other countries in the world. For the most part, it only concerned them insofar as it either facilitated or stifled their chance to build a business and thus a life out of their art. Such findings are consistent with the distinction I drew earlier between registers of economic and national anxiety, the latter being more characteristic of government administrators whose job it is to support Japanese industry at large. For administrators, economic success and cultural anxiety become fused under a rhetoric of soft power that imagines pop culture as an antidote to a seemingly nationwide malaise. For creators I spoke with, however, art has little to do with national status or prestige.

Although the Contents Market represents a site where government bureaucracy under a soft power logic intervenes administratively into the relationship between culture and economy, there is little evidence to suggest that soft power ideology directly affects creators' decisions in regard to their art. In general, the only site where an explicit ideological formation of soft power *did* seem to bear on the work of these creators was in its role as interpellator (Althusser 1972).[10] In other words, the term *soft power* obliged artists to reframe their art in relation to its status as culturally "Japanese" where they had not considered the point before. In the same way that several (often female) officials at the Japan Foundation express uneasiness at the pairing of kawaii culture and national identity to which they feel pressure to respond (see Maeda's comments in chapter 1), some artists feel the pressure to contextualize their work in response to an increase of government interest in the fields of anime, manga, and video games.

I spoke about this concern with a Japanese sculptor. Shigematsu Hisashi is not by many measures a well-known or well-publicized artist, but at the time of our meeting in 2009, he did have a growing number of patrons from Japan and a few from abroad. He was forty-eight years old at the time we first spoke. Eight years prior he had quit his job as a "salary man" (*sararī man*) for a public relations company to devote his attention to art full time. He is gentle and humble but also outgoing, and when talking about his art and the inspiration for it, he becomes increasingly animated. He cares deeply about his work. He also cares deeply about the state of Japanese society and the sense of malaise that he thinks increasingly characterizes it. His art gives this malaise a tactile palpability. He works mostly in clay that is the color of gray ash. And in fact, it is this ash color (*hai'iro*) that he thematizes in his work. In the introduction to his *Ash* series presented in Yokohama in June 2009, Shigematsu (2011) writes:

Gray is something difficult to express
As a color close to black it expresses darkness
As a color close to white it resembles crushed bones
At the base of all the colors there is gray
Color expresses happiness, anger, sadness and sorrow
But gray expresses nothing
Gray has only silence.

In this series Shigematsu sculpts life-size human figures out of desolate ash-colored clay. One work in the series shows an aging couple seated at a traditional Japanese hearth, the color and texture of their bodies the same as the ash of the fire at their feet. Another figure is of a boy, lying almost flat on his back, with his head propped up just enough by a wall to let him see the TV screen on which he is playing a video game. The boy and the washed-out picture on the TV are the same gray. Next in the exhibition is a drunken salary man, the gray color of both his face and suit matching that of the vomit he has just expectorated on the sidewalk. Another figure, a woman, is at a desk with her head slumped over her arm, exhausted and asleep. She holds in her hand an open cell phone—the screen, again, gray.[11]

Shigematsu described to me at length how he imagined the installation. The dreariness and evacuated affect represented in some of the work and expressed in his line "Gray has only silence" contrasts with the passion that animates his vocal criticism of contemporary Japanese society. Shigematsu bemoans the attenuation of human ties and face-to-face communication he sees as characteristic of contemporary Japan, a condition often referred to as "connectionless society" (*muen shakai*). And he laments what he sees as a consequential lack of empathy. He also regrets what he described as an ahistorical consciousness among Japanese, expressing admiration in our conversation at an exceptional young girl from Okinawa he recently saw on TV who was advocating for protecting the war memories of Okinawa's elderly. Shigematsu expressed disappointment that there seemed to be no desire in people today to carry on traditions from the past nor motivation to impart them to future generations, a feeling he thought especially lacking in Japan and that distinguished it from other countries. He blamed Japan's contemporary malaise on a culture of self-contempt resulting from the war, specifically instilled through the public shame of the International Military Tribunal for the Far East (Kyokutō Kokusai Gunji Saiban). Shigematsu once wrote to me in an email, "From the Meiji Restoration forward Japan had a wonderful culture and traditions. However, since the Tribunal, all of it, everything seemed to vanish like mist [*unsan mushō*]! What was left was only historical masochism." Shigematsu considers this new Japan born after the Pacific War only sixty-five years old, a short but thoroughly disappointing period compared to the nostalgic portraits through which he imagines his country's history.

In bringing up Japan's contemporary popular culture—its anime, manga, and the government's branding of it in Cool Japan campaigns—the patient and pleasant Shigematsu closed his eyes, seeming to suffer viscerally from his consideration of the topic. After a pause and a deep breath, he tells me that he knows all about it and is troubled at what he sees as a steady inundation of all things pop into a more diversely and richly composed field of Japanese art. He mentions the artist Murakami Takashi—the representative of Super Flat mentioned in the previous chapter—as an example of how art has become commodified to extreme degrees in the present. However, Shigematsu is less concerned about the commodification of art than he is about its inundation by images of Cool Japan. Artists like Murakami, he clarified, do not influence or affect his own art, which he is happy to pursue while feeling little pressure to acquiesce to market demands. But he bemoaned the conflation of Japanese culture with anime and manga that he sees celebrated in Murakami Takashi's work and expressed by officials. In a voice heavy with lament but calmed by what appeared as a practiced patience he said, "I want to ask these officials, is that really all Japan is?"

Shigematsu experiences the images of Pop-Culture Japan—of which Murakami Takashi's work is representative for him—viscerally. They seem to produce in him a disappointed feeling tone that he experiences just slightly too intensely to be called malaise. The intensity is, after all, irksome enough to compel him to action—to produce his art. Like a few of the other artists I spoke with and like a great many of the eclectic groups of creators, business executives, and other people with whom I spoke about Cool Japan in Tokyo's endless alleyways of small bars and eateries, Shigematsu does not take the government's support of popular culture very seriously. He does not feel much connection with it nor recognize his values reflected in its images. In these sites of government-sponsored representations, the state, from Shigematsu's perspective (and in social philosopher Ernest Gellner's [1983] terms) fails to secure a particular image of the nation for which one feels affinity. The result is a sense of alienation from those political representatives and bureaucratic administrators of state affairs stereotypically criticized, both in Japan and elsewhere (Herzfeld 1992), as inept and emotionally detached from average citizens.

It may not be fair to cite Shigematsu's attitude as indicative of a widely spread cultural ostracism due to Pop-Culture Japan. Perhaps the most imposing case of interpellation he experienced, in fact, came from me. However, I suspect these moments of dissonance take place far more often than official or typical academic accounts of Cool Japan suggest they might. I suspect this moment of interpellation happens with Shigematsu each time he hears a story about Cool Japan or soft power—or a government proposal to fund a manga and anime museum (see chapter 1). I assume this because of Shigematsu's physical response to my question about Cool Japan: the closed eyes, the deep sigh, and the palpable displeasure his body, voice, and words expressed. Such a physically troubling response was not likely generated by my question alone. What this indicates, I think, is that the particular register of bureaucratic anxiety out of which excitement over soft power is produced has very different effects outside government. It certainly produces in many subjects a kind of hope similar to that experienced by government administrators. But for many others, it engenders a sense of disconnection between the official and the everyday citizen, even to the extent of eliciting embarrassment or modest disgust. The narratives of nationalism circulated among officials in response to global pressures and perceived at the same time to be both in line with and in the service of Japanese publics can also at times evoke further anxiety over the status of Japanese culture. In this way, anxiety proliferates in processes of its administration. Under conditions like these, state policy does not touch people in daily life directly, like a dial administering a voltage of national hope, but rather like a winch raising a precarious load up a hill, steadily torquing sentiment against administrators' best intentions.

Higher Education

Given the proliferation of Cool Japan discourses through government and media, it is no wonder that academic accounts of it, in addition to the already increasing studies of Japanese popular culture in general, have been on the rise the last two decades. Where Japan's decreasing population of young people has pressured universities to compete for both domestic and international students, programs featuring popular Japanese culture have often served as strategies to broaden appeal. While these courses take many different forms, some fitting quite squarely within established curriculums, others are more clearly the product of a new consciousness surrounding Pop-Culture Japan. In 2010 I took part in a four-day "field research program" at a prestigious university in Tokyo, which I keep anonymous for the sake of collegiality. The course syllabus for the program states the following: "Some say that in the 21st century, Japan should make its living by its 'soft' industries. This year we will visit some sites of anime production, observe the manufacturing process for these products and consider the new support industries that form the back-up for anime production." The course was run by two instructors in the school's Department of International Relations and invited a number of guest lecturers from the field of anime and manga. The course also included a trip to an anime production studio, where participants could observe and speak with artists and producers.

Although the course included Japanese students among its forty-some participants, it was overwhelmingly attended by Chinese, Korean, and Southeast Asian students coming from those countries often identified as composing Japan's regional political economic bloc of "Japanese popular culture in Asia" (Otmazgin 2013). By sharing some experiences from the course, I illustrate the general assumptions upon which a framework for understanding Japan's "soft industries" was constructed.

In one notable experience, a Japanese media studies expert on anime and manga was invited to give a guest lecture to the class. He described the general state of the anime industry in Japan, noting economic challenges the industry and its employees faced. Demonstrating what he characterized as an increasingly dilapidated state of anime production studios, the lecturer showed a slide indicating the growing number of illustrator jobs that were being sent overseas, most specifically to China and South Korea. The purpose of the slide was, first, to demonstrate the increasing loss of profit in the industry to overseas markets through foreign distributors and, second, to show how insufficient capital within the industry resulted in comparatively low wages for Japanese employees. This example was just one of many provided in the class to illustrate the current challenges facing Japanese industries and to stimulate ideas among students on how to address and overcome them.

The assumption on which this and other similar case studies in the course relied is that international students should be concerned with revitalizing "Japanese" industries and note the dangers of industry jobs being sent overseas—in some cases to the very countries that these students called home. The instructor's presentation of the case of outsourcing within the manga industry was particularly revealing of this assumption, as the example, somewhat insensitively I felt at the moment, asked Chinese and South Korean students to think how Chinese and South Korean jobs could be returned to Japan. Given that the course was offered by an international relations department, and not the university's economics department or business school, the lecturer's point seemed to lack some critical distance. Additionally, that the global dimensions of a "national" company or industry were left unproblematized by the speaker, despite the multinational composition of many content production studios, seemed to cast the lecturer's point within a logic of soft power that imagines the role of Japan's content industries as an engine for driving a singularly "Japanese" economy.

In a related example, concluding the course was a final essay assignment with a simple instruction: "Offer your analysis on how Japanese industries can be revitalized for the 21st century." Subsequently, Chinese, South Korean, and a host of other students from various countries set out to strategize how Japan could best build its content industries, precisely the approach taken by Japan's Ministry of Economy, Trade and Industry in realizing a strategy of soft power cultivation streamlined to stimulate economic growth.

The course I took on Japan's soft industries provides one example for the ideological alignment of industry and higher education in some newly established academic departments in Japan. This alignment channels narratives of Pop-Culture Japan into education, which is welcomed and reproduced by some and resented and rejected by others. Many of these departments have emerged out of the Ministry of Education's investments in internationalizing its universities. For example, the department in which I took the fieldwork course discussed above is part of one of thirteen universities in Japan receiving funding from the Ministry of Education's Global 30 Project, which ran from 2009 through 2014. The program's purpose was stated as follows:

> The Ministry of Education, Culture, Sports, Science and Technology has launched the "Global 30" Project for Establishing Core Universities for Internationalization, for the purpose of selecting universities that will function as core schools for receiving and educating international students. In 2009, thirteen universities were selected. These core universities will play a major role in dramatically boosting the number of international students educated in Japan as well as Japanese students studying abroad. (MEXT 2009)

The key word *Internationalization* (*kokusaika*), as Roger Goodman (1990, 2007) has extensively documented, has played a central role in higher education for the last three decades in Japan. In combination with subsequent and related terms such as *globalization* (*gurōbaruka*) or *global* (*gurōbaru*), *internationalization* functions as an operative term organizing and guiding an array of programs that claim to open Japan to the world and make it more competitive internationally. Given Japan's declining workforce and the increase in the elderly population stretching the state's pension system to its limits, welcoming foreign workers to Japan has been proposed as one inevitable if also largely begrudged solution. Increasing the number of foreign students to Japan through education facilitates this aim in part while also increasing university revenue. As the same announcement from MEXT cited above states,

> Japan formulated the 300,000 International Students Plan in July of 2008, with the aim of receiving 300,000 international students by 2020. The "Global 30" Project for Establishing Core Universities for Internationalization is being implemented to realize this goal by selecting measures for the internationalization of universities including the recruitment of international students, along with forming Japan's centers of internationalization. Selected universities will receive prioritized financial assistance of 200 to 400 million yen per annum [about $2.1–$4.2 million at the time] over the next 5 years. Endowed with this aid, each university will strive to recruit 3,000 to 8,000 international students. (MEXT 2009)

Programs emerging from this project are often academically broad, incorporating several disciplines under one department. Admission standards are generous, as departments aim to meet international student enrollment goals established by the ministry's policy. Curriculums vary from one program to another but reveal thematic integration between ministry objectives and university course offerings. One prominent university department I observed, for example, included faculty members who had previously worked in the Ministry of Economy, Trade and Industry; the Ministry of Foreign Affairs; the Ministry of General Affairs and Telecommunications; and the Japan Foundation. Given this revolving door between state bureaucracy and higher education, I should perhaps not have been surprised when a Japanese MA student who, upon hearing that I conducted work on soft power, came to me with his research proposal for his seminar in international relations. His research proposed to explore how to boost Japanese soft power through the training of instructors teaching Japanese to foreign students at Japanese universities.[12] Although I was surprised at the direct reflection of government policy in a student's research project, I was also reminded of my own project's complicity with the growth of soft power ideologies in Japanese government agencies—a point I return to below.

At another prominent university in Tokyo receiving funding through Japan's Global 30 project, a department took an even more assertive approach in cultivating a shared partnership with the government in building Pop-Culture Japan. In 2011 the university established an English track within its School of Global Japanese Studies, which offered students the opportunity to earn all their credits in English toward a Bachelor of Arts degree. The description of the program traces a line connecting soft power ideology, education policy, and curriculum design:

> This program features a curriculum that concentrates on traditional and modern Japanese culture, as well as Japanese society in the global community, all of which are currently attracting worldwide attention. The Cool Japan.
>
> The school also provides total support for students' careers in Japan or in Japan-related fields. They will have opportunities to learn Japanese as a second language, which will be included in the credits necessary for graduation. They will also have hands-on experience in the real world through workshops, extracurricular activities, and internships.

If in the example of NHK's dramatic shift in communications policy cited above we witness a transposition of a transnational consciousness into a nationalist one, here there is little transposition at all as government policy is directly inscribed into educational curriculums featuring Japan-based popular culture studies. In conjunction with this program, the university also set up a Cool Japan Summer Program. For two weeks in August, the university planned to invite twenty international students for a series of lectures, field trips, and workshops with Cool Japan specialists. Lectures had such titles as "Akihabara and Japanese Pop Culture," "Manga Literacy," and "Movie, Music, and Fashion." Students made field trips to Akihabara, Harajuku, the Suginami Animation Museum, a manga studio, the comic market in Odaiba, and the Ghibli Museum (Studio Ghibli is the production studio of director Miyazaki Hayao's widely celebrated animated features).[13]

One could argue that curriculums are one thing and classes another, the latter leaving room for critique and critical discussion. And in both knowing and speaking with some of the course instructors, I can attest that some of the content was as critical as it was celebratory of Cool Japan. However, what most interests me here is the process by which the imaginary of Pop-Culture Japan is constructed institutionally—a process that happens not through streamlining a particular message but in building infrastructure in which general themes become dominant, even if they engender as much room for critique as they do for the publicity of Cool Japan. For administrators, particularly of MOFA, the more these narratives surrounding Japanese popular culture circulate and establish dominance, the more potential they have to capture the hearts of foreign publics.

Since the Global 30 project, the Ministry of Education has adopted additional strategies for globalizing Japanese universities. In 2012 it launched the Project for Promotion of Global Human Resource Development (Gurōbaru Jinzai Ikusei Puroguramu). This time the focus was not only on bringing foreign students to Japan but also on building the global skills of Japanese students in order to overcome what the ministry described as the "Japanese younger generation's 'inward tendency'" (*uchimuki shikō*) and "to foster human resources who can positively meet the challenges and succeed in the global field as the basis for improving Japan's global competitiveness and enhancing the ties between nations" (MEXT 2012). Shortly thereafter, the Ministry of Education launched yet another major initiative, combining both the Global 30 and Global Resource Development Program. The

Super Global University Project (Sūpā Gurōbaru Daigaku Sōsei Shien), running from 2014 through 2023, aims to "provide prioritized support to those universities that are leading the internationalization of Japan's education" (MEXT 2014). Less officially, the program was reportedly motivated by Prime Minister Abe Shinzō's hope to advance ten Japanese universities into the list of those ranked top one hundred in the world.[14] Given the government's focus on its own students as "human resources" (*jinzai*) of global competitiveness, it is easy to see how courses focusing on Japanese subcultures become easily entangled with soft power pursuits of building national cultural resources.

These latest developments suggest that despite several discussions of the end of Cool Japan (Kelts 2010; Abel 2011; Favell 2011; Mori 2011; Hijiya-Kirschnereit 2013; McLelland 2017b), the figure of Pop-Culture Japan has acquired an institutional robustness that is likely to outlive the nation's more targeted branding campaigns. As I have aimed to illustrate, one reason for this is that the ambiguity of soft power ideologies supporting Pop-Culture Japan has proven effective in uniting heterogeneous fields of knowledge—media, art, education—toward a common purpose. To the degree that soft power continues to become inscribed in administrative structures of education, economy, politics, and the everyday, its assemblages approach the status of what Foucault (1980) and Deleuze and Guattari (1987) called an "apparatus."[15] In processes of inscription and institutionalization, Pop-Culture Japan thus acquires increased capacities to naturalize discourses like soft power and the nationalist consciousness upon which it depends. At the same time, while the institutional integration of government and society in Japan helps circulate images of Pop-Culture Japan, it also creates tensions and anxiety among citizens who feel less excited about their country represented overwhelmingly through images of manga, anime, and kawaii culture.

Reflexivity and Complicity in Pop-Culture Japan

To summarize the above, state investments in Pop-Culture Japan prove capable of affecting citizens through the institutionalization of media platforms, through creating economic opportunities for artists contributing to Cool Japan, and through investment and structural adjustments in higher education. Just as Japan's government agencies establish links with counterpart agencies in other states, creating an infrastructure that generates geopolitical points of comparison and contest (see chapter 1), the administrative connections bureaucrats make with subjects in everyday life enable varying flows and impacts of affect. Given the integration of government and mass media, the popular imagery of Pop-Culture Japan can inundate public discourse, naturalizing images of Japan as an increasingly pop-culture nation. In METI's Tokyo Contents Market, these connections prove weaker and more ambiguous, allowing most creators to engage with Pop-Culture Japan on their own terms and for their own interests. On the other hand, for independent artists like Shigematsu, Cool Japan rhetoric can nonetheless feel alienating and even offensive. Finally, in higher education, Pop-Culture Japan might have found its most accommodating partners yet, where state money can be directly invested in universities serving a growing number of young students interested in Japanese popular culture. Observing these inscriptions of soft power through academia and higher education and recognizing my own decision to focus my research on the politics of Japan's popular culture, however, begs questions of the researcher's reflexivity (Clifford and Marcus 1986) and complicity (Marcus 1998b) in the production of critiques of the state.[16]

The globalization of Japanese popular culture and the government's various investments in it have sparked massive interest from academics. Japanese and, increasingly, Korean pop culture are hot topics in East Asian studies and anthropology. Whereas popular culture was still considered a marginalized topic in anthropology in the 1970s and '80s, in the anthropology of Japan today, popular culture is arguably at its center. The enormous number of monographs and articles on popular culture in Japan are almost too numerous to keep track of, and there are respected journals now dedicated exclusively to Japanese popular culture.[17] Furthermore, conferences and panels focusing on Japan's popular culture make up a large portion of Japan Studies content, even after the rise and fall of a tide of studies on Cool Japan over the last two decades.[18]

Most significantly, there continues to be a strong demand for university courses on Japanese popular culture. While some quantitative data suggests a majority of students around the world are indeed studying Japanese out of an interest in popular culture,[19] even more instructive than statistics are observations from instructors of these courses. Professor of Comparative Media Studies at MIT Ian Condry provides one exemplary account through personal communication:

I felt like most of my classmates in Japanese language at Harvard in the mid-1980s were interested in Japan as a business opportunity (i.e., many were Econ majors in my cohort). Now, my sense is that students come to classes on Japan because they were introduced to the country through popular culture, especially manga, anime, and games. Of course, there is always a percentage (10–20 percent perhaps) of my classes where students come to Japan through other interests: martial arts, literature, family connections, and so on.

Condry's story of a shift in interest from Japan Inc. to popular Japanese culture is unsurprising to those with even a casual familiarity with Japan. And yet, what might be most surprising in his observation is not the narrative itself but how long the story has endured. Even as recently as 2019, Oyama Shinji writes of his seven years teaching at a college in London, "I am surprised by the number of international applicants, mostly from East and Southeast Asia, who would like to come to Japan to study Cool Japan at a graduate level so that they can emulate it in their home countries" (2019, 2). For Oyama, these students reflect not the success of Japan's creative industries, of which he is rather pessimistic, but rather the success of Cool Japan as a projected "image of the nation where the creative industries . . . are taken seriously and are supported generously and aggressively by the government to seize opportunities opened up by globalization and digitalisation" (2019, 8).[20] Among the many things these observations reveal is the commensurability between a genuine interest among foreign youth in the creative subcultures of Japan and the expedience of subcultural images to the centralized production of Pop-Culture Japan. That academics can find almost endless topics of critique on both of these themes and often government funding to support them makes popular Japanese culture both a legitimate topic of sociological study and a resource that feeds the ideological aims and affective hopes for Pop-Culture Japan.

While my own decision to study Japan came many years ago from an interest in Japanese language, I was exposed to popular Japanese culture through courses of the kind Condry teaches. Subsequently, I developed an interest in the politics and ethics of consuming popular media and art, most specifically of popular Japanese literature. In ways that are inescapable but revealing, then, much of my academic training, as well as this very book, are entangled with the assemblage of Japan's economic policy, soft power ideology, and regimes of higher education. For example, the finances to support my fieldwork for this study came in large part from the Japanese state through a Ministry of Education research grant; most of my solicitations for speaking or publishing are from scholars or government officials interested in Japanese popular culture; and my first university position upon completing my PhD was in a global studies department, teaching media and cultural studies courses that catered to foreign students and English-speaking Japanese students. As such, both this study and my professional subjectivity are part of a self-perpetuating cycle that, while offering a critique of Pop-Culture Japan, also feed it with energy, attention, and publicity. In this manner soft power becomes accommodated and naturalized within structures of higher education, reflecting again the sociologist Pierre Bourdieu's observation that "matters of culture . . . are constituted as such by the actions of the state which, by instituting them both in things and in minds, confers upon the cultural arbitrary all the appearances of the natural" (1993, 55). What I endeavor to add to this otherwise well-established observation is an illustration of how the assemblage of Pop-Culture Japan is held together by an affective administrative sensitivity to Japan's geopolitical status in the world.

I emphasize affect because it illustrates how, as suggested in the book's introduction, the worlds that state administrators manage become the feelings others embody but seldom make explicit. While I have aimed to show throughout this book how geopolitical anxiety is cultivated within Japan's structures of national cultural administration, in this chapter I have tried to show how this anxiety can refract outward as well, sometimes meshing and melding with feelings of economic and social precarity and other times eliciting other forms of anxiety based in a distaste for the government endorsement of popular culture. At the risk of pushing reflexivity beyond its methodological limits and current interests, I feel obliged to admit to a certain anxiety of my own.[21]

At times during this study I have felt the energy and excitement surrounding soft power moving through social spaces in Japan like a typhoon, collecting and assembling new constellations of language, policy, and aesthetic production in ways that have made me admittedly uneasy given soft power's top-down management efforts. Additionally, I have at times stumbled through research, self-consciously concerned about being labeled an "anime person," a "pop-culture person," or a "Cool Japan person" out of an awareness for how government interests have structured my own. While I like to think my anxiety has on occasions emerged as a product of fieldwork itself, and as such has served as evidence for tapping into and running up against a geopolitically organized assemblage of affect, I find it hard to know. Thus, I too find myself facing an epistemological gap between an anxiety that I may or may not share in part with my interlocutors and the stories I draw on to make it known and manageable. Such observations point to both the difficulty of incorporating affective introspection into fieldwork and the importance of grappling with it despite that difficulty.[22] Reflections on the "researcher's affects" (Stodulka 2015; Stodulka, Selim, and Mattes 2018) can show how a powerfully productive pairing of anxiety and hope in government administration is able to spawn other kinds of anxiety. So, although the anxiety found among political elites may not be the same that NHK describes in the "Japan Syndrome" or that Ivy (1995) outlines in her study on nostalgia, or that Allison (2013) articulates in her work on precarity, or that Genda (2005) or Miyazaki (2006) have identified in studies on hopelessness, or that I felt myself in fieldwork, these different kinds of anxiety can nonetheless affectively feed and cannibalize each other in ways that are hard to trace through discourse alone, but nonetheless demand the effort.

Another reason to interrogate the anxious affect that my interlocutors and I may or may not share is to help evaluate to what degree academic works like this one perpetuate Pop-Culture Japan even by critiquing it. Genealogies of anxious affect are not easy to trace. The social structures and histories that engender a commensurability in anxiety between the researcher and interlocutors likely run more deeply than what is observable through fieldwork. For example, such anxiety may also likely draw from long disciplinary histories that frame academic work on Japan. As scholars like Masao Miyoshi, Harry Harootunian, and many others have noted, a sense of researcher anxiety pervades area studies. This has been the case at least since World War II, after "the organization of area knowledge was fixed" in North-American and North-Atlantic academic institutions, with only "periodic adjustments to the changing political realities" (Harootunian 2000, 27). Anxiety over the legitimacy of area studies as a discipline was, continues Harootunian, expressed in an ongoing sense of crisis and an "obsessive search for money here and abroad" (2000, 27). Comparing the sense of economic-generated anxiety and crisis over the representation of Japan in area studies with that in the Japanese government raises important questions about the overlapping endeavors of cultural scholarship on Japan and Japanese government investments in "culture." From this perspective, the investment in anxiety by anthropologists and government officials and their respective efforts to fix its meaning across the affect-emotion gap may have much in common.[23]

Perhaps Sianne Ngai is right and anxiety has become not only a common feature of interconnected modernities but also a dominant intellectual mode of interrogating them (2005, 212–15), composed of Western, increasingly global, and gendered patterns that require ongoing scrutiny. Maintaining a critical ethnographic perspective, I hold out the possibility that my own anxiety, and of the ethnographer's affects in general, can in some contexts serve as an empirically *adequate* metric of ethnographic verifiability.[24] Spinoza defined *adequacy* in relation to power and truth: to the degree that one's ideas were adequate, he suggested, one established a relation to the world that facilitated his or her ability to act in and upon it. From this point of view, the power of ideas are reflected in their ability to guide subjects effectively through social space. As Michael Hardt posits, "One importance of the adequate idea, then, is that through the expression of its causes it increases our power of thought; the more adequate ideas we have, the more we know about the structure and connections of being, and the greater our power to think" (1993, 90). While I hesitate to focus too much on "power," given what sounds dangerously close to a romantic celebration of individual agency over and against one's surroundings, there is ample material in the idea of adequacy for thinking about how ideas or representations of one's social embeddedness are generated through affective capacities to feel one's way through social space—what Andrea De Antoni and Paul Dumouchel (2017) call "practices of feeling with the world." In other words, feeling anxious in anxious worlds can be a sign of ethnographic understanding in somatic terms. Like in my discussion of meiwaku in chapter 3, I suggest that it takes bodies time to accommodate to places where new sign systems, material objects, and discursive rules circulate unfamiliar sensations. The affect theorist Teresa Brennan famously remarked, "Is there anyone who has not, at least once, walked into a room and 'felt the atmosphere'?" (2004, 1). We might add to this resonant question another one that I think is just as illustrative of Brennan's main point: Is there anyone who has not walked into a room and *not* felt the atmosphere? The number of times foreigners and foreign anthropologists have recalled to me feeling out of place in Japanese rooms (admittedly a kind of atmosphere-reading) suggests the experience is not uncommon. And in many ways, the best of anthropology is often nothing more and nothing less than a long practice of accommodating the body to different rooms in order to listen to, hear, and amplify what its occupants have to say.

I felt that the government rooms I entered in Japan were both hopeful and anxious places, but because of the different histories and affiliations one brings into these rooms, I unsurprisingly felt more anxious than hopeful. I like to think that feeling this way was a sign of Brennan's (2004) "transmission of affect," even if its transmission can happen in uneven, accidental, and unexpected ways. The transmission of anxiety in Japan draws on the shared experience of dominant discourses, such as those of geopolitical fear that feed Pop-Culture Japan as tool of either government or academic politics, but they equally draw on those infinitely complex personal histories through which we differently meet and frame those discourses. In the final chapter, I explore a few of these complex personal histories from subjects in Japan who have encountered the anxiety that seems so inextricably tied to imagining Japan's national welfare and have attempted to narrate a way out of it.

Conclusion

Melancholic Belonging and the Future of Pop-Culture Japan

So far in this book I have described how by investing in and managing a hopeful future for Pop-Culture Japan, state administrators simultaneously draw from and amplify affects of national cultural anxiety in the present. I have argued that in contrast to previous forms of national imagining in Japan's history, largely focused on tropes of nostalgia and tradition, the image of Pop-Culture Japan in the eyes of Cool Japan promoters is future oriented, propelling the nation forward through fantastic worlds created and commodified by its pop-culture content producers. Although such a committed state investment in fantasy, fiction, and play is clearly for many publics in Japan uplifting, I have also suggested that in its narrow appeal to generic and highly gendered portraits of youth cute culture, it can marginalize and disappoint many who feel such depictions do not represent their own experiences, feelings, and hopes for the future.

That discourses of soft power and nation branding play a central role in creating the imagery and narratives of Pop-Culture Japan, as well as in shaping its future possibilities, points to the political power of storytelling—that crystalizing side of the affect-emotion gap, where feelings take literal shape through practices of representation and art. From this perspective, although artists clearly inspire the administrators of Pop-Culture Japan, administrators also resemble artists in the way they tell stories about the meaning, value, and future trajectories of the nation. Because this intersecting synergy between storytelling and policymaking proves so constitutive of Pop-Culture Japan, I want to conclude the book by evaluating how fiction and politics connect in Japan's cultural policy, how values are contested and accommodated therein, and what this implies for the possible futures of Pop-Culture Japan. In short, I ask, If Pop-Culture Japan is also the future of Japan, is it inevitable? Are there alternatives? If so, who is best positioned to offer them? While I started this book by suggesting that, for better or worse, state administrators are the actual articulators of dominant national imaginaries, I end the book by considering how artists—Dewey's favored articulators—also play a considerable role, especially when they are targeted by state administrators for appropriation.

Most specifically, I examine in this final chapter practices of producing popular culture—namely of writing, reading, and commenting on it by Japan's contemporary fiction writers—that resist the anxiety tied to the administrative manufacturing of national hope and, in doing so, create alternative pairings of national imagining and affective belonging. I focus on these alternative practices of producing popular culture not to exercise anthropology as a kind of therapy for those who feel ill at ease with Cool Japan nor to politicize ethnography by citing examples of an alternative and elusive moral paradigm of state resistance and personal freedom. Rather, I do so to explore understudied ways of living affectively and effectively in and with a national community whose most dominant forms of national identity can feel to some uncomfortable.

Historically marginalized subjects in Japan, whether women, ethnic minorities, gay, transgender, indigenous, disabled, mentally ill, or other individuals—including certain men—not readily spoken for by the state's traditionally patriarchal elite, may today find ample material for expression and solidarity in the wide variety of Japan's popular art, media, and culture. But what happens when those spaces of popular alterity themselves become appropriated by the state? How do those who are perceived as legal or cultural citizens of Japan but nonetheless feel themselves affectively marginalized from it nonetheless construct a sense of belonging or of coping from within? To address these questions, I think through examples from popular fiction writers and their readers that illustrate how popular culture seen as cool and coveted abroad and thus potentially regenerative of national culture at home also serve as a source for alienated subjects to cultivate resistance, antagonism, and ultimately an affectively detached accommodation to national identity that I call *melancholic belonging*. I suggest that melancholic belonging is cultivated as an alternative to a state-driven manufacturing process that politically interlocks a "cruel optimism" (Berlant 2011) for a difficult future—whether of the "American dream" in Berlant's case or of national resurgence via pop culture in Japan's—to various socioeconomic anxieties in the present.

The Cosmopolitan Cool of Murakami Haruki

For many who would identify as either critics or crusaders of Cool Japan, the popular Japanese fiction writer Murakami Haruki is quintessentially cool. Literary scholar Matthew Strecher (1998b, 61) said of Murakami, "With a style that admits the influence of no single previous Japanese author, and an approach to the world around him that has been detached at best, Murakami has built a reputation as one of Japan's 'coolest' writers of fiction." Masao Miyoshi (1991, 234) described Murakami as "always cool, never ruffled" and noted that the extensive references to pop culture and "everyday trivia" in his stories produce a world where "all the players come off cool and clean." Jay Rubin credited Murakami's coolness for his broad regional appeal in East Asia, "where his cool, detached, often comical narrator seems to offer an alternative to life lived in the grim Confucian envelope of State and Family" (2003, 5). Finally, in my own interview with him, Murakami conceded he had considered his popular status as cool, connecting the coolness of his characters to his personal life and referring to a moment of heightened political consciousness when he was at university in Tokyo: "I used to be an idealistic person in 1968 or 1969. And I became kind of passive or kind of independent, kind of cool."[1]

By all accounts Murakami is as cool as a cucumber. As if to punctuate the fact, when I met the author at the University of Hawai'i in 2006 for a couple of informal interviews about the intersections of consumerism and postmodern critique in his literature, Murakami was wearing a T-shirt with an actual picture of a cucumber on it. Cool. Although I had not considered myself a fan of his literature at the time, and neither would I easily admit to it today, especially considering aspects of gender I return to later in this chapter, I was nevertheless quickly enamored of Murakami in person. Like a 1990s teenager with an embarrassing crush, at our next meeting I gave him a mixtape of songs I liked; I mentioned my availability for a local jog or bike ride, activities I knew he enjoyed; and I drafted a research proposal exploring the reasons for Murakami's regional popularity in East Asia.[2] Although neither then nor now did I ever link an interest in Murakami with an interest in Japan, given that I was far more interested in the reasons for his discomfort with his cultural home, I realize that administrators interested in

Murakami as a resource of soft power could read this story very differently. This awkward and even at times antagonistic commensurability of parallel worlds—the ability to read one story of consuming popular Japanese culture in multiple ways—is, I think, key to understanding the anxiously complex present and hopefully anticipated future of Pop-Culture Japan.

Today, Murakami Haruki could be considered a literary poster child for Cool Japan and a beloved representative of the nation's literary culture, but this has not always been the case. Even more importantly, the feeling is far from mutual. In his early career, when he began to gain attention abroad faster than he did at home, Murakami was viewed by the Japanese literary establishment (*bundan*) as an Americanized, international, and resolutely un-Japanese writer. The mouthpiece for the literary establishment as it stood in the late 1980s and early '90s was the Nobel Prize laureate Ōe Kenzaburō, who famously wrote, "Murakami Haruki writes in Japanese, but his writing is not really Japanese. . . . I suspect that this sort of style is not really Japanese literature" (cited in Strecher 1998a, 374). Ōe and other old guard critics relegated Murakami to the realm of mass or pop literature (*taishū bungaku*). Ōe further lamented, "I believe that any future resuscitation of "pure literature" (*junbungaku*) will be possible only if ways are found to fill in the wide gap that exists between Murakami and pre-1970 postwar literature" (1989, 200). Murakami's cosmopolitanism—his informal writing style, his references to American and British popular culture, his direct translation of English idioms into Japanese—provoked a nostalgic response from the old guard who defended pure literature on the grounds of its Japaneseness. Murakami represented at the time the popular, and the popular was not Japanese but Western.

Such criticism from an establishment that had in part shaped Murakami's early desire to write elicited animosity in the writer. In an interview with literary scholar Jay Rubin (2003, 47), Murakami explained, "The literary establishment was nothing but a pain for me, which is why I have stayed by myself, writing my novels. This is also why I went off to Europe for three years, and after a year in Japan, went to live in America for a little over four years." Reflecting this sense of alienation, themes of escape feature prominently in Murakami's literature and interviews.[3] Looking back on this period later in his career, Murakami admitted, "All I could think about when I began writing fiction in my youth was how to run as far as I could from the 'Japanese condition.' I wanted to distance myself as much as possible from the curse of Japanese" (cited in Rubin 2003, 47). In retrospect, it was clear that Murakami saw himself as an outcast from the start. This antagonism toward mainstream Japanese society manifested in his literature as a sense of detachment, ambivalence, and melancholy.

Melancholic Belonging

For many people in Japan who feel that their relationship to the nation in general and to Pop-Culture Japan in particular is less a source of pride and more one of burden, belonging in mainstream Japanese society can feel melancholic. While appeals to melancholy in academic literature often trigger thoughts of Freud's "Mourning and Melancholia" (1918), I want to jump to a creative adaptation of Freud that is, while possibly at first surprising, ultimately well suited to understanding melancholy's geopolitical dimensions. In his critique of the racial and colonial legacies embedded in the multicultural project of the United Kingdom, Paul Gilroy examines a state of "postcolonial melancholy" that seems fated to reproduce feelings of "discomfort, shame, and perplexity" in regard to Britain's end to empire, coupled with "apprehension of successive political and economic crises" (2005, 90). Seeking an alternative structure of feeling in relation to multiculturalism, Gilroy writes,

> We need to know what sorts of insight and reflection might actually help increasingly differentiated societies and anxious individuals to cope successfully with the challenges involved in dwelling comfortably in proximity to the unfamiliar without becoming fearful and hostile. (2005, 3)

Although the racial histories and politics Gilroy analyzes do not neatly map onto Japan, his diagnosis of melancholia-after-empire in Great Britain sheds light on how legacies of the "loss of imperial prestige" (2005, 90) continue to haunt a present in which Japan, given its own imperial legacy and that legacy's resurfacing in celebration of "Japan as number one," is implicated. Gilroy draws on Freud's ([1918] 1957, 245) notion of a melancholia that can arise as "the reaction to the loss of a loved object" when "one cannot see clearly what it is that has been lost" to elucidate a contemporary form of national imagining tied inextricably but vaguely to British empire. Gilroy's melancholia-after-empire helps us understand not only reactions to a sense of loss and at times shameful prestige but also to practices in the present that seek a distanced accommodation to an uncomfortable history that is not going away. In this sense, adapted to Japan, subjects like Murakami seek not to directly confront a problematic past tied to a sense of lost prestige in order to construct new forms of convivial living that might transcend it but rather to find a space of measured distance alongside that past.[4] In this sense, melancholy can serve as a skillful response to living within but at a distance from state systems that administratively inscribe patterns of pursuing national prestige in practices of everyday life.

Despite the increasing "internationalization" of Japanese society, despite the growing flows of global culture in and of local culture out, and despite even the genuine diversity of Japan's popular cultures irrespective of Pop-Culture Japan, there is nonetheless for many a palpable sense that little of social life in Japan is left untouched by state administration. From highly, if secularly, ritualized systems such as education to those of job hunting, corporate culture, marriage, home ownership, childcare, tourism, leisure, retirement, pensions, and even death, one feels the weight of a highly integrated system of state and society that has prefigured and substantially narrowed the conditions for living well in Japan. It is tempting but ultimately misleading to read a kind of cultural uniformity into this system, as well as to generalize the effects of this system's breakdown since the collapse of Japan's bubble economy in the early 1990s. But as a story about a singular "system" told about diverse structural effects, it is a powerful one that is repeated both in and outside Japan. As Genda Yūji (2005); Hirokazu Miyazaki (2009, 2013); Anne Allison (2013), and others have argued, the fracturing of a highly integrated system of economic growth, lifetime employment, mass consumption, and social, familial, and biological reproduction known as Japan Inc. has engendered a sense of precarity and hopelessness. As a highly circulated discourse of despair, this story's depressing effects—whether in discursive or socioeconomic terms—are hard to escape. For some in Japan, however, the very systematicity of the Japanese state project had already produced a sense of unease even before the collapse of the country's asset bubble and the start of its "lost decades" in the 1990s.

This antagonism to systematicity itself has thematically defined Murakami's literature in the past, thus making his stories into resources that acknowledge and invite melancholic forms of coping with an overbearing presence of the state in the present. Illustrating this is a feeling of foreboding that permeates Murakami's works, which is often represented in powerful characters like the "boss" (*bossu*) of *A Wild Sheep Chase* ([1982] 1989) or in organizations like the "System" (*shisutemu*) of *Hard-Boiled Wonderland and the End of the World* ([1985] 1991). In *Hard-Boiled Wonderland*, Murakami's protagonist says, "This System of yours is big, too big. The right hand never knows what the left hand is doing. Too much information, more than you can keep track of" (1991, 217).[5] In *Kafka on the Shore* ([2002] 2005), in discussing the possible perpetrators of a crime, a colleague tells the main character, "Narrow minds devoid of imagination. Intolerance, theories cut off from reality, empty terminology, usurped ideals, inflexible systems. Those are the things that really frighten me" (2005, 181–82).[6] In a speech accepting the Jerusalem Prize for literature, Murakami spoke more literally of one particularly violent manifestation of the "System":

> The System is supposed to protect us, but sometimes it takes on a life of its own, and then it begins to kill us and cause us to kill others—coldly, efficiently, systematically. I have only one reason to write novels, and that is to bring the dignity of the individual soul to the surface and shine a light upon it. The purpose of a story is to sound an alarm, to keep a light trained on The System in order to prevent it from tangling our souls in its web and demeaning them. (2009)

These foreboding characters and systems in Murakami's literature are frightening figures from which one seeks escape but often struggles to do so as they are too large, too complex, or too thoroughly integrated into those structures of the social world in which one—even in formulating projects of resistance—is implicated.

Given Murakami's articulation of his desire to "escape from the curse of Japanese," it is reasonable to reflect on the role of the state in manufacturing a sense of unease among some of its citizens in relation to mainstream sociality. The state's integration of economic, legal, and bureaucratic structures into everyday life discussed in the previous chapter is in its systematicity—Murakami's *shisutemu*—too complex to hold in one's head. As such it manifests affectively—as a sense of something out there beyond oneself: ambiguous yet systematic, intangible but palpably real. Dewey's ([1927] 1954, 131) observation that the consequences of collective living can be felt but not always readily perceived thus presents not only a more pragmatic interpretation of Durkheim's ([1912] 2008) classic theory of collective effervescence but also a practical problem to the contemporary anthropologist of affect: How can one articulate the effects of social life that, because of their complexity, manifest not as preformulated problems but as preconscious affects? If, again, as Dewey says, artists are the "real purveyors" of these problems, the ones who best combine a sensitivity to the social world with a skill to articulate it ([1927] 1954, 183–84), then analyzing the reception of one of the most widely read artistic articulators of those problems in writer Murakami Haruki should serve as a useful subject of anthropological inquiry.[7] As Jay Rubin says, borrowing a line from Murakami's *Hear the Wind Sing* ([1979] 1987), "Murakami is an epistemologist. He wants to investigate the 'gaping chasm [that] separates what we try to be aware of and what we actually are aware of'" (2003, 46). Such an author would serve as a valuable source for navigating the affect-emotion gap as it plays out in Pop-Culture Japan.[8]

Reading and Feeling Murakami

In an English conversation class I taught for staff and professors at a prestigious university in Tokyo, the day's exercise called for each student to list three possible "heroes" for a mock magazine that would feature the "World's Hero of 2010." I also participated in the exercise and, feeling it salutary to include a Japanese nominee in my list, chose the popular author Murakami Haruki. In explanation of my choice, I suggested that Murakami wrote narratives of such a cosmopolitan character that people from almost any nation could appreciate them. Despite the directions of the assignment calling for nominees for a "global" hero, perhaps I was not surprised that eight out of the nine nominees submitted by the Japanese participants were Japanese, including the sociologist Satō Kaoru and the sixteenth-century feudal lord Oda Nobunaga, who is credited with unifying—not exactly nonviolently—Japan. (The remaining nominee, incidentally, submitted by the only woman in the group, was John F. Kennedy). If I were not surprised at the number of Japanese nominees, I *was* surprised that nearly all the submission lists also included Murakami Haruki.

In one participant's explanation for his nomination, I found a curious description of the affective quality of Murakami's work. In response to a colleague who suggested that upon reading Murakami, one simply wanted to *keep* reading, the participant offered the following counterpoint: "I actually don't *want* to keep reading his books. But when I read his stories I'm left with this kind of strange feeling. I don't really understand what's happening in the story but somehow I'm attracted to it." He elaborated, "Many authors can write a story that makes you feel very strongly one way or another, but it's very difficult to write a story that leaves you with just such a strange feeling that compels you to read more."

Murakami seems to affect readers without their being able to convey exactly how or why. That this is so even among university professors and experts in cultural administration with whom I spoke, articulate and intelligent individuals who read and discuss literature for pleasure and some for their profession, makes this fact especially illustrative of affect's resistance to description. Murakami's novels are admittedly praised as much for their mesmerizing atmosphere as for their creative narratives, likely one reason it is difficult for fans to explain precisely why they like him. Still, the inability to articulate the source of Murakami's appeal in the face of such an enormous consensus of his popularity is suggestive of an affective power that is, as my English student called it, "strange." Today, fans anticipate this feeling in Murakami's stylistically consistent works and are regularly drawn to each new release from the author. The marketing campaign launched by the publisher Shinchōsha for the release of his latest novel in 2009, during an early period of my fieldwork, displayed nothing more than the title, *1Q84*, with a large green *Q* filling Shinchōsha's posters.[9] There was no description of the story, nor even a catchphrase or slogan. The reputation of the name Murakami alone accounted for the nearly 400,000 copies purchased in the first week by fans.[10] When I asked a number of friends who had recently read the first two installments what kind of story it was, they were at a loss to say. "It's kind of about religion," one said. "I didn't really understand the story," said another. "It doesn't really have an ending," claimed a third, "and I heard Murakami decided to write an additional volume to the story!" he enthusiastically added.

As mentioned above, at one point in the past I had contemplated doing a research project on fans of Murakami. I was interested in how readers incorporated his narratives into individual practices of self-development and ethical growth—a kind of case study in the anthropology of ethics for Foucault's "technologies of the self" (1997), or of what James Faubion has called "literature as a technology of self-formation" (1993, 184). One of the several reasons why I did not ultimately pursue the project was the variety and ambiguity of answers I received upon asking readers the admittedly naive question, Why do you like Murakami? Some liked Murakami's protagonist Boku (an informal and masculine way to say "I" or "me" in Japanese); some liked the mysterious and otherworldly elements of his stories, what literary critics call "magical realism"; others liked his short and direct style. Many people told me they liked the "feeling" (*kimochi*) of his stories. But the answer I received the most was "*nantonaku suki*" (somehow I just like him).[11] How does one talk about Murakami's somewhat esoteric power to leave people so "somehow" affected?

In his study of ambient media in Japan, Paul Roquet suggests that Murakami's novels prefigure a rise in mood-regulating media technologies associated with the late 1990s healing (*iyashi*) boom. For Roquet, a critical feature of ambient media in general and ambient literature in particular is "subtractivism, a smoothing of the self by designing out the need for strong emotional attachments, whether to other people or to the past itself" (2016, 127). "Ambient media," Roquet suggests, "both aestheticize the peaceful dissolution of identity and mark the loss of what had to be subtracted to get there" (148). "Ambient literature," then, "is an aesthetic response to the demand for transposable calm. . . . [It] rethinks the novel as a mood-regulating device" (154). While Murakami's literature predates the rise of what Roquet identifies as purposeful practices of writing literature as a mode of mood regulation, he credits Murakami for in part popularizing a style of "ambivalent calm" (18) that distinguishes both his protagonists and the affective impact of his stories.

Roquet's incisive analysis of the "low-affect living" (133) exemplified in Murakami's fiction helps identify Murakami's mysterious effect on readers. I suggest it is this low-level register of alluring but melancholic affect that attracts people to Murakami's work and that is mobilized by both Murakami and his fans in crafting a relationship of minimum investment in a highly systematized society with decreasing returns for social security. Under such conditions, literature that is cool and detached can also be enticing. Murakami's protagonists exhibit this disenchanting appeal by making efforts to seek something distinctively meaningful but always only with limited motivation and ultimately never quite getting anywhere special in the end. They are notoriously calm, sometimes even outwardly content, but often in ways that read as inwardly empty, lost, or lonely. They are usually thirty- or forty-something-year-old males, single, and often engaged in monotonous but intellectual work, such as translation. They are moderately confident and sometimes witty but more often just isolated and individualistic, spending time at home enjoying pasta with a can of beer. They are not impassioned single-minded heroes but are more modest, investing only moderately in projects of self-exploration and engaging in only half-inspired protests against imposing social structures. Yet, it is precisely through this low-level affectivity—and not infrequently in combination with interventions from mysterious female characters (a point I return to below)—that protagonists find strength. While maintaining only just enough anxiety to push them forward in their search for something other, they cultivate a kind of affective disinterest that proves productive in their search for something they have lost and helpful in their struggle with forces that are always looming and lurking close by.

This detached and melancholic tone resonates with many of the dwellers of hyper-consumer-driven urban centers, not only in Japan's Tokyo and Osaka but also in cities abroad where Murakami is extremely popular: Hong Kong, Seoul, Beijing, New York, Berlin, Paris, London. More praised for style than structure or story, Murakami's ability to capture the mood of the urban everyday while offering subtle glimpses of something slightly better and somewhat more satisfying appeals to readers. That readers find satisfaction in this resonance of ambience and melancholic mood rather than in the development of a narrative that overcomes it also accounts, I think, for much of the ambiguity in the descriptions of my interlocutors' admiration for Murakami.

In contrast to Murakami's narratives, those of Pop-Culture Japan strike a far more melodramatic tone. For many inside government, the effect is resounding, as self-authored and self-circulated stories (Hamano 2005; Nakamura and Onouchi 2006) of Japan's popularity abroad instill an optimism that negates any evidence suggesting that hopes for Pop-Culture Japan are misplaced. For those outside government, however, or for administrators outside their role in government, stories of Pop-Culture Japan are more dissonant. The Japanese pop singer Gackt famously criticized Cool Japan in a 2015 blog post, saying, "The Japanese government made a new attempt at this [promoting Japan's creative industries] in the name of Cool Japan, but while they have set up a huge budget for it, they have no idea where that money should go" (RocketNews 24 2015). And megastar artist Murakami Takashi called Cool Japan "stupid, too stupid to even discuss" (*Aho desu yo. Aho sugite hanashi ni naranai*) (Sasaki 2012). For many people in Japan, the soft power rhetoric and hyper-kawaii images of Pop-Culture Japan feel discomforting, inspiring ridicule and parody.[12] And some who feel this way or who feel conflicted about Pop-Culture Japan, such as the many male and many more female administrators among whom I worked in the Japan Foundation, even occupy those national bureaucracies in which Pop-Culture Japan is promoted and sustained, complicating a uniform picture of state administration.

Appropriating Cool, Cultivating Disaffection

That those seeking to escape Pop-Culture Japan exist uncomfortably alongside those promoting it is not surprising given the multiple dimensions and "faces" (Navaro-Yashin 2002) of the modern state. But the fact that it is at times precisely those narratives that best represent an opposition to mainstream Japan that are taken up as most representative of Cool Japan uniquely captures the appropriative power of Pop-Culture Japan. In 2006 the Japan Foundation sponsored a symposium on Murakami Haruki's literature, which the foundation titled in English, "'A Wild Haruki Chase': How the World Is Reading and Translating Murakami" (*Haruki o meguru bōken: Sekai wa Murakami bungaku o dō yomu ka*).[13] An online announcement for the symposium described the Japan Foundation's intentions:

> The Japan Foundation will hold a symposium and two workshops focusing on the novels and their translations of Haruki Murakami, one of the most popular contemporary novelists in the world. It is aimed at exploring the secret of this Murakami boom and considering what is common and different when his novels are read by people of different nations and of various generations. (Japan Foundation 2006)

The symposium took place over two days at the University of Tokyo and invited literary scholars, critics, translators, and fans from, according to the Japan Foundation (2006), "16 countries or territories." As suggested in the advertisement, the administrators sought to find a common thread in Murakami's appeal across diverse communities, likely hoping to discover something that could be distilled from the responses as illustrative of Murakami's—and now Japan's—contemporary charm. The symposium marked the official consecration of Murakami, previously the quintessential cosmopolitan author in an enduringly postwar culture, as the representative par excellence of Pop-Culture Japan.

Despite his recognition by the Japan Foundation, Murakami was himself characteristically leery of the symposium. When I asked him about it in a conversation, he said he was indeed contacted by the Japan Foundation and told them he had no objections to their hosting it, but he preferred not to attend himself. The response is typical of Murakami's apprehension about state endorsements of his work. In a rare public appearance by the author, in the speech for the 2009 Jerusalem Prize quoted above, the author offered a less-than-subtle condemnation of exercises of state power in general and of recent activities in the region in particular:

> A fair number of people advised me not to come here to accept the Jerusalem Prize. Some even warned me they would instigate a boycott of my books if I came. . . . Finally, however, after careful consideration, I made up my mind to come here. . . . Please do, however, allow me to deliver one very personal message. It is something that I always keep in mind while I am writing fiction. I have never gone so far as to write it on a piece of paper and paste it to the wall. Rather, it is carved into the wall of my mind, and it goes something like this: "Between a high, solid wall and an egg that breaks against it, I will always stand on the side of the egg."
>
> Yes, no matter how right the wall may be and how wrong the egg, I will stand with the egg. Someone else will have to decide what is right and what is wrong; perhaps time or history will decide. If there were a novelist who, for whatever reason, wrote works standing with the wall, of what value would such works be? (Murakami 2009)

Murakami's analogy, although clearly referencing Israel-Palestine relations, could also likely apply to his feelings toward the Japanese government, to mainstream society, and, retrospectively, to the Japan Foundation symposium featuring his work. Interestingly, his speech gained wide popularity in Japan, and I encountered several officials who expressed admiration for it. That an official for Japan's state administration of culture might show sympathy for the egg or, even further, align herself with it against a "system" she herself represents is neither ironic nor contradictory. It is, rather, exemplary of an obligatory nationalism by which an administrator recognizes that despite one's uneasy ambivalence toward discourses of the nation, one cannot deny one's subjectivity as, for better and for worse, indebted to it.

The measured engagement that characterizes the feelings of many of my Japan Foundation colleagues for national cultural administration (in contrast to those in MOFA) resonates with feelings evoked by Murakami's literature. Colleagues who adopt a distanced position in relation to Pop-Culture Japan embody not antagonism or pessimism so much as accommodation. For them and other subjects engaged in projects that in some form or another aim to establish a healthy distance from the state, Murakami's literature serves as a useful space where a melancholic mood of ambivalence feels welcoming and tempers the more impassioned rhetorics of nationalism that dominate soft power discourse. In its evocations of disaffection, his literature offers at the very least a moderate space of refuge within the dominant and continually recycled national narratives of "Japan as number one," as former economic giant, or of pop-culture powerhouse.

After many years of intermittent travel abroad, Murakami has now made Japan his permanent home. He continues to write voraciously, perhaps still in part motivated by an unabated desire for escape and difference. But he seems also to have forfeited the possibility of complete liberation from the "curse of Japanese." In another interview, Murakami provides what I think is an ideal articulation of the conflicted position in which many people in Japan, including my Japan Foundation colleagues, find themselves:

> No matter how much of an independent individual I am, and even though I think I live a life unrelated to Japanese literature, day after day I have to squarely face up to the objective reality that I am a Japanese writer who writes novels in Japanese. (Seats 2006, 65)

If one draws an analogy between the establishment (*bundan*) of Japanese literature and the rhetorics of soft power and nation branding, Murakami's comment helps illustrate how the nation-state participates in crafting many of the discourses through which people growing up and living in Japan inevitably make sense of their lives, as well as of the mixed feelings the state evokes in them.

As the Cool Japan discourse circulates, propelled by powerful state institutions and national coffers, Japanese citizens are increasingly required to give an account of themselves in relation to it. While certain government officials and content producers who seem likely to benefit from it might embrace the broader image of Pop-Culture Japan, for many others it is felt as a figure imposed from above: something uneasy, something to be wary of and resisted. Murakami's literature, in an affective disinterestedness that feels comforting because it feels familiar, proves effective as one form of this resistance. It is not a resistance materialized in conscious political projects of opposition and refusal but one simply confirmed and legitimated in the melancholic affects of affinity that many readers of Murakami feel when reading his work—resistance as resonance. For these readers, Murakami's literature captures the complex reality of their social worlds more than stories of soft power and Cool Japan do. Generalizing what James Faubion says in constructing a sociology of Greek writer Margarita Karapanou's literature, while a novel may not "cure," may not help one "live more easily in the world," it can nonetheless give "form to it" (1993, 195). Murakami's works impact readers not through stories that more accurately represent the world nor merely through forms of escape from it, but rather through a style that affects them in a way similar to how the realities of their urban worlds *feel*. The affective resonance readers discover and the strange attraction they feel to continually turn the page confirm not the accuracy but the *authenticity* of his stories. Stories of Cool Japan do not. They feel comparatively uneasy and discordant, less true, something to avoid. That said, like the forms of anxiety among my administrator interlocutors that I've endeavored to articulate, such affective responses are hardly uniform. And many, just like Pop-Culture Japan at large, similarly refract through shards of gender.

The (Gendered) Future of Anxiety after Pop-Culture Japan

While popular culture in Japan is ever-changing, always flexibly adaptive and sensitive to the social structures and strictures it encounters, Pop-Culture Japan has over the last two decades proven a more fixed and formidable figure. Built in part through the branding efforts of Cool Japan, whose publicity and popularity have risen and fallen through waves of investment and criticism, Pop-Culture Japan has endured. In this sense, Pop-Culture Japan shows itself irreducible to Cool Japan, formative of an arrangement of affect that feels simultaneously hopeful and anxious and that through practices of administration advances the claim that Japan increasingly *is* its popular culture. In this book I have endeavored to show how this process is facilitated not merely through ideology, government structures, and discourse (i.e., stories of Pop-Culture Japan), but also and more importantly through a circuitous looping effect with the affects those discourses condition and cultivate. That these affects have primarily manifested as anxious and have been sustained in the assemblage of Pop-Culture Japan through soft power, nation branding, and pop-culture diplomacy begs the question of whether that anxiety is destined to reproduce itself indefinitely in the future. While state apparatuses prove capable of maintaining current patterns of affect through national narratives, there is also reason to believe that alternative structures of feeling, such as those articulated through Murakami's melancholic belonging, may be growing among Japanese publics.

Consider the Japanese government's zealous bid to host the 2020 Olympics. When the government began its campaign in earnest in 2011 and 2012, the circuitry connecting anxious affect and emotional hope in a perpetual feedback loop seemed as energized as ever. The reasons were understandable. As noted in the introduction, Japan's economy was still recovering both from its 1992 asset bubble collapse and the 2008 global financial crisis; China had surpassed Japan as the second largest economy in the world in the fourth quarter of 2010; and Japan had suffered a dev-astating triple disaster of earthquake, tsunami, and nuclear meltdown in March 2011. The promotional material for Tokyo's 2020 Olympic bid clearly broadcasted the feelings of state administrators. The official slogan for the campaign organized by Japan's Liberal Democratic Party (LDP) read, "Now, what is needed in Japan is this power to dream" (*Ima, Nippon ni wa kono yume no chikara ga hitsuyō da*). As media scholar Yamada Kenta (2015, 39, 49) argued, the slogan originated out of the LDP's primary motivation to turn Tokyo 2020 into a "restorative Olympics" (*fukkō Gorin*), leveraging a sense of collective will in the face of the 2011 disasters in order to rebuild both national and party power.

Despite the sense of public optimism that the government projected through its campaign for Tokyo 2020, in reality, enthusiasm for hosting the global event was low. With meager early turnouts to volunteer recruit-ment and growing criticism over the plan to hire over 110,000 volunteers to work in scorching heat without compensation, the government considered incentives such as 1000-yen (US$9.00 at the time) gift cards for each day of volunteering (Takeshita 2018) and course credit for university students who volunteered (Koishikawa 2018). In a BBC discussion with contemporary female fiction writers Itō Hiromi, Sawada Tomoko, Motoya Yukiko, and translator Shibata Motoyuki, Itō Hiromi—well known as someone who, like Murakami, both sought and managed to escape from Japan for many years—responded to a question about whether there might be people in Japan hoping for a renaissance of Japanese culture in conjunction with the Olympics. Itō remarked with conviction, "I can't believe that kind of per-son is [in Japan]. We don't expect anything! And I don't really want them to have the Tokyo Olympics now." Translator Shibata Motoyuki agreed, "Yeah, I think we are pretty cynical about the Olympic games." Seeking to represent an alternative point of view that he imagined must be concurrently circulating in Japan, the British interviewer countered, "The Olympics often mark a shift in a culture's history, as the Beijing Olympics did in China in 2008, so Tomoko, do you think things will change in Japan after the Olympics?" Writer Sawada Tomoko responded, "I don't think much will change really. . . . There is always this excitement and buildup [in Japan] but no one really thinks about what happens next, and that's what concerns me more. . . . These kinds of events: I always feel a bit removed from them" (BBC Radio 3 2020).

In addition to what these artists—the "real purveyors of news" (Dewey [1927] 1954, 183–184)—had sensed as the mood of the public toward the Olympics, a string of very real problems seemed to plague Olympic preparation. In 2015 there were claims that the selected logo for the Olympics was plagiarized from a theater in Belgium (McCurry 2016), and managers of the logo design committee selected another. The stadium, originally selected to be built by world famous architect Zaha Hadid (who passed away in 2016), exceeded its budget by twice the originally estimated amount in the process of development and was replaced with a more economical design by Japanese architect Kuma Kengo. This subsequent design was also criticized for plagiarism, with claims that it borrowed too heavily from Hadid's design (McCurry 2016). Ultimately, the ongoing controversy was sidelined by a global pandemic, COVID-19. And only after swelling criticism did Japan's Olympic organizing committee agree to delay the games for a year, but *only* for one year (Nikkei 2020), casting the prospect of hosting the games altogether into doubt. In a poll taken among Tokyo residents by Kyodo News and Tokyo MX Television in the midst of the pandemic, 52 percent of respondents reported that they did not think the Olympics should be held in 2021, hoping for either further delays or cancellation (AFP 2020). Just a week before the opening ceremonies, an Ipsos Global Advisor poll recorded this number at 78 percent (Cancian 2021). And a poll conducted by Japan's Asahi News (2021) at the same time found that 68 percent did not believe a "safe and secure Olympics" (*anzen anshin Gorin taikai*) could be held at all. Although the Olympics ultimately went ahead with many successes given the unprecedented conditions, the empty stadiums, measured ceremonies, and strict restrictions on athletes' movements obviously and understandably fell far short of the LDP's original soft power ambitions.

Whether in failing to recreate the ambitiously imagined figure of Japan as number one, or simply in succumbing to the complex realities of a globally integrated economic system as sensitive to systematic failure as to severe respiratory syndromes, hopes for Japan's resurgence seem inevitably bound to fall short of its managers' expectations. Given the form of obligatory nationalism cultivated within state agencies of culture, however, it is hard to see how administrators could do anything less than strive to build an image of the nation's culture that, in finding approval abroad, would alleviate anxieties at home.

However, as suggested by critics of Tokyo 2020, of Cool Japan, and of state-sanctioned systems structuring Japanese society in general, while melodramatic stories of the nation may be appealing to administrators (Leheny 2018), they may not best serve their audience. In fact, such stories often prove to *administer* anxiety as much as to alleviate it. That many of Pop-Culture Japan's administrators operate in a traditionally male-dominated system of bureaucracy, where stories of Japan's decline from historical prominence are repeatedly recycled among colleagues, there is good reason to pursue a critique of the gendered dimensions of Pop-Culture Japan further. The criticism of the Ambassadors of Cute program from one female interlocutor cited earlier lingers in my mind: "I never know what those bureaucrats are thinking!" I have tried to show in this book to some degree what these (mostly) male administrators are not only thinking but also feeling, and how the coupling of feeling and thinking across a somatic-semiotic gap of intelligibility produces and sustains the sentimental circuitry of Pop-Culture Japan.

For how long Pop-Culture Japan will sustain this circuitry remains to be seen. However, the fact that affect is always responsive to interventions, reflections, and, most of all, to new artistic representations of it is suggestive that Pop-Culture Japan in both its narratives and affective evocations is vulnerable to change—a point as relevant to analyzing the affective politics of popular culture as to critiquing affect theory at large.[14] While the literature and reception of Murakami Haruki represents one alternative form of disaffected coping alongside and within a national imaginary that feels vaguely wrong, there is reason to ask to what degree even those artistic forms of escape from a nationalized culture are as masculinized as the state's promotion of it. While Murakami's endings to his novels and short stories have felt consistently and anticlimactically melancholic, a feeling Japanese readers would describe as *munashii*, he has also at times experimented with more emotionally evocative endings. In a short story titled "Kino" in a collection called *Men without Women* (*Onna no inai otokotachi*), Murakami writes:

> The willow branches swayed in the early summer breeze. In a small
> dark room somewhere inside Kino, a warm hand was reaching out

to him. Eyes shut, he felt that hand on his, soft and substantial. He'd forgotten this, had been apart from it for far too long. Yes, I am hurt. Very very deeply. He said this to himself. And he wept. In that dark, still room.

    All the while the rain did not let up, drenching the world in a cold chill. ([2014] 2017, 13)

Murakami's conclusion to a story about a man losing his wife and only just barely coping by, as one character tells him, using "that blank space as a kind of loophole" (202) is admittedly melancholic. But it is a melancholy that, in pointing specifically to an object lost, takes on a more emotionally punctuated form, almost sentimental.

    In a conversation with Murakami, titled in English "A Feminist Critique of Murakami's Novels," the fiction writer Kawakami Mieko challenges Murakami on his depictions of women:

> It's common for my female friends to say to me, "If you love Haruki Murakami's work so much, how do you justify his portrayal of women?" The notion being that there's something disconcerting about the depiction of women in your stories. It irks some people, men and women alike. . . . There are many cases where women are presented as gateways, or opportunities for transformation. . . . On the one hand, your work is boundlessly imaginative when it comes to plots, to wells, and to men, but the same can't be said for their relationships with women. It's not possible for these women to exist on their own. . . . A common reading is that your male characters are fighting their battles unconsciously, on the inside, leaving the women to do the fighting in the real world. (2020, para. 14, 22, 30)

Murakami seemed somewhat surprised and unprepared for the critique: "I think any pattern is probably coincidental. At a minimum, I never set things up like that on purpose. I guess it's possible for a story to work out that way, on a purely unconscious level. . . . I'm not making excuses. I'm speaking from feeling and experience" (Kawakami 2020, para. 32). As Yat Him Tsang has observed in reference to Murakami's speech in Jerusalem quoted above, although Murakami aims to depict the "dignity of the individual soul" against a "system" that sometimes "'takes on a life of its own' and 'begins to kill us,'" these depictions of the individual can be critiqued as "masculinized" (2011, ii), even if embedded in, in Murakami's words, "feeling and experience" and working out on a "purely unconscious level."

While Murakami's literary responses to systems like the state represent just one of many atmospheric spaces for affective refuge, care, and comfort (*iyashi*) in contemporary Japan (Roquet 2016), those spaces may, just like Pop-Culture Japan at large, also nonconsciously leverage stereotypical representations of women to treat historically masculinized concerns. For male administrators, the practice of drawing on scripted national histories in order to transform anxiety over what was lost into hope for something new feels imperative. For many others, however, such as Japan Foundation officials, female cultural administrators, and authors like Itō Hiromi, Kawakami Mieko, as well as for Murakami Haruki himself, this seemingly never-ending circuitry of anxiety and hope tied to national imagining is exhausting. Interlocking representations of the nation with gendered patterns of history, Pop-Culture Japan leverages images of the young, feminine, popular, and cute in order to make the nation politically mature, masculine, successful, and strong. While some male administrators may cultivate a sensitivity to national anxiety as a form of obligatory nationalism and find hope in Pop-Culture Japan through the fantasized images of youthful and commodifiable femininity, such images also reproduce anxieties for real women. As Kawakami Mieko ([2019] 2020, 88) writes in her novel published in English as *Breasts and Eggs*, which rapidly gained global popularity, "Prettiness means value. But some people never experience that personally."[15] If Pop-Culture Japan is for the time being one highly promoted possible future for the nation and one heavily invested in selective depictions of pretty (*kirei*) and cute (*kawaii*) femininity, it will continue not only to be contested ideologically but also to be accommodated affectively by those marginalized and appropriated and even by those who feel administratively obliged to manage it.

Feeling Ethnographically Better

Reflecting on Pop-Culture Japan's potential futures and of other possible futures for Japan naturally raises questions about the role of nationalism at large today, as well as of anthropology's role in assessing it. As I have endeavored to show throughout this book, at least in the way it is administered today, the state is something that impacts affectively—often whether one wants it to or not, whether one celebrates it or not, whether one even, sometimes, *knows* it or not. This latter point in particular makes *affect* a key conceptual term to keep close at hand for cultural analysis. That affect itself is amenable through the way it is represented in narrative, depicted in art, or administered through policy also makes its emotional counterparts—those on the semiotic side of the affect-emotion gap—just as important to analyze. This is what makes the affect-emotion gap/circuit/ nexus/interchange—choose your metaphor—a dynamic and mutable figure as I have tried to describe it. There is an important reflexive component to consider here as well.

Just as the figure of Pop-Culture Japan shapes how people feel about their relation to Japan, whether one identifies as Japanese or not, ethnographic depiction also has its affective consequences. Although what Thomas Stodulka (2013) and Stodulka, Dinkelaker, and Thajib (2019) have called the "researcher's affects" may not fall within the traditional purview of anthropological analysis or of the ethnographic record as we typically know it now, I and others who write about it certainly have our own feelings about what "Japan" means as figure, place, concept, idea, and effect. And whether we try or not to exclude those feelings from our writing, they inevitably sneak back in through the frames of our analysis. From this perspective, one may wonder just how anxious I am myself about the future of Japan or of Pop-Culture Japan. A commitment to my readers, to the affect theory I've engaged with here, and to a certain anthropological reflexivity in which I was trained likely justifies a reply.

After spending more than a decade living in and through that shifting and amorphous but nevertheless tangible figure we call "Japan," and much longer researching it, I cannot help but think I share with my interlocutors a certain anxiety about *how* Japan can best mean for those who, either out of professional obligation or unexpected happenstance, come to care for it. If, as Durkheim proposed, collective representations such as the nation are made of those collaborative feelings to which we give conceptual shape, do those representations also call for our collective care and responsibility? And if so, how should the anthropologist best write on nations and nationalism with this in mind? While I have, admittedly, purposefully performed a certain analytical distance for communicative effect, my own *feelings* remain largely unchanged: one cares for the interlocutors he studies and for the figures that for better or worse shape their sentiments. In this respect, feelings always already in part condition our objects of research, as well as, as James Faubion has argued (2009, 155–56), the ontological and interpretive frames we apply to make sense of them. From this perspective, articulating the affect-emotion gap operating through Pop-Culture Japan demands that the researcher make the project, like all ethnographic projects, necessarily personal to be sufficiently "thick," as Geertz (1973) famously called good ethnographic description.

In this sense, I wonder if there is not a way for those more connected to Japan than I am—or indeed for those connected to or disconnected from a nation anywhere, whether by cultural fate or cultivated choice—to feel better in relation to it. Accordingly, I wonder how anthropologists can feel *ethnographically* better—methodologically, analytically, theoretically—toward this end, given, again, the inescapable realities of ethnographic reflexivity. Should Pop-Culture Japan have come and quickly gone like any other national figure or fad, I might be less concerned about the kinds of anxiety I found to undergird it. Should it have less affective impact on less global a scale, I might be less committed to analyzing its antecedents and likely trajectories. However, for those deeply affected by a global anxiety that intersects politically with national figures on multiple fronts at the moment, I sense there is some value in recognizing in it a shared vulnerability—an increased susceptibility to simple narratives that either too quickly or too rashly push people together or pull them apart. Capturing these affective sensations remains a challenge for the anthropology of affect. What that challenge also importantly reveals, I think, is not only anthropology's role in understanding feeling but in feeling's role in affecting anthropology.

Moments of intellectual rupture brought about by dramatic global events, such as Japan's triple disaster, a global pandemic, resurgent calls for racial justice, or even a decade-long research project that inevitably hits close to home, unveil the importance of cultivating feeling toward the diagnosis of social celebration and social pain—toward, in other words, feeling ethnographically better. While one may feel discomforted or disillusioned by leveraging affect to anthropological analysis, perhaps it is precisely *because* many in times of national anxiety or dramatic global upheaval are so personally affected that one might also find solace in admitting that ethnographic practice has not recently, nor has it ever, done otherwise. Whether carried out by an anthropologist or government administrator, managing or administering affect inevitably *administers* affect of another sort. Perhaps the recognition of our shared conditions, contradictions, and complicities in this process may lead to feeling collaboratively better through future anthropological experiments with affect.

Notes

Introduction

1. In his classic study of popular culture, John Fiske (1989) distinguishes between "mass culture," referring specifically to products made by dominant commercial industries (or what John Storey [2018, 8] eloquently called "hopelessly commercial culture"), and "popular culture," referring to the organic practices, material objects, and semiotic systems through which people create meaning. Importantly for Fiske, although the latter was embedded with forces of "domination and subordination," which were the forces of most concern to early critics of mass culture (Horkheimer and Adorno [1944] 1998), the field of popular culture also afforded "signs of resisting or evading these forces" (Fiske 1989, 4–5). I use *popular culture* to refer similarly to this zone of contradictory forces and practices where subordination, resistance, and a wide variety of identity practices are exercised through material culture.

2. In her expert analysis of popular culture in relation to the all-female theater troupe Takarazuka, Jennifer Robertson (1998) notes the difficulty of maintaining Fiske's "popular culture" versus "mass culture" distinction when translating these terms into Japanese. The more relevant distinction in Japanese, according to Robertson, drawing from Kawazoe (1980), is between *taishū* and *minshū* culture. While *minshū bunka* (culture of the masses) refers more to folk and regional cultures, *taishū bunka* is a more "transcendent category— occasioned by certain forces, such as industrialization and modernization—that is virtually synonymous with the nation in its superclass, superregional orientation and its affective reach" (Robertson 1998, 34). Robertson's description points to the difficulty of distinguishing mass from popular culture forces in Japan, while also suggesting that given the reach of and accessibility to *taishū bunka,* it can also be understood as "national culture." While acknowledging Robertson's insight into the mixing of dominant and resistant forces of mass and popular culture in Japan, I highlight the category of "national culture" as a contested figure, disproportionately defined by state administrators and sometimes enthusiastically accepted by and rejected by Japanese citizens.

3. The philosopher and social anthropologist Ernest Gellner's classic distinction between nation and state proves useful for thinking about how soft power is mobilized toward varying "sentimental" and "instrumental" ends, terms originally used by the social psychologist Herbert Kelman (2001) to denote two different ways individuals emotionally invest, or "cathect," in political systems. As the nation is imagined culturally, through shared symbols, imagery, and stories, the state serves as the political entity whose responsibility it is to administer and secure the integrity of it. "Nationalism," Gellner explains, "is primarily a political principle, which holds that the political and the national unit should be congruent" (1983, 1). This splitting of the state from the nation engenders strong sentiments. Gellner (1983, 1) writes, "Nationalist sentiment is the feeling of anger aroused by the violation of the principle [that the political and the national unit should be congruent], or the feeling of satisfaction aroused by its fulfillment."

4. I make two additional notes here on terminology in relation to "Pop-Culture Japan" and the "assemblage" respectively. First, while *Pop-Culture Japan* is an analytical term that I apply to identify this assemblage of soft power, nation branding, cultural diplomacy, and geopolitical anxiety at play in Japan, it is also applied in emic instances among those I consider its advocates. Examples include references to pop-culture diplomacy (*poppu karuchā gaikō*) and pop-culture communicators (*poppu karuchā hasshinshi*) by administrators in the Ministry of Foreign Affairs (MOFA 2017); the establishment of a pop-culture team within the Japan Foundation; and descriptions by popular authors of Japan's "Pop Power" (*Poppu pawā*; Nakamura and Onouchi 2006) and of pop culture's ability to "save the world through manga, anime, and characterization" (Koyama 2004).

Second, my use of the term *assemblage* draws on the work of Deleuze and Guattari (1987); Foucault (1980); and more recently, De Landa (2016). It also draws on overlapping definitions of what Foucault calls the "apparatus" (*dispositif*), which he defined as "a thoroughly heterogeneous ensemble consisting of discourses, institutions, architectural forms, regulatory decisions, laws, administrative measures, scientific statements, philosophical, moral and philanthropic propositions—in short, the said as much as the unsaid. Such are the elements of the apparatus. The apparatus itself is the system of relations that can be established between these elements" (Foucault 1980, 194). I find Foucault's emphasis on the apparatus as characterized by the "*relations* that can be established between these elements" useful for what I aim to describe with the phrase "Pop-Culture Japan." My preference for *assemblage* as opposed to *apparatus* comes only from what Paul Rabinow notes is a temporal dynamic that can distinguish between the two: "Assemblages are secondary matrices from which apparatuses emerge and become stabilized or transformed" (Rabinow 2003, 56).

5. The "Lippmann-Dewey debate" has become a conventional reference in communication studies today, highlighting the endurance of a problematization since at least the 1920s of how to facilitate democratic participation given the increasing technological complexity of communication in large-scale societies. In reality, there was never an actual debate between Lippmann and Dewey. Rather, the journalist and critic Walter Lippmann outlined a critique of democracy in his books *Public Opinion* (1922) and *The Phantom Public* (1925), arguing that the institutionalization of a group of experts was the only way

to enable the legitimate characterization of social problems and solutions. In favorable reviews of Lippmann's books and in a series of lectures later published as *The Public and Its Problems*, Dewey praised Lippmann's critique of the threats facing democracy but disagreed with his answer, instead proposing to seek an ethos as well as a practice of democracy. What made this discourse into a debate, argues Schudson (2008, 1032), "were liberal intellectuals in the 1980s and 1990s, writing at another moment of democratic disillusion as they sought to take stock and seek hope."

6. An important but less-cited exception to Weber's otherwise largely affectless characterization of bureaucracy is a point he makes on sentiments of status: "A strong status sentiment among officials not only is compatible with the official's readiness to subordinate himself to his superior without any will of his own, but—as in the case with the officer—status sentiments are the compensatory consequence of such subordination, serving to maintain the official's self-respect" ([1922] 1978, 968).

7. While few anthropological studies address bureaucratic sensitivity as a specific ethnographic focus, several works have emerged that analyze the affective dimensions of the state, such as Ann Stoler's "Affective States" (2007) and *Along the Archival Grain* (2008); Matthew Hull's *Government of Paper* (2012); Laura Bear's *Navigating Austerity* (2015); Nayanika Mathur's *Paper Tiger* (2015); Bear and Mathur's "Remaking the Public Good" (2015); the collection of works on "affective states" by Laszczkowski and Reeves (2015); Jason Dittmer's *Diplomatic Material* (2017); Maria Rashid's *Dying to Serve* (2020); and most importantly, Yael Navaro-Yashin's *The Make-Believe Space* (2012).

8. Anderson famously writes, "Communities are to be distinguished, not by their falsity/genuineness, but by the style in which they are imagined" ([1986] 2006, 6).

9. Cosplay is derived from the Japanese *kosupurei*, a portmanteau of "costume" and "play." In cosplay conventions, participants dress up as admired characters from manga, anime, and games.

10. The *Economist* article also features in NHK's promotional video for the new series (NHK 2011b).

11. In September 2014, Prime Minister Modi made a statement to the UN General Assembly in which he proposed an International Yoga Day on June 21: "Yoga is an invaluable gift from our ancient tradition. Yoga embodies unity of mind and body, thought and action . . . a holistic approach [that] is valuable to our health and our well-being. Yoga is not just about exercise; it is a way to discover the sense of oneness with yourself, the world and the nature" (United Nations 2015). While quickly adopted around the world and officially announced by the United Nations the next year, the announcement also strained tensions in India between Hindus and Muslims over the religious status of yoga (Burke 2015).

12. These figures are gathered from "China GDP Growth Rate," Trading Economics, accessed June 11, 2020, https://tradingeconomics.com/china/gdp-growth.

13. In 2010, there were 282 centers operating in 88 countries (Dawson 2010). At the time of writing in 2020, there were 530 in 149 countries (Xinhua 2019).

14. For a few representative book-length studies, see Nye (2004); Matsuda (2007); Kurlantzick (2007); Otmazgin (2013); Watanabe and McConnell (2008); Snow (2016); Hub-

bert (2019); and Bhutto (2019). Also see Ulf Hannerz's (2016) chapter on soft power in his *Writing Future Worlds* (2016).

15. This argument builds on the work of others who have recognized similar functions of the soft power and Cool Japan discourse in Japan, such as Leheny (2006a, 2018); Lam (2007); Otmazgin (2008, 2013); Choo (2009, 2010, 2013); Daliot-Bul (2009); Valaskivi (2013); and Iwabuchi (2015).

16. See in particular Watanabe and McConnell's (2008) volume in which multiple authors refer to this point.

17. Author Kawaguchi Morinosuke has made a recent attempt to quantify soft power in his 2016 book *Nihonjin mo shiranakatta Nihon no kokuryoku (sofuto pawā)*. However, the book is even more editorial than the English title suggests. The English translation printed on the cover of the book reads, "Gross National Talent: A Quantitative Analysis of Amazing Japanese Soft Power." A literal translation would better read, "The Soft Power of Japan That Even Japanese Don't Know."

18. The most detailed studies of Japan's content industries are provided by Japan's Digital Content Association in the annual *Digital Content Report (Dejitaru kontentsu hakusho)*. The Ministry of Economy, Trade and Industry regularly incorporates data from these reports and other sources in ministry summaries, such as *The Current State of the Content Industry and Future Development Trends (Kontentsu sangyō no genjō to kongo no hatten no hōkōsei)*, *Content Industry International Market and Domestic Market Overview (Kontentsu no sekai shijō Nihon shijō no gaikan)*, and several white paper reports (*hakusho; hōkokusho*) included in the content industries (*kontentsu sangyō*) and the Cool Japan/creative industries (*kūru Japan/kurieitibu sangyō*) section of the ministry's website (www.meti.go.jp/policy/index.html). These summaries show mixed trends, with certain sectors like games and character development slowly increasing but others like music and publishing in decline. Fluctuation and the global financial crisis in 2008 make broad estimates difficult, but in the anime industry, for example, the industry most often cited as evidence for Cool Japan's appeal abroad, the industry declined from 31 billion yen ($310 million) earned from exports in 2005 to less than 20 billion yen ($200 million) in 2015 (Kawashima 2018, 25). Highlighted in METI's latest summary of content industry exports is Japan's decline in its total share of the global content market from 8.25 percent in 2016 to 8.22 percent in 2019 and an estimated 7.98 percent for 2023 (METI 2020a, 2). As Oyama Shinji (2019, 7) summarizes, "Creative industries in the US generate more than 17% of its annual turnover in the overseas market, while Japan's remains low at 2.8%. . . . If one looks at the size of actual revenue inflow for media and content—character goods ($315 million), animation ($130 million), and manga ($120 million)—it becomes apparent that they are not enough to have a substantial influence on employment and growth." Kawashima argues that "the available data strongly suggest the lack of income from abroad" (2018, 24) and "the economic policy of the Japanese government specifically targeting these [content] industries does not seem to have been impressive in its results" (20). Also see Otmazgin (2013) for a more comprehensive review.

19. Yasukuni Shrine, in Tokyo's Chiyoda ward, commemorates soldiers and victims of Japan's military conflicts. Its enshrining of the deceased as *kami* (deities), including not only

Japanese but also non-Japanese involved in relief efforts, such as Korean and Taiwanese, has become a flashpoint for contesting Japan's military incursions in East and Southeast Asia.

20. In a similar analysis of the circulation of "Cool Japan" through government offices, Kukhee Choo traces "Cool Japan" vocabulary in governmental proceedings on anime and the content industries, finding a sudden and significant proliferation in the early 2000s of proceedings in which the words *content* (*kontentsu*) and *anime* are cited (2009, 122).

21. The official website for the Cool Japan Fund explains that the "Cool Japan Fund was founded in November 2013 as a public-private fund with the aim of supporting and promoting the development of demand overseas for excellent Japanese products and services" (https://www.cj-fund.co.jp/en/about/cjfund.html, accessed July 16, 2020).

22. For studies on the role of "characters" in Japanese popular culture, see also Allison (2006); Azuma (2009); Condry (2009); Manning (2009); Steinberg (2009); Occhi (2010, 2012); Nozawa (2013); Yano (2013b); and Galbraith (2019).

23. Although styles of anthropological thought, particularly North American, have long attended to how "culture" shapes emotional capacities, most notably in what came to be called the Culture and Personality school attributed to American anthropologists Margaret Mead and Ruth Benedict in the early to mid twentieth century, "emotion" most crystallized into an object of ethnographic observation and theoretical discussion in the 1970s and '80s. Robert Levy aimed to capture the "interior" experiences or "ethnopsychology" of the "Tahitians" in his prominent 1973 ethnography. Writing a few years later, Michelle Rosaldo (1980) and Renato Rosaldo (1989) analyzed emotional experiences of the Ilongot in the northern Philippines, with the latter famously characterizing a feeling called *liget* that, although not having an exact equivalent in anglophone cultures, was best described in the idiomatic expression by locals when they said, "It makes us want to 'cut off human heads'" (Rosaldo 1989, 168). Catherine Lutz, in her study of the Ifaluk in Micronesia (1982, 1988), famously leveraged local words that combined moral reflection and sentiment, such as *fago* (loneliness/sadness) and *song* (justified anger), to build a critique of the highly contextual and gendered division between reason and emotion in Western cultures. Other important works on emotion from this period followed a similar approach (Levy 1984; Abu-Lughod 1986; Lutz and White 1986; Lutz and Abu-Lughod 1990; Wikan 1990; Myers 1991).

These works found evidence for different arrangements of emotional experiences in emotion words that did not neatly map onto words in other languages and the cultures in which they were presumably bound. In this sense, anthropologists of emotion added important cultural and discursive context to classic sociological debates on how collective life engenders sentiments, or what Émile Durkheim classically called "collective effervescence" ([1912] 2008). As processes of global movement and capital exchange rendered these culture-bound emotional words less distinct and the 1980s critique of the production of anthropological knowledge challenged an us-them model of culture on both epistemological and ethical grounds, a culture- and language-bound approach to emotion faced limitations. According to some critics of the period, who would later label a shift away from this approach the "affective turn" (Clough 2007), missing in early approaches to emotion was attention to those aspects of emotional energy and intensity that could never be quite captured in language and that often exceeded and confounded it. Although scholars associated with the affective turn have often overlooked the degree to which anthropologists in the 1980s did, in fact, engage with non-linguistic aspects of emotion (see Lutz 2017; White 2017), they nonetheless drew important attention to the role that nonconscious intensities of feeling and sensation played in the conditioning of emotion and productively asked how anthropologists could incorporate "affect" into their conceptual toolkit.

24. Affect theory grows generally out of two genealogical trajectories, with yet a third deserving recognition. The first is psychological, rooted in evolutionary debates inspired by Darwin's *The Expression of the Emotions in Man and Animals* (1872), passing through a critical debate focused on William James's "What Is an Emotion" (1884), then relegated to the realm of instincts and the unconscious in Freud. Most important to this genealogy is the work of Silvan Tomkins and his momentous *Affect Imagery Consciousness* (2008), which captured renewed interest among critical theorists with Eve Kosofsky Sedgwick and Adam Frank's essay and volume on Tomkins (1995). The second and more often-cited trajectory is philosophical, beginning with Spinoza's *Ethics* in 1677, rekindled in Deleuze's materialism, and most popularized today in the work of Brian Massumi (2002). The plethora of scholars within the humanities and social sciences recently taking up projects that at least in part address affect are indebted to this latter tradition, even if critical of it (Fisher 2002; Terada 2003; Brennan 2004; Thrift 2004, 2008; De Landa 2016; Clough 2007; Stewart 2007; Gregg and Seigworth 2010; Berlant 2011; Mazzarella 2013, 2017; Anderson 2014; Berlant and Stewart 2019). A third body of work deserving attention includes studies from geography, literature, women's studies, critical race studies, and anthropology that have more directly criticized the citational practices that have inflated the prominence of the Deleuze-Massumi nexus and overlooked important work that aimed to situate affect not in universalizing figures of the body and biology but rather in social and cultural contexts. Examples of these works include Ahmed (2004a, 2004b); Ngai (2005); Thien (2005); Navaro-Yashin (2009, 2012); Muehlebach (2011); Leys (2011, 2017); Martin (2013); Berg and Ramos-Zayas (2015); and Boler and Zembylas (2016). For additional genealogical summaries of affect theory, see Navaro-Yashin (2012); and De Antoni (2019).

25. This philosophical debate between the semiotics and somatics of sensation is also reflected in psychological genealogies. See in particular Stanley Schachter and Jerome Singer's "two factor theory of emotion" (1962).

26. Throughout this book, I follow Massumi's (2002) use of the term "nonconscious" rather than "unconscious" to distinguish affect theory's engagement with nonconscious modes of socially coding a body's responses that are not grounded in a Freudian model of the unconscious.

27. I appeal to the metaphor of "circuitry" no more than is necessary to illustrate these three dimensions of the relationship between affect and emotion I wish to feature: feedback, transduction, and gapping. I do not suggest to extend the metaphor of "circuitry" into an even more ambiguous notion of "energy." Indeed, I am sympathetic to scholars like William Mazzarella (2017) and Jonas Bens (2020), who critique the overdetermination of the energy metaphor from nineteenth-century studies of mana all the way to contemporary affect

theory. As Mazzarella (2017, 52), citing Ulf Hannerz (1992, 264), reminds us, "Whenever one takes an intellectual ride on a metaphor, it is essential that one knows where to get off."

28. My articulation of this "gap" draws from others writing about affect who have made similar observations, such as Tim Ingold (2000); Sara Ahmed (2004a); William Mazzarella (2008); Emily Martin (2013); Lauren Berlant (2011); Margaret Wetherell (2012); and Sasha Newell (2018).

29. In her wide-ranging and multidisciplinary analysis of affect, Margaret Wetherell (2012) discusses the role that "affective discursive loops" (34–36, 53) play in problematizing any clean, ontological distinctions between affect and emotion while also allowing for an analysis of their interactivity. In one particularly insightful passage, she writes, "Spiralling affective discursive loops can be set in motion as initial affect is narrated, communicated, shared, intensified, dispersed, modified and sometimes re-awoken even decades later" (53).

30. In electromechanics, a transducer is a machine or mechanism, such as a sensor, that translates one kind of energy, such as kinetic, into another, such as a digital signal. In his application of the concept of transduction to social analysis, Tim Ingold gives a simple example: "In drawing . . . the pencil serves as a transducer, converting the kinaesthetic awareness of the draughtsman into the flow and inflection of the line" (2013, 131). This notion of transduction effectively describes what I mean by the administrative translation of affective anxiety into pop-culture projects of national hope for Japan.

31. This perspective on power draws from Foucault's work on knowledge and power (1991, 1994).

32. Also see Lam (2007), Leheny (2006a, 2006b, 2018), Bouissou (2008), Watanabe and McConnell (2008), and Bouissou et al. (2010).

33. In this sense, hope also functions as what Hirokazu Miyazaki has described as an affective "method" of knowledge production (2004), a dimension that becomes particularly salient in conditions of the "unknown and the unknowable" (2013, 143). The incorporation of hope into an entire field of research called "hope studies" (*kibōgaku*) at the University of Tokyo also attests to the power of uncertainty and precarity in this particular moment in Japan (Genda 2005; Allison 2013; Leheny 2018).

34. For Wittgenstein, *family resemblances* (*Familienähnlichkeiten*) refers to a shifting set of characteristics that different things have in common but that cannot, because of their commonality, be said to categorically constitute a similarity ([1953] 2009, 36–38). While in his most cited instance, Wittgenstein exemplified the concept in reference to games, and although he applied it as part of his critique of language, it can also help explain the resemblance of anxious affects. From this perspective, anxiety takes on multifaceted dimensions that an ethnographic approach is particularly well suited to tease apart.

35. Two important exceptions worth nothing are David Leheny's (2018) analysis of sentimental national narratives of hope and Katarzyna Cwiertka and Miho Yasuhara's (2020) critique of *washoku* (Japanese food) branding. While these works are not explicitly ethnographic, they directly address the production of national culture, including Cool Japan, from the point of view of state administrators.

36. Anthropologists such as Csordas (1993), Howes (2005), and Pink (2015) have discussed the value of and methods for integrating attention to sensory experience as an important part of the fieldworker's toolkit.

37. *Yakunin*, sometimes combined with the honorific prefix "o" (*oyakunin*), consists of two characters: "役" (*yaku*), which means "duty" or "office," and "人" (*nin*), which means "person." Also see works by Garon (1987) and Shimizu (2020) for historical descriptions of the development of bureaucracy in Japan and of the exceptional role bureaucrats came to play in policymaking relative to other nation-states.

38. Notable examples of the important role that forms of obligatory socialization play in labor contexts in Japan can be found in Allison (1994); Roberts (1994); Ogasawara (1998); and Sedgwick (2007).

Chapter 1

1. For histories of soft power's policy adoption in Japanese politics, see Leheny (2006a, 2018); Lam (2007); Bouissou (2008); Watanabe and McConnell (2008); Daliot-Bul (2009); and Iwabuchi (2007, 2015).

2. Tomiko Yoda and others also refer to this as the "Japanese system," whereby "not only politics and economics but also the nation's social and cultural organizations . . . took shape in the process of [Japan's] modernization" (Yoda 2006a, 16–17).

3. My summary portrays the essential points of what has become a canonical narrative of postwar historical context-setting in ethnographic works on Japan. See Gabriella Lukács's superb ethnography of female entrepreneurs in Japan's digital economy for a more detailed and contextualized version of this postwar narrative (2020, 10).

4. Because of the increased affective toll on workers and the demand to provide friendly affect as a service, some critics have characterized this shift as one to "affective labor." Already in 1983, Arlie Hochschild had published *The Managed Heart*, introducing the concept of "emotional labor" (7) to both emphasize capital's dependence on and appropriation of emotion as well as to designate a set of industries in which, as in her example of the flight attendant, "the emotional style of offering the service is part of the service itself" (5). In their books *Empire* (2000) and *Multitude* (2004), Michael Hardt and Antonio Negri popularized the term "affective labor" to draw attention to the body's capacity to enact and undergo manipulation through labor, ascribing "emotion" to the conceptual field (Hardt and Negri 2004, 108). The similarities between critics like Hochschild, Hardt, and others point to a global shift in labor practices in which affect is increasingly made into an object of conscious management, creating opportunities for emotion-savvy consumers and administrators alike.

5. In an article titled "Japanamerica: Why 'Cool Japan' Is Over," academic and journalist of Japan's popular culture Roland Kelts writes, "The phrase 'cool Japan' is as convenient as it is vague. Does it refer to an aspect of the national or ethnic character that is fundamentally cool? Is it Japan's capacity to absorb and then reinvent a range of outside influences that makes it so au courant in our smorgasbord 21st century? And, perhaps most pressing: If Japan is cool now, can it possibly stay that way?" (2010, 1). Additional speculations about (Abel 2011; Mori 2011; McLelland 2017a) and proclamations of (Favell 2011, 47) the end of Cool

Japan in spite of almost twenty years of debate suggest a need to account for the emotional investments sustaining Pop-Culture Japan distinct from Cool Japan.

6. Such gendered framings of the US and Japan reflect a common historical pattern of discriminatory attitudes that follow, in Sylvia Yanagisako's words, "the symbolic equation that East is to West as female is to male" (2002, 185).

7. The joint Fulbright and US-Japan Conference on Cultural and Educational Interchange (CULCON) took place on June 12, 2009 and was titled "Japan & US Soft Power: Addressing Global Challenges."

8. In her work comparing religious and political discourses of international relations, Mika Luoma-Aho writes, "It needs to be said that theorizing on person-hood of the state is hardly a novelty. Body-politics is a remarkably persistent mode of representing the state, the history of which we can easily document from the Ancients to post-Modernity" (2009, 294). For additional studies evaluating anthropomorphism and the personification of the state, see Wendt (1999); Neumann (2004); Franke and Roos (2010); and Hall (2015). Also see Douglas (1984); and Anderson ([1986] 2006) for respective studies on the body, imagined communities, and their implications for the "body politic."

9. The affective energy surrounding Obama's rhetoric of hope has been described as a global phenomenon. Christine Yano's essay (2013a) on its permutations in Japan suggests how hopeful affect can take shape in multiple and varied discourses.

10. For an elegant study of the relevance of mana and magical thinking to contemporary politics, see William Mazzarella's *The Mana of Mass Society* (2017). For a discussion of the connection of dreams to sociomaterial environments, see Daniel Miller's *Materiality* (2005, 8–9).

11. Thomas Csordas calls "somatic modes of attention" the "culturally elaborated ways of attending to and with one's body in surroundings that include the embodied presence of others" (1993, 138).

12. In addition to anthropological work on embodiment by Csordas (1990, 1993, 1994) and Mascia-Lees (2011), see in particular Susan Lepselter's (2016) ethnography on repetition and resonance as the operative poetic mechanisms driving the anxious affects of UFO experiencers in the western United States.

13. In the translation of Shimizu's 2013 work (Shimizu 2020), Amin Ghadimi makes what I think is the correct rendering of "those bureaucrats" (*karera*) as "men." While *karera* can be a gender-neutral plural pronoun, when members of the group contain both men and women, translating *karera* as "men" draws attention to the fact that men have historically dominated Japan's modern bureaucracy, even if this point on gender is left unexamined by Shimizu in the original. Statistics suggest that this is still the case today. In the decades prior to 2015, female government officials (*kōmuin*) averaged 25 percent of the total. In 2015, when the cabinet introduced a plan for gender equality, this number increased to 31 percent and then to 35.4 percent in 2019 (data from Japan's Cabinet Secretariat, https://www.cas.go.jp/jp/gaiyou/jimu/jinjikyoku/jinji_w5.html, accessed May 26, 2020).

14. See David Leheny (2018, 115) for an eloquent reflection on an encounter with a state official that resembles my own experiences, wherein Japan's politicians compare their country with "advanced industrial nations" as a "natural" habit within administrative culture.

15. On this debate over Japan's legacy as copier versus innovator, Sheldon Garon (1987, 7) writes, "Japanese leaders, it is now argued, did not slavishly imitate; rather, they engaged in 'selective borrowing,' whereby they selected what was necessary from various Western models and then skillfully adapted it to their native culture." For an analysis of cultural adoption and adaptation discourses related to popular culture, see Craig (2000).

16. That the term *wakon yōsai*, commonly translated as "Japanese spirit, Western technology," has become one of the most common tropes of Japan's relationship with the West in histories of Japan's modernization further attests to the power of political elites and intellectuals to leverage state apparatuses to normalize their own articulations of national problems over others.

17. Further demonstrating the power of Vogel's legacy in the present, both Vogel and former Prime Minister Nakasone attended a symposium on *Japan as Number One* in October 2010 (Fukada 2010).

18. The "Overcoming Modernity" (*Kindai no chōkoku*) symposium assembled several of Japan's leading intellectuals in Tokyo for two days in July 1942 to envision a way forward for Japan's modernization that preserved Japan's traditional culture while also overcoming the influential threat of the West. Calichman (2008, ix) writes of the symposium, "In the Overcoming Modernity symposium, the modernity to be overcome was associated with the West itself, such that overcoming modernity and overcoming the West were seen as essentially the same thing. In this way, the symposium participants refused to acknowledge that Japan's course of modernization, with its nearly fifty-year history of colonial acquisition, already represented a certain fulfillment of modernity. . . . While the symposium largely focused on the need to restore Japan's traditional culture and spirit, it is important to grasp that this appeal to cultural nationalism and the country's military expansionism were in fact two sides of the same coin."

19. The characters for *kanmin* (官民) stand for "officials" and "people" respectively. As Hayashi Kaori explains (1999), in Japan the word *public* (*kōkyō*) most often refers to officials of state administration rather than to the people who, in the traditional Habermasian sense (1989), stand over and distinct from the state. *Yuchaku* (癒着), a medical term, means adhesion, healing up, or union (McVeigh 1998, 91).

20. See again Kukhee Choo's work (2009) on the emergence of Cool Japan as in large part stimulated by South Korea's own investments in its culture industries.

21. Japanese yen to US dollar exchange rates are calculated at the time of each citation during fieldwork from 2009 to 2010, where 100 JPY averaged US$0.90 (macrotrends.net/2550/dollar-yen-exchange-rate-historical-chart).

22. The leader of the Democratic Party of Japan, who in a rare shift in political control from the Liberal Democratic Party would serve as prime minister from September 2009 through June 2010, is quoted as saying about the Media Arts Center, "It's Taro Aso who likes anime. Now the bureaucracy has decided to build (a museum) for him. . . . It's nonsense and a terrible waste of money" (Corkill 2009, cited in Matsui 2014).

Chapter 2

1. Although this is a well-known and often-cited story among bureaucrats and politicians in Japan, I cite this version from a conversation with academic Watanabe Yasushi, a prominent scholar of public diplomacy in Japan.

2. I first heard of this phrase from a high-ranking official and researcher from the Japan Foundation.

3. Nye emphasized the independence of soft power from hard forms of power, such as military and economic power: "Soft power uses a different type of currency (not force, not money) to engender cooperation—an attraction to shared values and the justness and duty of contributing to the achievement of those values" (2004, 7).

4. Norma Field's brilliant analysis of Tanaka Yasuo's novel *Somehow, Crystal* (*Nantonaku, kurisutaru*, 1980) serves as a representative study of a dominant concern among Japan's intellectuals over the relationship between national identity and consumer culture. The concern is captured in the novel's character Masataka, who opines, "I guess in the end you have to say that we have no resistance to brand names. Our generation. Maybe it's not just our generation, maybe it's all Japanese" (cited in Field 1989, 174–75).

5. For critical studies of nation branding, see Dzenovska (2005); Allison (2009); Kaneva (2011); Aronczyk (2013); and Graan (2013, 2016).

6. Anne Allison has analyzed the reverberation of Cool Japan branding among youth, writing, "What is a form of biopower—the life of youth at play, in their imaginations and through the intimacies they form with others—becomes biocapital—making this productive of capital (and, as soft power, productive of national interests)" (2009, 94). In response to this trend, Allison argues that youth have increasingly invested in what she calls "affective activism," which "attempts to care for the wounds youth have incurred in a capitalist society where reserves of care have dried up" (92).

7. One prominent example of the postwar call to build Japan into a "nation of culture" came with Prime Minister Katayama Tetsu's address to the Diet in 1947, in which he advocated for "the construction of a democratic nation of peace, a nation of culture" (*minshuteki na heiwa kokka, bunka kokka no kensetsu*) (Dower 1993, 4).

8. Although the committee's explanation emphasizes traditional Japanese art, the logo itself, clearly emphasizing an association of the English letter *J* with the English word *Japan*, arguably draws heavily on the rise of J-pop as a signifier of Japanese popular culture at large. Referencing the work of postmodern critic Asada Akira (2000), Tomiko Yoda explains that "the 1990s were the decade of 'return to J' (*J kaiki*)," which includes J-pop, the popular music genre from Japan, as well as the branding of other popular culture such as the J-league, "a Japanese professional soccer league that was self-consciously created and marketed as a more pop, hip, and contemporary alternative to professional baseball, the traditional national sport of Japan" (2006a, 44). In resonance with my own argument on the creation of Pop-Culture Japan, Yoda argues that "we may understand the prefix *J-* as inscribing the subculturation of the national" (46).

9. See Kukhee Choo's work tracing the proliferation of the terms *content* and *anime* in government white papers in parallel with Cool Japan citation trends (2009, 122).

10. Boyer and Howe (2015) describe a "portable analytic" as a strategy by which anthropologists "develop analytic concepts from within specific ethnographic contexts, concepts that help us to objectify or to epitomize the forces and forms at work there, and then . . . dislocate and mobilize these concepts for experimental, analytical use in new research situations" (in Boyer and Yurchak 2010, 214n4).

11. Iwabuchi (2003, 22) explains that since 1970, 95 percent of Japanese television has been domestically produced.

12. William Mazzarella (2019) argues that this type of jouissance explains the pleasure and popularity of hegemonic discourses, such as those enacted by Donald Trump, in which the speaker in a sense "outparodies" his critics.

13. *Kata* refer to prescribed styles, movements, or instructions characteristic of arts and artistic pedagogies in Japan. In her ethnography of Japanese singers of sentimental folk ballads (*enka*), Christine Yano describes *kata* as "patterned forms," which in the context of *enka* provide not only a "language for expressing emotion, they also embody that emotion, sensually wrought and theatrically staged" (2002, 90).

14. The word *cool* here is left in English, pronounced in Japanese as *kūru*.

15. See chapter 3 for a discussion on the relation between cute and cool culture in the context of Pop-Culture Japan and the gender politics embedded in these terms. *Kawaii International* ran on NHK World for 9 years, broadcasting its final show in March 2021.

16. Kathleen Stewart describes world making, or "worlding," as "a sharpening of attention to the expressivity of something coming into existence. Here, affect is a gathering place of accumulative dispositions. What matters is not meaning gathered into codes but the gathering of experience beyond subjectivity, a transduction of forces, a social aesthetics attuned to the way a tendency takes on consistency, or a new regime of sensation becomes a threshold to the real" (2010, 340).

Chapter 3

1. Fujiko Fujio is actually a pen name for two manga artists collaborating on *Doraemon*, Fujimoto Hiroshi and Abiko Motoo. The original manga ran from 1969 to 1996, with additional volumes released in 2005 under the name *Doraemon+*. Anime, film, and merchandising adaptations of Doraemon have made the character a global figure, and the manga itself is one of the best selling in the world.

2. For related theoretical works on characterization and animation, see Silvio (2010, 2019), Manning and Gershon (2013), and Gershon (2015).

3. This view of affect posits the "environment" as a space where no explicit boundaries between "nature" and "culture" can be discerned at the level of the body. In other words, the "environment" is always already a socially coded space. Perspectives on affect and emotion from fields as diverse as neurology (Damasio 1994), psychology (Barrett 2017), and interpretive anthropology (Geertz 2012) offer similar models of affect.

4. For critical work on the relationship between affect and space not only in anthropology but also in geography, where work on affect has been overlooked and subject to processes of

what Yael Navaro-Yashin (2009) calls "ruination," see Thien (2005); Anderson and Harrison (2011); and Navaro-Yashin (2012).

5. The pop-culture team I worked with consisted of two women and two men, with one of the women employed as temporary staff (*haken*). Although the foundation did not publish any official statistics on gender ratios among employees then, my observations suggested that more women served in the Japan Foundation than in other government ministries, whose statistics on gender are published (National Personnel Authority 2010, 28). Nevertheless, men outnumbered women generally, and more obviously in senior management positions.

6. In describing the second of a four-part approach to ethics derived from what became Foucault's (1984) second volume in his *History of Sexuality, The Uses of Pleasure*, James Faubion (2001, 90) explains, "In introducing the mode of subjectivation as the way 'in which an individual establishes his relation to [a] rule and recognizes himself as obligated to put it into practice,' Foucault plainly seeks to direct our attention to the historical, cultural, and social diversity of the avenues through which actors might assess or be directed to assess the personal applicability of any given ethical standard." In Faubion's application of Foucault's analytic to anthropology and in the context of the anthropology of ethics that has developed alongside it (Zigon 2008; Faubion 2011; Robbins 2013; Laidlaw 2014; Mattingly and Throop 2018), Faubion offers a way to understand how an ethics of obligation can develop in organizational settings such as the Japan Foundation.

7. I use the generic term *advisor* to refer to presenters of Japan's anime diplomacy in this chapter and to the Ambassadors of Cute in the following chapter. In reality, many of the ideas and the promotion for these programs came from a single individual named Sakurai Takamasa, a pop-culture researcher, media producer, and Special Advisor to MOFA on Matters of Anime Diplomacy (Gaimushō Anime Bunka Gaikō ni kan suru Yūshikisha Kaigi Iin). Tragically, Sakurai-san passed away in a traffic accident in Tokyo in December 2015. Given this deeply sad and unexpected event, I hesitate to single out one individual, with whom I cannot engage in dialogue, within a program administered more broadly by MOFA and the Japan Foundation. Thus, I prefer to point to the administrative role that multiple individuals played in facilitating the program. My use of the term *advisor* and sometimes *administrator* when talking about those engaged with pop-culture diplomacy reflects my desire to balance the discussion of the institutional role that MOFA officials and advisors played in promoting animation and the Ambassadors of Cute with respect for Sakurai-san himself.

8. Brian Massumi (2002, 83) writes, "A bureaucracy participates in catalyzing the social or cultural. Furthermore, even bureaucracy has a culture specific to it: its separation from that to which it becomes-immanent constitutes it as a mini society." This can be as true of a state's bureaucratic system as a whole as it is of its constituent agencies.

9. Monji inserted black lines over the eyes of the Iraqi translators to protect their identity. I withhold the image here for the same reason.

10. *Kokutai* is written in Japanese with the characters for "country" (国) and "body" (体). The latter character also refers to one's physical body but is pronounced "*karada*."

11. Of course, this logical discordance between "national culture" and culture as "international public good" can be reconciled in several ways. See Michael Herzfeld's (2005)

discussion of "cultural intimacy" and Brian McVeigh's (2004, 187) description of "proprietary nationalism."

12. Ogoura ultimately adopts and adjusts the phrase *soft power* to fit his bureaucratic obligations, but this is not to say that such obligatory feelings are left unaffected in the process. Important to recognize in the emergence of the soft power discourse, and elucidated in William Connolly's observation that "to place a new word or phrase into an established network is also to alter the network itself in a small or large way" (2002, 72), is that introducing soft power into practices of administering national culture alters that administration.

13. This role was fulfilled and largely created by media producer Sakurai Takamasa (see note 7 from this chapter).

Chapter 4

1. I make this decision with some conflict, noting that there are many who would contest describing women in their twenties as "girls." However, aiming to represent the politics of girl culture and, in the words of Laura Miller (2011b, 103), "women who remain girls in their hearts," I use the word *girls* when describing the dominant representations of the Ambassadors of Cute.

2. I use the generic terms *advisor* or *special advisor* to refer to the presenter of the Ambassadors of Cute in this chapter. This role was most often filled by Special Advisor to MOFA Sakurai Takamasa. However, because of the special circumstances surrounding Sakurai-san (see note 7 in chapter 3) and my emphasis on the role rather than the personality of the special advisor, I use the term *advisor* here to focus attention on the administrative function and administrative affects of managing the Ambassadors of Cute.

3. That the ambiguity of superflat aesthetics and soft power narratives of national culture have similar potential to efface accounts of cultural diversity within Japan is, I would argue, not merely coincidental but typical of aesthetic styles applied to serve the interests of national identity branding.

4. See Reynolds (2009) and Ellwood (2010) for examples.

5. Anne Allison (2009, 92) sees this view on the political and economic productivity of female representations of Cool Japan as adapted from representations of female "reproduction" in more general terms, "not in the sense of whether . . . industry can reproduce, but rather, as the social crisis confronting the nation—and many of its citizens—of (not) being able to (biologically/socially) reproduce and even struggling to (physically/psychically) survive." Also see Sato (2003) and Yoda (2006b).

6. As explained by Mark Crawford, *womenomics* was first coined in 1999 by a "group of investment strategists at Goldman Sachs Japan led by Kathy Matsui" (2021, 1). The term described the group's "recommended strategy for revitalizing the stagnant Japanese economy by 'closing the gender employment gap' and promoting the better utilization of human capital through workplace equality."

7. See Lukács (2020, 16–17) for a brilliant summary of the many recent academic characterizations of recent transformations in labor that emphasize its affective dimensions.

8. See again Sato (2003) for an interwar history of the anxieties that the figure of the "new woman" (*atarashii onna*) elicited among Japan's mostly male managers of state.

9. This is not only a matter of language. Statistics from 2010 show agencies addressing welfare and labor (Kōsei Rōdōshō) employ roughly 24 percent women, comparatively high for state agencies in Japan, while officials and agencies such as the Cabinet Secretary (Naikaku Kanbō) and the National Public Safety Commission (Kokka Kōan Iinkai) employ only 8 percent and 10 percent respectively (National Personnel Authority 2010, 28). This suggests a gendering of agencies based not only on the issues they attend to (feminized welfare versus masculinized policing) but also on the hierarchy of prestige assigned to these agencies—a point I credit to Emma Cook.

10. It is worth noting that other kawaii characters also feature prominently in Pop-Culture Japan. In addition to Doraemon being selected as Anime Ambassador and the three women described in this chapter as Ambassadors of Cute, both Hello Kitty and Pikachu, the latter from the media mix Pokémon, were selected as Special Envoys for the 2025 World Expo to be held in Osaka (MOFA 2017).

11. The status of Hello Kitty's felinity has been cast into doubt by a media storm around Christine Yano's account of a conversation with Sanrio executives (Miranda 2014), who told her that "Hello Kitty is not a cat. She's a cartoon character. She is a little girl. She is a friend. But she is not a cat." In response to widespread surprise and dismay among fans, however, Sanrio subsequently qualified its statements, noting Hello Kitty's anthropomorphized features and leaving her status up to the imagination of fans (Mars 2020).

12. See Kinsella (2000, 19–20) for another example contesting Abe's perspective but from a conservative position, which argues that popular culture like modern manga signal a discrete break from traditional culture.

13. *Boys Love* (BL) refers to content within shōjo manga that emerged in the 1970s and featured homoerotic scenes between young men. Developing from a genre of *shōnen ai* (also translated as "boys love"), which featured young men in relationships that did and did not contain sexual content, BL has become a genre of its own within mainstream manga. BL fanzines (*dōjinshi*) are manga written by fans and feature similarly homoerotic scenes but are often parodic in nature. This amateur manga featuring homoerotic and parodic content is also referred to by fans as *yaoi*. The word is an "acronym for '*yama nashi, ochi nashi, imi nashi*,' or, roughly, 'no climax, no point, no meaning,' an apt description," James Welker arguably suggests, "of the relatively plotless narrative and parodies replete with implied or roughly depicted male-on-male sex" (2015, 55). Important to note about all of these genres is their overlapping nature, diverse content, and gender fluidity by which both women and men are writing for women, men, and nonbinary readers. (Also see the collection of essays on Boys Love in McLelland et al. [2015].)

14. Patrick Galbraith (2019) and Thomas Lammare (Galbraith and Lamarre 2010) make a strong argument that the diversity of practices falling under the category of "otaku" as well as the politicized nature of the term's emergence warrant leaving the term in quotation marks. Given that the term *otaku* has become commonplace today, making its multiple and

contested meanings more apparent now than in the recent past, I omit quotation marks or italics in subsequent references.

15. The verb *moeru* ("to bud") is written 萌える; the homophone *moeru* ("to burn") is written 燃える.

16. Patrick Galbraith writes that *nijigen* and *sanjigen* "mean the manga/anime world or 'dimension' and the human world or 'dimension,' rather than literally two-dimensional and three-dimensional. For example, a manga/anime character in the form of a figurine is still said to be two-dimensional. This is not a distinction between fictional and real, because a two-dimensional character is both fictional and real, but real in a different way than a three-dimensional human. Using the terms 'two-dimensional' and 'three-dimensional,' manga/anime fans talk about their interactions and relations with characters as separate and distinct from humans" (2019, 7).

17. Philosopher of affect Brian Massumi writes that affect "requires a complete reworking of how we think about the body. Something that happens too quickly to have happened actually is virtual. The body is as immediately virtual as it is actual" (1995, 91).

18. This image of otaku as abject and strange rather than cool, currently promoted in Cool Japan discourses, became amplified after reports emerged in 1989 of serial killer Miyazaki Tsutomu. Miyazaki, who had molested and killed four young girls, was also found to own a large collection of pornographic manga and anime. While this event highly stigmatized the word "otaku" at the time, and is still widely remembered today, "otaku" has been generally but not completely emptied of these negative connotations (Leheny 2018, 100).

19. Patrick Galbraith (2009, 100) defines *himote* as "unpopular, especially with females. *Himote* guys believe that the status of women is built on the backs of men, who must slave to earn money and win female attention." In her study of self-identifying *himote*, including an analysis of links between *himote* discourses and the violent attacks on a group of pedestrians in the otaku hub of Akihabara in 2008, Elizabeth Miles (2019) cites scholarship such as that of Ueno Chizuko (2010) that sees *himote* identities as symbolic of new forms of misogyny in contemporary Japan.

20. One of the best illustrations of this point is Patrick Galbraith's (2019, 227–60) discussion of the "Eshi 100" exhibits in Akihabara, featuring collections of bishōjo images and sponsored by representatives from bishōjo game companies as well as Japan's Ministry of Economy, Trade and Industry.

21. Fujioka Shizuka's Official Blog: https://ameblo.jp/shizuka3570/, accessed July 12, 2020.

Chapter 5

1. As Harry Harootunian observes in *History's Disquiet: Modernity, Cultural Practice, and the Question of Everyday Life* (2000, 5), the category of the "everyday" emerged in Japan as a historical moment (most specifically in the late nineteenth and early twentieth centuries), as a lived experience of modernizing and industrializing cities, as well as a "category of historical explanation that enlarged the perspective from which we can explore the contradictions of capitalist modernity." This "perspective" includes those of Japanese intellectuals like Tosaka Jun who, as Harootunian notes (2000, 5), described the centering of attention on the everyday

as "both a contemporary category identifying modernity and a philosophical method—what Tosaka Jun called the 'quotidianization of thought.'"

2. Miyadai is most concerned with the infamous sarin gas attacks on the Tokyo subway in 1995 launched by the cult Aum Shinrikyo. Miyadai interprets the cult's appeal as a dangerous consequence of people without the tools to live with the "endless everyday" (*owaranai nichijō*) that emerged in the 1980s in conjunction with a "godless society" (*kaminaki shakai*), the disappearance of Japan's traditional "community" (*kyōdōtai*), and a consequential "wandering conscience" (*samayoeru ryōshin*) (1995, 111–12). In response, Miyadai writes, "what we need today is 'wisdom to live with the endless everyday.' This means 'wisdom to live within the endless everyday holding a vague conscience without understanding what is good'" (*Watashitachi ni hitsuyō na no wa, 'owaranai nichijō o ikiru chie' da. 'Owaranai nichijō no naka de, nani ga yoki koto na no ka wakaranai mama, bakuzen to shita ryōshin o kakaete ikiru chie' da*) (1998, 113). I thank one of my astute anonymous reviewers for drawing my attention to Miyadai's argument on the endless everyday.

3. In a famous quote articulating the relationship between affect, its forms of articulation, and its transformation into public consciousness, Dewey ([1927] 1954, 183–84) writes, "The function of art has always been to break through the crust of conventionalized and routine consciousness. Common things, a flower, a gleam of moonlight, the song of a bird, not things rare and remote, are means with which the deeper levels of life are touched so that they spring up as desire and thought. This process is art. Poetry, the drama, the novel, are proofs that the problem of presentation is not insoluble. Artists have always been the real purveyors of news, for it is not the outward happening in itself, which is new, but the kindling by it of emotion, perception and appreciation."

4. Building on Dewey's philosophy of the public, Latour writes, "We might be more connected to each other by our worries, our matters of concern, the issues we care for, than by any other set of values, opinions, attitudes or principles" (2005, 4). Moreover, as "matters of concern" are not merely ideological but incorporate material realities, Latour's perspective helps the fieldworker trace how concerns and the affects that accompany them become inscribed through policy, administration, and institutional structures.

5. In his book *Soft Power*, Joseph Nye writes, "Converting [soft power] resources into realized power in the sense of obtaining desired outcomes requires well-designed strategies and skillful leadership" (2004, 3). And later, "Broadcasting is important but needs to be supplemented by effective 'narrow casting'—targeting of messages for particular groups—via the Internet" (2004, 111).

6. Such impositions of national interest appear even more surprising when contrasted with models of public broadcasting on which Japan's public broadcasting system is based, namely the United Kingdom's BBC. See Georgina Born's (2004) ethnography on the BBC for a comparison.

7. Abe's three arrows of economic reform include quantitative easing, stimulus packages, and structural reform. Colloquially known as Abenomics, evaluations of the policies have been mixed, with little evidence suggesting they will lead to substantial increases in growth (Hausman and Wieland 2014). With the delay and then scandals surrounding the

2020 Olympics, hope for Japan's economy seems continually elusive, with critics already claiming Japan has endured yet another lost decade and debating how to prevent a fourth (Iwasaki 2020).

8. Dentsū and Hakuhodo have long dominated as the top two advertising agencies in Japan. In 2018 Dentsū held 38 percent of Japan's total advertising sales compared to 24 percent for Hakuhodo (DigiMarJob 2019).

9. I use pseudonyms in this section for the creators and companies I spoke with.

10. Louis Althusser (1972, 174) famously describes interpellation through the example of a police officer hailing a subject, in which case the subject hailed is marked as both a subject of the law and, as such, is subjugated *to* the law. His model helps illustrate how ideological frameworks supported by the institutions of the state acquire the power of interpellation even over subjects who resist it.

11. Unfortunately, I could not ultimately reproduce images of the exhibition, and little is left of its publicity.

12. The student's project also reflects popular coverage around the world expressing fears, particularly in Japan and the US, over China's Confucius Institutes, which contribute substantial funding to universities and cultural institutes to offer courses on Chinese language and culture, taught by teachers trained at China's state Hanban agency (Hubbert 2019).

13. Some universities, in fact, are doing much more than simply offering courses on Cool Japan. Meiji University in Tokyo, for example, has invested in establishing a manga archive and museum in Akihabara, the Tokyo International Manga Museum (Tōkyō Kokusai Manga Toshokan), which will serve simultaneously as a museum, research center, and tourist attraction. See the project at www.meiji.ac.jp/manga/.

14. At the time of the program's launch in 2014, Japan had five universities ranked in the top one hundred in the world. In an effort to increase this number, MEXT has been aiming to boost the hiring of foreign faculty at Japanese universities, which in 2014 stood at around 4 percent of staff. These numbers can seem dramatically low when one compares them—as administrators do—to universities such as the University of Cambridge and Harvard University, which stood at 40 percent and 30 percent respectively (Kakuchi 2014). Incidentally, the name of the government initiative (Sūpā Gurōbaru Daigaku Sōsei Shien) is slightly adjusted in English. Recognizing the overzealous connotation of the word *super* in English, left as *sūpā* in the Japanese announcement, the program is typically listed in English as the Top Global University Project (Kakuchi 2014).

15. For more on the "apparatus," see note 4 in the introduction.

16. Notable critiques of the state to which I refer and am indebted include Stoler (2007, 2008); Hull (2012); Navaro-Yashin (2012); Mathur (2015); Laszczkowski and Reeves (2015); and Rashid (2020).

17. Just a few representative ethnographic works on Japanese popular culture include those addressing toys (Allison 2006), hip-hop (Condry 2006), anime (Condry 2013), TV drama (Lukács 2010), characters (Tobin 2004; Yano 2013b; Galbraith 2019), digital-economy entrepreneurs (Lukács 2020), and popular culture at large (Iwabuchi 2002). Prominent journals focusing on popular culture in Japan include *Mechademia* and the *East Asian Journal of Popular Culture*.

18. Despite a waning of attention by academics in the specific topic of Cool Japan, the managers of the Cool Japan Fund continue to increase their investment. Kodachi (2019) reports that the "Cool Japan [fund] will spend 40 billion yen more in fiscal 2020, a 120 percent increase from its planned 2019 spending."

19. In 2013 the Japan Foundation reported that 54 percent of Japanese language learners chose to study Japanese out of an interest in "manga, anime, and J-Pop."

20. Laura Miller makes similar observations about her own students, while also citing statistics (Landsberg 2011) that "over half of those studying Japanese in the United States said they wanted to be able to read manga and understand anime" (2017, 52). Also see McLelland (2017).

21. See Jennifer Robertson (2002) for a consideration of how to balance the analytical merits of reflexivity with a growing feeling among many cultural anthropologists that deliberate exercises of reflexivity in (particularly North American) ethnographies overemphasize positionality at the expense of detailed, empirical fieldwork accounts.

22. On specific discussions on affect and ethnographic method, see Howes (2005); Pink (2015); Knudsen and Stage (2015); and De Antoni and Dumouchel (2017). On introspection and method, see Reis (1998); Cook (2018); and White (2018).

23. I thank one of my careful anonymous reviewers for encouraging me to draw out this point on reflexivity and area studies even more here.

24. See again Thomas Stodulka's work on the ethnographer's affects (2015; Stodulka, Selim, and Mattes 2018).

Conclusion

1. This period of 1968–69 is cited by many writers and artists of Murakami's generation as a watershed moment, when students protested against, among other issues, the renewal of the US-Japan Mutual Cooperation and Security Treaty (Anpo jōyaku). These protests coincided with the civil rights movement and student-led protests in the United States against the Vietnam War, as well as with student protests across Europe. In my interview, Murakami described this moment as one of energizing hopefulness for genuine political change, contrasting it with the period that followed, when things essentially returned to the status quo, which he described as deeply depressing.

2. Our meetings took place while I was a graudate student in Japanese literature at the University of Hawai'i, in 2006. Murakami was a visiting professor during this period.

3. Blai Guarné and Paul Hansen (2018) have thematized the notion of escape in their impressive volume *Escaping Japan: Reflections on Estrangement and Exile in the Twenty-First Century*.

4. Many literary scholars would argue that Murakami's novel *The Wind-up Bird Chronicle* ([1994–1995] 1997) represents the kind of explicit engagement with Japan's troubled past, in particular with the Pacific War, that I suggest Murakami avoids. Like many of Murakami's novels, however, I ultimately read into the conclusion of this work (with its historical treatment by many measures an exception within his oeuvre) not a reconciliation with the past nor the charting of alternative future narratives, but rather precisely the kind of melancholic accommodation I describe in this chapter.

5. The more detailed Japanese version reads, "*Mottomo shisutemu to wa ittemo keisanshi no shisutemu to iu no wa amari ni mo han'i ga hirokute fukuzatsu de, shikamo osoroshii made no himitsushugi to kiteru kara, nani ga doko de dō natteru ka nante, hon no hitonigiri toppu ni shika wakaranain da. Yō suru ni migi te ga nani yatteru no ka hidari te ni mo wakaranai shi, migi me to hidari me ga chigau mono o miteru tte yōsu sa*" (Murakami 1985, 189).

6. The Japanese reads, "*Sōzōryoku o kaita kyōryōsa, hikanyōsa. Hitoriaruki suru tēze, kūso na yōgo, sandatsu sareta risō, kōchoku shita shisutemu. Boku ni totte hontō ni kowai no wa sō iu mono da*" (Murakami 2002 I, 385).

7. In fact anthropology has long benefitted from engaging with literature as both a method and object for ethnographic inquiry. See Clifford and Marcus (1986); Dennis and Aycock (1989); De Angelis (2002); Daniel and Peck (1996); Faubion (2003); and Reed (2018).

8. See Hirokazu Miyazaki's (2009) excellent and resonant discussion of ambivalence toward hope in another Murakami (Ryū), writing his famous work *Exodus in a Country of Hope* (2000) in the same period.

9. In Japanese the number 9, pronounced "kyū," is a homophone with the English *Q*, thus making the work a deliberate reference to George Orwell's *Nineteen Eighty-Four* and another allusion to the theme of overbearing systems and systematicity.

10. Oricon News (2009), which compiles statistics on Japan's media industry, stated that 349,513 copies of volume 1 and 2 of the novel were sold in its first week. Asahi News (2019), one of Japan's leading daily newspapers, selected the book as first in its "30 Books of Heisei" list, evaluating books published from 1989 to 2019.

11. The phrase *nantonaku suki* will elicit for many readers a reference to another novel praised for its atmospheric pleasure, Tanaka Yasuo's *Somehow, Crystal* (*Nantonaku, kurisutaru*, 1980). See Norma Field (1989) for an insightful examination of the text.

12. See Silverberg's (2009) historical study of the "erotic grotesque"; Yano's (2013b) work on parodies of Hello Kitty; or any of the many artworks of Nara Yoshitomo featuring young, cute, but often cigarette- or weapon-toting girls.

13. The title plays off Murakami Haruki's popular novel *A Wild Sheep Chase* ([1982] 1989).

14. In other words, as I have endeavored to show throughout the book, I suggest that both anthropologists and administrators of affect engage in similar practices of investing in representations of affect in order to advance individual aims and interests (theoretical positions, professional associations, personal careers).

15. *Breasts and Eggs* (*Chichi to ran*) was originally the title of a short story written by Kawakami in 2007. The story was later rewritten and incorporated into a longer novel titled *Natsuko's Story* (*Natsuko monogatari*) in 2019. The quote from the latter work reads in Japanese, "*Kirei na mono ni wa kachi ga aru. Shikashi sono kireisa ni en ga nai ningen ga iru no da*" (2019, loc. 801).

References

Abe, Shinzō. 2007. "Prime Minister of Japan and His Cabinet. Establishing Japan as a Peaceful Nation of Cultural Exchange." Accessed February 12, 2011. http://www.kantei.go.jp/foreign/policy/bunka.

Abel, Jonathan. 2011. "Can Cool Japan Save Post-Disaster Japan? On the Possiblities and Impossibilities of a Cool Japanology." *International Journal of Japanese Sociology* 20 (1):59–72.

Abu-Lughod, Lila. 1986. *Veiled Sentiments: Honor and Poetry in a Bedouin Society*. Berkeley: University of California Press.

AFP (Agence France-Presse). 2020. "Half of Tokyo Residents Oppose Olympics in 2021: Poll." *Unseen Japan*, June 29, 2020. https://unseenjapan.com/half-of-tokyo-residents-oppose-olympics-in-2021-poll/.

Ahmed, Sara. 2004a. "Collective Feelings: Or, the Impressions Left by Others." *Theory, Culture & Society* 21 (2):25–42.

———. 2004b. *The Cultural Politics of Emotion*. New York: Routledge.

Allison, Anne. 1994. *Nightwork: Sexuality, Pleasure, and Corporate Masculinity in a Tokyo Hostess Club*. Chicago: University of Chicago Press.

———. 2006. *Millennial Monsters: Japanese Toys and the Global Imagination*. Berkeley: University of California Press.

———. 2009. "The Cool Brand, Affective Activism and Japanese Youth." *Theory, Culture & Society* 26 (2–3):89–111.

———. 2013. *Precarious Japan*. Durham, NC: Duke University Press.

Althusser, Louis. 1972. "Ideology and Ideological State Apparatuses: Notes toward an Investigation." In *Lenin and Philosophy, and Other Essays*, 127–86. New York: Monthly Review Press.

Anderson, Ben. 2014. *Encountering Affect: Capacities, Apparatuses, Conditions*. Farnham, Surrey: Ashgate.

Anderson, Ben, and Paul Harrison. 2011. *Taking-Place: Non-Representational Theories and Geography*. London: Routledge.

Anderson, Benedict. [1986] 2006. *Imagined Communities: Reflections on the Origin and Spread of Nationalism.* London: Verso.

Anholt, Simon. 2007. *Competitive Identity: A New Model for the Brand Management of Nations, Cities and Regions.* Hampshire: Palgrave Macmillan.

———. 2013. "Beyond the Nation Brand: The Role of Image and Identity in International Relations." *Exchange: The Journal of Public Diplomacy* 2 (1):1–7.

Aoyama, Tomoko. 2005. "Transgendering *Shōjo Shōsetsu*: Girls' Inter-Text/Sex-Uality." In *Genders, Transgenders and Sexualities in Japan*, edited by Mark McLelland and Romit Dasgupta, 65–80. New York: Routledge.

Appadurai, Arjun. 1996. *Modernity at Large: Cultural Dimensions of Globalization.* Minneapolis: University of Minnesota Press.

Arai, Hisamitsu. 2005. "Intellectual Property Strategy in Japan." *International Journal of Intellectual Property-Law, Economy and Management* 1 (1):5–12.

Aronczyk, Melissa. 2013. *Branding the Nation: The Global Business of National Identity.* Oxford: Oxford University Press.

Asada, Akira. "J-kaiki no yukue" [The future of the return to J]. *Voices* 267:58–59.

Asahi News. 2019. "Asahi Shinbun 'Heisei no 30 Satsu' o happyō 1-i 'IQ84' 2-i 'Watashi o hanasanaide' 3-i 'Kokuhaku'" [Asahi News' "30 Books of Heisei" reports first place "1Q84," second place "Never Let Me Go," third place "Confession"]. *Asahi Shinbun*, March 7, 2019. https://book.asahi.com/article/12182809.

———. 2021. "Anzen anshin no Gorin taikai 'dekinai' 68% Asahi yoron chōsa" [Safe and secure Olympics "cannot be done" 68% Asahi poll]. *Asahi Shinbun*, July 19, 2021. https://www.asahi.com/articles/ASP7L7H2PP7HUZPS006.html.

Ashcraft, Brian, and Shoko Ueda. 2010. *Japanese Schoolgirl Confidential: How Teenage Girls Made a Nation Cool.* Tokyo: Kodansha International.

Ashkenazi, Ofer. 2005. "The Image of the United States in German Film." In *Germany and the Americas: Culture, Politics, and History: A Multidisciplinary Encyclopedia*, edited by Thomas Adam and Will Kaufman, 347–53. Santa Barbara: ABC-CLIO.

Asō, Tarō. 2006. "Speech at the Digital Hollywood University." Ministry of Foreign Affairs of Japan, April 28, 2006. https://www.mofa.go.jp/announce/fm/aso/speech0604-2.html.

Azuma, Hiroki. 2001. "Superflat Japanese Postmodernity." Lecture, MOCA Gallery, Pacific Design Center, West Hollywood, April 5, 2001. https://pdfcoffee.com/azuma-hiroki-superflat-pdf-free.html.

———. 2009. *Otaku: Japan's Database Animals.* Minneapolis: University of Minnesota Press.

Barrett, Lisa Feldman. 2017. *How Emotions Are Made: The Secret Life of the Brain.* Boston: Houghton Mifflin Harcourt.

Baudrillard, Jean. [1970] 2016. *The Consumer Society: Myths and Structures.* Thousand Oaks, CA: Sage.

BBC Radio 3. 2020. "Free Thinking." In *Japan Now 2020*, edited by Philip Dodd. February 19, 2020. https://www.bbc.co.uk/programmes/m000fgyj.

BBC World Service. 2008. "Tracking Poll." Accessed December 11, 2009. www.globescan.com/news_archives/bbccntryview08/.

Bear, Laura. 2015. *Navigating Austerity: Currents of Debt on a South Asian River*. Stanford, CA: Stanford University Press.

Bear, Laura, and Nayanika Mathur. 2015. "Introduction. Remaking the Public Good: A New Anthropology of Bureaucracy." *Cambridge Journal of Anthropology* 33 (1):18–34.

Befu, Harumi. 2001. *Hegemony of Homogeneity: An Anthropological Analysis of "Nihonjinron."* Melbourne: Trans Pacific Press.

Bell, Michael. 2000. *Sentimentalism, Ethics and the Culture of Feeling*. London: Palgrave Macmillan.

Benedict, Ruth. [1946] 2005. *The Chrysanthemum and the Sword: Patterns of Japanese Culture*. Boston: Houghton Mifflin.

Bens, Jonas. 2020. "Vitalism and Its Discontents: Use and Misuse of the Energy Metaphor in Affect and Emotion Research: A Reply to Hicks." *Global Discourse: An Interdisciplinary Journal of Current Affairs* 10 (1):37–40.

Berg, Ulla D., and Ana Y. Ramos-Zayas. 2015. "Racializing Affect: A Theoretical Proposition." *Current Anthropology* 56 (5):654–77.

Berlant, Lauren Gail. 2011. *Cruel Optimism*. Durham, NC: Duke University Press.

Berlant, Lauren Gail, and Kathleen Stewart. 2019. *The Hundreds*. Durham, NC: Duke University Press.

Berndt, Jaqueline, Kazumi Nagaike, and Fusami Ogi. 2019. *Shōjo across Media: Exploring "Girl" Practices in Contemporary Japan*. Cham, Switz.: Palgrave Macmillan.

Bhutto, Fatima. 2019. *New Kings of the World: Dispatches from Bollywood, Dizi and K-Pop*. New York: Columbia Global Reports.

Billig, Michael. 1995. *Banal Nationalism*. London: Sage Publishers.

Boler, Megan, and Michalinos Zembylas. 2016. "Interview with Megan Boler: From 'Feminist Politics of Emotions' to the 'Affective Turn.'" In *Methodological Advances in Research on Emotion and Education*, edited by Michalinos Zembylas and Paul A Schutz, 17–30. Switzerland: Springer.

Born, Georgina. 2004. *Uncertain Vision: Birt, Dyke and the Reinvention of the BCC*. London: Random House.

Bouissou, Jean-Marie. 2008. "Popular Culture as a Tool for Japanese 'Soft Power': Myth or Reality?" Paper presented at Popular Culture Co-productions and Collaborations in East and Southeast Asia Center for Southeast Asian Studies, Kyoto National University, December 10–11.

Bouissou, Jean-Marie, Ariane Beldi, Marco Pellitteri, and Bernd Dolle-Weinkauff. 2010. "Manga in Europe: A Short Study of Market and Fandom " In *Manga: An Anthology of Global and Cultural Perspectives*, edited by Toni Johnson-Woods, 253–66. London and New York: Continuum.

Bourdieu, Pierre. 1977. *Outline of a Theory of Practice*. Cambridge: Cambridge University Press.

———. 1993. *The Field of Cultural Production*. New York: Columbia University Press.

Boyer, Dominic, and Cymene Howe. 2015. "Portable Analytics and Lateral Theory." In *Theory Can Be More Than It Used to Be: Learning Anthropology's Method in a Time of Transition*, edited by Dominic Boyer, James D. Faubion and George E. Marcus, 15–38. Ithaca, NY: Cornell University Press.

Boyer, Dominic, and Alexei Yurchak. 2010. "American Stiob: Or, What Late-Socialist Aesthetics of Parody Reveal about Contemporary Political Culture in the West." *Cultural Anthropology* 25 (2):179–221.

Brennan, Teresa. 2004. *The Transmission of Affect*. Ithaca, NY: Cornell University Press.

Burke, Jason. 2015. "Modi's Plan to Change India and the World through Yoga Angers Religious Minorities." *Guardian*, June 6, 2015. https://www.theguardian.com/world/2015/jun/06/narendra-modi-yoga-india.

Calichman, Richard. 2008. *Overcoming Modernity: Cultural Identity in Wartime Japan*. New York: Columbia University Press.

Cancian, Dan. 2021. "2020 Olympics: 78 Percent of Japanese Oppose the Tokyo Games, Poll Reveals." *Newsweek*, July 14, 2021. https://www.newsweek.com/olympics-2020-tokyo-games-78-percent-japanese-oppose-ipsos-poll-1609534.

Chang, Gordon. 2009. "Humiliating Japan." *Forbes*, October 30, 2009. http://www.forbes.com/2009/10/29/okinawa-japan-china-diplomacy-barack-obama-opinions-columnists-gordon-g-chang.html.

Choo, Kukhee. 2008. "Girls Return Home: Portrayal of Femininity in Popular Japanese Girls' Manga and Anime Texts during the 1990s in *Hana Yori Dango* and *Fruits Basket*." *Women: A Cultural Review* 19 (3):275–96.

———. 2009. "The Making of Cool Japan: The Japanese Government's Cultural and Economic Policies towards the Anime Industry in the Global Age." PhD diss., University of Tokyo.

———. 2010. "'Kūru Japan' nēshon: Nihon no popyurā karuchā shinkyō seisaku" ["Cool Japan" nation: The promotional policies of Japan's pop culture]. In *Sabukaru de yomu nashonarizumu: Kashika sareru aidentiti* [Reading nationalism through subculture: Visualized identity], edited by Tanikawa Takeshi et al., 50–71. Tokyo: Seikyusha.

———. 2013. "Playing the Global Game: Japan Brand and Globalization." In *Asian Popular Culture: The Global (Dis)Continuity*, edited by Anthony Y. H. Fung, 213–27. Abingdon: Routledge.

Clarke, Kamari M. 2013. "Notes on Cultural Citizenship in the Black Atlantic World." *Cultural Anthropology* 28 (3):464–74.

Clifford, James, and George E. Marcus. 1986. *Writing Culture: The Poetics and Politics of Ethnography*. Berkeley: University of California Press.

Clough, Patricia Ticineto. 2007. "Introduction." In *The Affective Turn: Theorizing the Social*, edited by Patricia Ticineto Clough with Jean Halley, 1–33. Durham, NC: Duke University Press.

Condry, Ian. 2006. *Hip-Hop Japan: Rap and the Paths of Cultural Globalization*. Durham, NC: Duke University Press.

———. 2009. "Anime Creativity: Characters and Premises in the Quest for Cool Japan." *Theory, Culture & Society* 26 (2–3):139–63.

————. 2013. *The Soul of Anime: Collaborative Creativity and Japan's Media Success Story.* Durham, NC: Duke University Press.

Connolly, William E. 2002. *Neuropolitics: Thinking, Culture, Speed.* Minneapolis: University of Minnesota Press.

Cook, Emma E. 2016. *Reconstructing Adult Masculinities: Part-Time Work in Contemporary Japan.* London: Routledge.

Cook, Joanna. 2018. "Paying Attention to Attention." *Anthropology of This Century* 22 (May). http://aotcpress.com/articles/paying-attention-attention/.

Corkill, Edan. 2009. "Is a National 'Manga Museum' at Last Set to Get Off the Ground?" *Japan Times*, June 14, 2009. https://www.japantimes.co.jp/life/2009/06/14/general/is-a-national-manga-museum-at-last-set-to-get-off-the-ground/#.Xs5vly2ZMWo.

Cornyetz, Nina, and Keith Vincent. 2010. *Perversion and Modern Japan: Psychoanalysis, Literature, Culture.* Routledge Contemporary Japan Series. London: Routledge.

Craig, Timothy J. 2000. *Japan Pop! Inside the World of Japanese Popular Culture.* Oxon: M. E. Sharpe.

Crawford, Mark. 2021. "Abe's Womenomics Policy, 2013–2020: Tokenism, Gradualism, or Failed Strategy?" *Asia-Pacific Journal: Japan Focus* 19 (4):1–16.

Csordas, Thomas J. 1990. "Embodiment as a Paradigm for Anthropology." *Ethos* 18 (1):5–47.

————. 1993. "Somatic Modes of Attention." *Cultural Anthropology* 8 (2):135–56.

————, ed. 1994. *Embodiment and Experience: The Existential Ground of Culture and Self.* Cambridge: University of Cambridge Press.

Cwiertka, Katarzyna J., and Miho Yasuhara. 2020. *Branding Japanese Food: From Meibutsu to Washoku.* Honolulu: University of Hawai'i Press.

Daliot-Bul, Michal. 2009. "Japan Brand Strategy: The Taming of 'Cool Japan' and the Challenges of Cultural Planning in a Postmodern Age." *Social Science Japan Journal* 12 (2):247–66.

Damasio, Antonio R. 1994. *Descartes' Error: Emotion, Reason, and the Human Brain.* New York: Putnam.

Daniel, E. Valentine, and Jeffrey M. Peck. 1996. *Culture/Contexture: Explorations in Anthropology and Literary Studies.* Berkeley: University of California Press.

Darwin, Charles. [1872] 2018. *The Expression of the Emotions in Man and Animals.* Mineola, NY: Dover.

Dawson, Kelly Chung. 2010. "Confucius Institutes Enhance China's International Image." *China Daily*, April 23, 2010. http://www.chinadaily.com.cn/china/2010-04/23/content_9766116.htm.

De Angelis, Rose. 2002. *Between Anthropology and Literature: Interdisciplinary Discourse.* London: Routledge.

De Antoni, Andrea. 2019. "Affect." In *The International Encyclopedia of Anthropology*, edited by Hilary Callan, 1–8. New Jersey: John Wiley and Sons.

De Antoni, Andrea, and Paul Dumouchel. 2017. "Practices of Feeling with the World." *Japanese Review of Cultural Anthropology* 18 (1):91–98.

De Landa, Manuel. 2016. *Assemblage Theory.* Edinburgh: Edinburgh University Press.

Deleuze, Gilles, and Félix Guattari. 1983. *Anti-Oedipus: Capitalism and Schizophrenia*. Minneapolis: University of Minnesota Press.

———. 1987. *A Thousand Plateaus: Capitalism and Schizophrenia*. Translated by Brian Massumi. Minneapolis: University of Minnesota Press.

Dennis, Philip Adams, and Wendell M. Aycock. 1989. *Literature and Anthropology*. Lubbock: Texas Tech University Press.

Dewey, John. [1927] 1954. *The Public and Its Problems*. Athens: Swallow Press.

DigiMarJob. 2019. "Kōkoku dairiten uriagedaka rankingu" [Advertising agencies top sales ranking]. *DigiMarJob*, October 25, 2019. https://digimarjob.com/column_job_transfer/ad-agency-ranking-2019-4.

Dinnie, Keith. 2008. *Nation Branding: Concepts, Issues, Practice*. Oxford: Butterworth-Heinemann.

Dittmer, Jason. 2017. *Diplomatic Material: Affect, Assemblage, and Foreign Policy*. Durham, NC: Duke University Press.

Douglas, Mary. 1984. *Purity and Danger*. London: Routledge.

Dower, John W. 1993. "Peace and Democracy in Two Systems: External Policy and Internal Conflict." In *Postwar Japan as History*, edited by Andrew Gordon, 3–33. Berkeley: University of California Press.

———. 1999. *Embracing Defeat: Japan in the Wake of World War II*. New York: Norton.

Durkheim, Émile. [1912] 2008. *The Elementary Forms of the Religious Life*. Translated by Joseph Ward Swain. Mineola, NY: Dover.

Dzenovska, Dace. 2005. "Remaking the Nation of Latvia: Anthropological Perspectives on Nation Branding." *Place Branding* 1 (2):173–86.

Economist. 2010. "The Future of Japan: The Japan Syndrome." November 18, 2010. https://www.economist.com/leaders/2010/11/18/the-japan-syndrome.

Ellwood, Mark. 2010. "Japan's 'Ambassadors of Cute'." *Financial Times*, March 27, 2010. https://www.ft.com/content/06978f58-384d-11df-8420-00144feabdc0.

Faubion, James D. 1993. *Modern Greek Lessons: A Primer in Historical Constructivism*. Princeton, NJ: Princeton University Press.

———. 2001. "Toward an Anthropology of Ethics: Foucault and the Pedagogies of Autopoiesis." *Representations* 74 (1):83–104.

———. 2003. "Cavafy: Toward the Principles of a Transcultural Sociology of Minor Literature." *Modern Greek Studies (Australia and New Zealand)* 11:40–65.

———. 2011. *An Anthropology of Ethics*. Cambridge: Cambridge University Press.

Favell, Adrian. 2011. *Before and after Superflat: A Short History of Japanese Contemporary Art, 1990–2011*. Hong Kong: Blue Kingfisher.

Featherstone, Mike. 1991. *Consumer Culture and Postmodernism*. London: Sage Publications. Published in association with *Theory, Culture & Society*.

Field, Norma. 1989. "Somehow: The Postmodern as Atmosphere." In *Postmodernism and Japan*, edited by Masao Miyoshi, Harry Harootunian, Fredric Jameson, and Stanley Fish, 169–88. Durham, NC: Duke University Press.

Fisher, Philip. 2002. *The Vehement Passions*. Princeton, NJ: Princeton University Press.

Fiske, John. 1989. *Understanding Popular Culture*. Boston: Unwin Hyman.

Foucault, Michel. 1980. "The Confession of the Flesh." In *Power/Knowledge: Selected Interviews and Other Writings, 1972–1977*, edited by Colin Gordon and translated by Colin Gordon, Leo Marshall, John Mepham, and Kate Soper, 194–228. Brighton, Sussex: Harvester Press.

———. 1984. *The Use of Pleasure*, vol. 2 of *The History of Sexuality*. Translated by Robert Hurley. New York: Vintage.

———. 1991. *Discipline and Punish: The Birth of a Prison*. London: Penguin.

———. 1994. "Truth and Power." In *Michel Foucault: Power (Essential Works of Foucault 1954–1984)*, edited by James Faubion, 111–33. New York: New Press.

———. 1997. "Self Writing." In *Michel Foucault: Ethics: Subjectivity and Truth*, edited by Paul Rabinow, 207–22. New York: New Press.

Franke, Ulrich, and Ulrich Roos. 2010. "Actor, Structure, Process: Transcending the State Personhood Debate by Means of a Pragmatist Ontological Model for International Relations Theory." *Review of International Studies* 36 (4):1057–77.

Fraser, Nancy. 2016. "Contradictions of Capital and Care." *New Left Review* 100 (July–Aug.):99–117.

Freedman, Alisa, Laura Miller, and Christine Reiko Yano. 2013. *Modern Girls on the Go: Gender, Mobility, and Labor in Japan*. Stanford, CA: Stanford University Press.

Freud, Sigmund. [1918] 1957. "Mourning and Melancholia." In *The Standard Edition of the Complete Psychological Works of Sigmund Freud*. Vol. 14 (1914–1916), *On the History of the Psycho-Analytic Movement, Papers on Metapsychology and Other Works*, edited by James Strachey, 237–58. London: Hogarth Press.

Frevert, Ute, Monique Scheer, Anne Schmidt, Pascal Eitler, Bettina Hitzer, Nina Verheyen, Benno Gammerl, Christian Bailey, and Margrit Pernau. 2014. *Emotional Lexicons: Continuity and Change in the Vocabulary of Feeling 1700-2000. Emotions in History*. Oxford; New York: Oxford University Press.

Fukada, Takahiro. 2010. "Looking Back at 'Japan as No. 1.'" *Japan Times*, November 11, 2010. https://www.japantimes.co.jp/news/2010/11/11/national/looking-back-at-japan-as-no-1/#.XsvX6y2ZMWo.

Fukuyama, Francis. 1992. *The End of History and the Last Man*. New York: Simon and Schuster.

Gabrakova, Dennitza. 2018. *The Unnamable Archipelago: Wounds of the Postcolonial in Postwar Japanese Literature and Thought*. Leiden: Brill.

Galbraith, Patrick. 2009. *The Otaku Encyclopedia: An Insider's Guide to the Subculture of Cool Japan*. Tokyo: Kodansha International.

———. 2010. "Akihabara: Conditioning a Public 'Otaku' Image." *Mechademia* 5 (1):210–30.

———. 2012. "Idols: The Image of Desire in Japanese Consumer Capitalism." In *Idols and Celebrity in Japanese Media Culture*, 185–208. London: Palgrave Macmillan UK.

———. 2019. *Otaku and the Struggle for Imagination in Japan*. Durham, NC: Duke University Press.

Galbraith, Patrick, and Jason G. Karlin. 2012. *Idols and Celebrity in Japanese Media Culture.* London: Palgrave Macmillan UK.

Galbraith, Patrick, and Thomas Lamarre. 2010. "Otakuology: A Dialogue." *Mechademia* 5:360–74.

Garon, Sheldon. 1987. *The State and Labor in Modern Japan.* Berkeley: University of California Press.

Geertz, Clifford. 1973. "Thick Description: Toward an Interpretive Theory of Culture." In *The Interpretation of Cultures,* 3–30. New York: Basic Books.

———. 2012. "Culture, Mind, Brain / Brain, Mind, Culture." In *Available Light: Anthropological Reflections on Philosophical Topics,* 203–17. Princeton, NJ: Princeton University Press.

Gellner, Ernest. 1983. *Nations and Nationalism, New Perspectives on the Past.* Ithaca, NY: Cornell University Press.

Genda, Yūji. 2005. *A Nagging Sense of Job Insecurity: The New Reality Facing Japanese Youth.* Tokyo: International House of Japan.

———. 2016. "An International Comparison of Hope and Happiness in Japan, the UK, and the US." *Social Science Japan Journal* 19 (2):153–72.

Gershon, Ilana. 2015. "What Do We Talk about When We Talk about Animation." *Social Media + Society* 1 (April–June):1–2.

Gilroy, Paul. 2005. *Postcolonial Melancholia.* New York: Columbia University Press.

Goodman, Roger. 1990. *Japan's "International Youth": The Emergence of a New Class of Schoolchildren.* Oxford: Clarendon Press.

———. 2007. "The Concept of Kokusaika and Japanese Educational Reform." *Globalisation, Societies and Education* 5 (1):71–87.

Gottfried, Heidi. 2009. "Japan: The Reproducitve Bargain and the Making of Precarious Employment." In *Gender and the Contours of Precarious Employment,* edited by Leah F. Vosko, Martha MacDonald, and Ian Campbell, 76–91. London: Routledge.

Graan, Andrew. 2013. "Counterfeiting the Nation? Skopje 2014 and the Politics of Nation Branding in Macedonia." *Cultural Anthropology* 28 (1):161–79.

———. 2016. "The Nation Brand Regime: Nation Branding and the Semiotic Regimentation of Public Communication in Contemporary Macedonia." *Signs and Society* 4 (S1):S70–S105.

Gregg, Melissa, and Gregory J. Seigworth. 2010. *The Affect Theory Reader.* Durham, NC: Duke University Press.

Guarné, Blai, and Paul Hansen. 2018. *Escaping Japan: Reflections on Estrangement and Exile in the Twenty-First Century.* London: Routledge.

Habermas, Jürgen. 1989. *The Structural Transformation of the Public Sphere.* Translated by Thomas Burger. Cambridge, MA: MIT Press.

Hall, Ivan P. 1998. *Cartels of the Mind: Japan's Intellectual Closed Shop.* New York: Norton.

Hall, Todd H. 2015. *Emotional Diplomacy: Official Emotion on the International Stage.* Ithaca, NY: Cornell University Press.

Hamano, Yasuki. 2005. *Mohō sareru Nihon—eiga, anime kara ryōri, fasshon made* [Imitating Japan: From film and anime to food and fashion]. Tokyo: Shōdensha.

Hanada, Tatsurō. 1997. "Can There Be a Public Sphere in Japan?" *Review of Media, Information and Society* 2:1–23.

Handelman, Don. 2007. "The Cartesian Divide of the Nation-State: Emotion and Bureuacratic Logic." In *The Emotions: A Cultural Reader*, edited by Helena Wulff, 119–40. Oxford: Berg Publishers.

Handler, Richard. 1988. *Nationalism and the Politics of Culture in Quebec*. Madison: University of Wisconsin Press.

Hannerz, Ulf. 1992. *Cultural Complexity: Studies in the Social Organization of Meaning*. New York: Columbia University Press.

———. 2016. *Writing Future Worlds: An Anthropologist Explores Global Scenarios*. New York: Palgrave Macmillan.

Hardt, Michael. 1993. *Gilles Deleuze: An Apprenticeship in Philosophy*. Minneapolis: University of Minnesota Press.

Hardt, Michael and Antonio Negri. 2000. *Empire*. Cambridge, MA: Harvard University Press.

———. 2004. *Multitude: War and Democracy in the Age of Empire*. New York: Penguin.

Harootunian, Harry D. 2000. *History's Disquiet: Modernity, Cultural Practice, and the Question of Everyday Life*. New York: Columbia University Press.

Harvey, David. 2005. *A Brief History of Neoliberalism*. Oxford: Oxford University Press.

Harris, Daniel. 2000. *Cute, Quaint, Hungry, and Romantic: The Aesthetics of Consumerism*. New York: Basic Books

Hausman, Joshua K., and Johannes F. Wieland. 2014. "Abenomics: Preliminary Analysis and Outlook." *Brookings Papers on Economic Activity* 2014 (1):1–63.

Hayashi, Kaori. 1999. "Reflections on Japan's Public Sphere and Journalism from a Historical Perspective." *Review of Media, Information and Society* 4:89–114.

Hayashi, Yoshimichi. 1996. *Fusei no fukken* [The restoration of fatherhood]. Tokyo: Chūō Kōronsha.

Herzfeld, Michael. 1992. *The Social Production of Indifference*. Chicago: University of Chicago Press.

———. 2005. *Cultural Intimacy: Social Poetics in the Nation-State*. New York: Routledge.

Hijiya-Kirschnereit, Irmela. 2013. "Is Japan Cool?" In *The Cultural Career of Coolness: Discourses and Practices of Affect Control in European Antiquity, the United States, and Japan*, edited by Ulla Haselstein, Irmela Hijiya-Kirschnereit, Catrin Gersdorf, and Elena Giannoulis, 155–80. Lanham, MD: Lexington Books.

Hochschild, Arlie Russell. 1983. *The Managed Heart: Commercialization of Human Feeling*. Berkeley: University of California Press.

Holbraad, Martin. 2012. *Truth in Motion: The Recursive Anthropology of Cuban Divination*. Chicago: University of Chicago Press.

Holbraad, Martin, and Morten Axel Pedersen. 2017. *The Ontological Turn: An Anthropological Exposition*. Cambridge: Cambridge University Press.

Honda, Tōru. 2005. *Moeru otoko* [Man, bursting into bud]. Tokyo: Shinshō.

Horkheimer, Max, and Theodor W. Adorno. [1944] 1998. *Dialectic of Enlightenment*. New York: Continuum Publishing.

Howes, David. 2005. *Empire of the Senses*. Oxford: Berg Publishers.

Hubbert, Jennifer Ann. 2019. *China in the World: An Anthropology of Confucius Institutes, Soft Power, and Globalization*. Honolulu: University of Hawai'i Press.

Hubbert, Jennifer Ann, and Theodore Powers. 2020. "China, Soft Power, and Confucius Institutes with Jennifer Hubbert." *Anthropology News*, March 18, 2020.

Hull, Matthew S. 2012. *Government of Paper: The Materiality of Bureaucracy in Urban Pakistan*. Berkeley: University of California Press.

Ingold, Tim. 2000. *The Perception of the Environment: Essays on Livelihood, Dwelling and Skill*. London: Routledge.

———. 2011. *Being Alive: Essays on Movement, Knowledge and Description*. London: Routledge.

———. 2013. *Making: Anthropology, Archaeology, Art and Architecture*. London: Routledge.

Ishihara, Shintarō. 1997. *Chichi nakushite kuni tatazu* [No father, no nation]. Tokyo: Kōbunsha.

Ivy, Marilyn. 1995. *Discourses of the Vanishing: Modernity, Phantasm, Japan*. Chicago: University of Chicago Press.

Iwabuchi, Koichi. 2002. *Recentering Globalization: Popular Culture and Japanese Transnationalism*. Durham, NC: Duke University Press.

———. 2003. "Feeling Glocal: Japan in the Global Television Format Business." In *Television across Asia: TV Industries, Programme Formats and Globalisation*, edited by Michael Keane and Albert Moran, 21–35. London: Routledge.

———. 2007. *Bunka no taiwaryoku: Sofuto pawā to burando nashonarizumu o koete* [Culture's power of dialogue: Overcoming soft power and brand nationalism]. Tokyo: Nihon kezai shinbun shuppansha.

———. 2015. "Pop-Culture Diplomacy in Japan: Soft Power, Nation Branding and the Question of 'International Cultural Exchange.'" *International Journal of Cultural Policy* 21 (4):419–432.

Iwasaki, Hiromitsu. 2020. "Nihonjin wa 'ushinawareta 30 nen' no honshitsu o wakattenai" [Japanese people do not understand the nature of "three lost decades"]. *Toyo Keizai Online*, January 26, 2020. https://toyokeizai.net/articles/-/325346.

Jaggar, Alison M. 1989. "Love and Knowledge: Emotion in Feminist Epistemology." *Inquiry* 32 (2):151–76.

James, William. 1884. "What Is an Emotion?" *Mind* 9 (34):188–205. http://www.jstor.org/stable/2246769.

Japan Foundation. 2006. "Haruki o meguru bōken: Sekai wa Murakami bungaku o dō yomu ka" ["A wild Haruki chase": How the world is reading and translating Murakami]. Accessed April 7, 2007. http://www.jpf.go.jp/j/intel_j/topoics/murakami/index.html.

———. 2009. "Japan's Kawaii Ambassador in Brazil." Accessed November 2, 2009. http://www.jpf.go.jp/e/culture/new/0911/11_02.html.

———. 2010. "Dokuritsu gyōsei hojin kokusai kōryū kikin hō" [Independent administrative agency Japan Foundation law]. Accessed December 17, 2010. http://www.jpf.go.jp/j/about/outline/admin/guide/kikinhou/kikinhou.html.

———. 2013. "400-man nin ni semaru! Sekai de Nihongo o manandeiru no wa donna hito?" [Approaching four million people! What kinds of people are studying Japanese?] *Wochi Kochi Magazine*, December 2013.

Japanesque Modern. 2006a. "Raison d'être." Accessed February 10, 2010. Project archived at https://web.archive.org/web/20131206011755/http://www.tepia-infocompass.jp/japanesque-modern/about.html.

———. 2006b. "Shin Nihon yōshiki 100 sen" [New Japan style: 100 selections]. Accessed February 10, 2010. Project archived at https://web.archive.org/web/20131206011755/http://www.tepia-infocompass.jp/japanesque-modern/about.html.

Kakuchi, Suvendrini. 2014. "Not Just International but 'Super Global Universities.'" *University World News*, November 21, 2014. https://www.universityworldnews.com/post.php?story=20141120233337379.

Kaneva, Nadia. 2011. "Nation Branding: Toward an Agenda for Critical Research." *International Journal of Communication* 5:117–41.

Kantei [Cabinet Office], Intellectual Property Headquarters. 2004. *Kontentsu bijinesu shinkō seisaku: Sofuto pawā jidai ko kokka senryaku* [The policy for promotion of content business: National strategy in the age of soft power]. https://www.kantei.go.jp/jp/singi/titeki2/tyousakai/contents/houkoku/040409houkoku.pdf.

———. 2009. *Keizai zaisaku kaikaku no kihon hōshin* [Annual policy plan for the Japanese economy]. http://www.kantei.go.jp/jp/singi/keizai/kakugi/090623kettei.pdf.

Kawakami, Mieko. 2019. *Natsuko monogatari* [Natsuko's story]. Kindle ed. Tokyo: Bungeishunjū.

———. 2020. *Breasts and Eggs*. New York: Europa Editions. (Originally published as *Natsuko monogatari*, 2019).

Kawamata, Keiko. 2005. "Nihon no kontentsu sangyō no genjō" [Outlook for the Japanese content industry]. *Kyoto Management Review* 7:107–32.

Kawasaki, Yasushi. 1997. *NHK to seiji* [NHK and politics]. Tokyo: Asahi Shinbunsha.

Kawasaki, Yasushi, and Tetsuji Shibata. 2004. *Kenshō Nihon no soshiki jānarizumu: NHK to Asahi Shinbun* [Japan's systematized journalism examined: NHK and Asahi News]. Tokyo: Iwanami Shoten.

Kawashima, Nobuko. 2018. "'Cool Japan' and Creative Industries: An Evaluation of Economic Policies for Popular Culture Industries in Japan." In *Asian Cultural Flows*, edited by Nobuko Kawashima and Hye-Kyung Lee, 19–36. Singapore: Springer.

Kawazoe, Noboru. 1980. "Nihon bunmei to taishū bunka" [Japanese enlightenment and mass culture]. *Jurisuto* [Jurist] 20:6–12.

Kelman, Herbert. 2001. "The Role of National Identity in Conflict Resolution: Experiences from Israeli-Palestinian Problem-Solving Workshops." In *Social Identity, Intergroup Conflict, and Conflict Reduction*, edited by R. D. Ashmore, L. Jussim, and D. Wilder, 187–212. Oxford: Oxford University Press.

Kelts, Roland. 2010. "Japanamerica: Why 'Cool Japan' Is Over." *3:AM Magazine*, May 17, 2010. https://www.3ammagazine.com/3am/japanamerica-why-cool-japan-is-over/.

Kinsella, Sharon. 1995. "Cuties in Japan." In *Women, Media and Consumption in Japan*, edited by Lise Skov and Brian Moeran, 220–54. Honolulu: University of Hawai'i Press.

———. 2000. *Adult Manga: Culture and Power in Contemporary Japanese Society*. Honolulu: University of Hawai'i Press.

———. 2014. *Schoolgirls, Money and Rebellion in Japan*. London: Routledge.

Klein, Naomi. 2000. *No Logo*. London: Flamingo.

Knudsen, Britta Timm, and Carsten Stage. 2015. *Affective Methodologies: Developing Cultural Research Strategies for the Study of Affect*. Basingstoke: Palgrave Macmillan.

Kodachi, Hisao. 2019. "Cool Japan and Other State-Backed Funds Hit by Huge Losses." *Nikkei Asian Review*, October 12, 2019. https://asia.nikkei.com/Business/Business-trends/Cool-Japan-and-other-state-backed-funds-hit-by-huge-losses.

Koishikawa, Shinichi. 2018. "Tōkyō Gorin, boranteia fuzoku kennen de daigaku ni jugyō nittei henkō . . . shōchūkōsei mo 'mushō dōin'" [Tokyo Olympics, with fear of volunteer shortage, request for change to university schedules . . . also for elementary, junior, and high schools with "uncompensated mobilization"]. *Business Journal*, September 19, 2018. https://biz-journal.jp/2018/09/post_24825.html.

Komatsu, Sakyō. 1973. *Nihon chinbotsu* [Japan sinks]. Tokyo: Kōbunsha.

Kotani, Mari. 2007. "Doll Beauties and Cosplay." *Mechademia* 2 (1):49–62.

Koyama, Masahiro. 2004. *Poppu karuchā wa sekai o sukuu ka—manga, anime no kyarakutā ka to shōhin kachi* [Will pop culture save the world? The characterization of manga and anime and their merchandise value]. Tokyo: Shōtensha.

Krauss, Ellis S. 2000. *Broadcasting Politics in Japan: NHK and Television News*. Ithaca, NY: Cornell University Press.

Kurlantzick, Joshua. 2007. *Charm Offensive: How China's Soft Power Is Transforming the World*. New Haven, CT: Yale University Press.

Kusuda, Minoru. 1996. "Remarks by the Honorable Minoru Kusuda Former Chief Secretary to Prime Minister Eisaku Sato U.S.-Japanese Relations and the Nixon Shocks, 1969–1976." Woodrow Wilson International Center for Scholars, Smithsonian Institution, March 11, 1996. Accessed December 4, 2021. https://nsarchive2.gwu.edu/japan/kusuda.htm.

Laidlaw, James. 2014. *The Subject of Virtue: An Anthropology of Ethics and Freedom*, New Departures in Anthropology. Cambridge: Cambridge University Press.

Laidlaw, James, and Paolo Heywood. 2013. "One More Turn and You're There." *Anthropology of This Century* 7. http://aotcpress.com/articles/turn/.

Lam, Peng Er. 2007. "Japan's Quest for 'Soft Power': Attraction and Limitation." *East Asia* 24 (4):349–63.

Lamarre, Thomas. 2009. *The Anime Machine: A Media Theory of Animation*. Minneapolis: University of Minnesota Press.

Landsberg, Eddie. 2011. "Demand for Japanese Language Instruction in US Skyrocketing." *Japan Today*, October 8, 2011. https://japantoday.com/category/features/opinions/demand-for-japanese-language-instruction-in-u-s-skyrocketing.

Laszczkowski, Mateusz, and Madeleine Reeves. 2015. "Introduction." *Social Analysis* 59 (4):1–14.

Latour, Bruno. 2005. "From Realpolitik to Dingpolitik." In *Making Things Public: Atmospheres of Democracy*, edited by Bruno Latour and Peter Weibel, 4–31. Cambridge, MA: MIT Press.

Leheny, David. 2006a. "A Narrow Place to Cross Swords: Soft Power and the Politics of Japanese Popular Culture in East Asia." In *Beyond Japan: The Dynamics of East Asian Regionalism*, edited by Peter J. Katzenstein and Takashi Shiraishi, 211–33. Ithaca, NY: Cornell University Press.

———. 2006b. *Think Global, Fear Local: Sex, Violence, and Anxiety in Contemporary Japan.* Ithaca, NY: Cornell University Press.

———. 2018. *Empire of Hope: The Sentimental Politics of Japanese Decline.* Ithaca, NY: Cornell University Press.

Lepselter, Susan. 2016. *The Resonance of Unseen Things: Poetics, Power, Captivity, and UFOs in the American Uncanny.* Ann Arbor: University of Michigan Press.

Levy, Robert I. 1973. *Tahitians: Mind and Experience in the Society Islands.* Chicago: University of Chicago Press.

———. 1984. "The Emotions in Comparative Perspective." In *Approaches to Emotion*, edited by Klaus R. Scherer and Paul Ekman, 397–412. Mahwah, NJ: Lawrence Erlbaum Associates.

Leys, Ruth. 2011. "The Turn to Affect: A Critique." *Critical Inquiry* 37 (3):434–72.

———. 2017. *The Ascent of Affect: Genealogy and Critique.* Chicago: University of Chicago Press.

Lippmann, Walter. [1922] 1997. *Public Opinion.* New York: Free Press Paperbacks.

———. [1925] 1927. *The Phantom Public.* New York: Macmillan.

Looser, Thomas. 2006. "Superflat and the Layers of Image and History in 1990s Japan." *Mechademia* 1 (1):92–109.

Lukács, Gabriella. 2010. *Scripted Affects, Branded Selves: Television, Subjectivity, and Capitalism in 1990s Japan.* Durham, NC: Duke University Press.

———. 2015. "The Labor of Cute: Net Idols, Cute Culture, and the Digital Economy in Contemporary Japan." *Positions* 23 (3):487–513.

———. 2020. *Invisibility by Design: Women and Labor in Japan's Digital Economy.* Durham, NC: Duke University Press.

Luoma-Aho, Mika. 2009. "Political Theology, Anthropomorphism, and Person-hood of the State: The Religion of IR." *International Political Sociology* 3 (3):293–309.

Lutz, Catherine. 1982. "The Domain of Emotion Words on Ifaluk." *American Ethnologist* 9 (1):113–28.

———. 1988. *Unnatural Emotions: Everyday Sentiments on a Micronesian Atoll and Their Challenge to Western Theory.* Chicago: University of Chicago Press.

———. 2017. "What Matters." *Cultural Anthropology* 32 (2):181–91.

Lutz, Catherine, and Lila Abu-Lughod. 1990. *Language and the Politics of Emotion.* Studies in Emotion and Social Interaction. Cambridge: Cambridge University Press.

Lutz, Catherine, and Geoffrey M. White. 1986. "The Anthropology of Emotions." *Annual Review of Anthropology* 15 (1):405–36.

Malinowski, Bronislaw. [1922] 1966. *Argonauts of the Western Pacific: An Account of Native Enterprise and Adventure in the Archipelagos of Melanesian New Guinea.* London: Routledge.

Manning, Paul. 2009. "Can the Avatar Speak?" *Journal of Linguistic Anthropology* 19 (2):310–25.

Manning, Paul, and Ilana Gershon. 2013. "Animating Interaction." *HAU: Journal of Ethnographic Theory* 3 (3):107–37.

Marcus, George E. 1998a. "Ethnography in/of the World System: The Emergence of Multi-Sited Ethnography" (1995). In *Ethnography through Thick and Thin,* 79–104. Princeton, NJ: Princeton University Press.

———. 1998b. "The Uses of Complicity in the Changing Mise-en-scene of Anthropological Fieldwork" (1997). In *Ethnography through Thick and Thin,* 85–108. Princeton, NJ: Princeton University Press.

Marres, Noortje. 2005. "Issues Spark a Public into Being: A Key but Often Forgotten Point of the Lippmann-Dewey Debate." In *Making Things Public,* edited by Bruno Latour and Peter Weibel, 208–17. Cambridge, MA: MIT Press.

Mars, Roman. 2020. "Return of the Yokai," episode 403. 99% Invisible, podcast, edited by Roman Mars and Vivian Le. https://99percentinvisible.org/episode/return-of-the-yokai/.

Martin, Emily. 2013. "The Potentiality of Ethnography and the Limits of Affect Theory." *Current Anthropology* 54 (S7):S149–58.

Maruyama, Masao. 1974. *Studies in the Intellectual History of Tokugawa Japan.* Translated by Mikiso Hane. Tokyo: University of Tokyo Press.

Marx, Karl. [1867] 1976. *Capital: A Critique of Political Economy,* vol. 1. London: Penguin.

Mascia-Lees, Frances E., ed. 2011. *A Companion to the Anthropology of the Body and Embodiment.* Oxford: Wiley-Blackwell.

Massumi, Brian. 1995. "The Autonomy of Affect." *Cultural Critique* (31):83–109.

———. 2002. *Parables for the Virtual: Movement, Affect, Sensation.* Durham, NC: Duke University Press.

Mathur, Nayanika. 2015. *Paper Tiger.* Cambridge: Cambridge University Press.

Matsuda, Takeshi. 2007. *Soft Power and Its Perils: US Cultural Policy in Early Postwar Japan and Permanent Dependency.* Stanford, CA: Stanford University Press.

Matsui, Takeshi. 2014. "Nation Branding through Stigmatized Popular Culture: The 'Cool Japan' Craze among Central Ministries in Japan." *Hitotsubashi Journal of Commerce and Management* 48 (1):81–97.

Mattingly, Cheryl, and Jason Throop. 2018. "The Anthropology of Ethics and Morality." *Annual Review of Anthropology* 47 (1):475–92.

Mauss, Marcel. [1925] 1954. *The Gift: Forms and Functions of Exchange in Archaic Societies.* Glencoe, IL: Free Press.

Mazzarella, William. 2003. *Shoveling Smoke: Advertising and Globalization in Contemporary India.* Durham, NC: Duke University Press.

———. 2008. "Affect: What Is It Good For?" In *Enchantments of Modernity: Empire, Nation, Globalization,* edited by Saurabh Dube, 291–309. London: Routledge.

———. 2013. *Censorium: Cinema and the Open Edge of Mass Publicity*. Durham, NC: Duke University Press.

———. 2017. *The Mana of Mass Society*. Chicago: University of Chicago Press.

———. 2019. "Brand(ish)ing the Name; or, Why Is Trump So Enjoyable?" In *Sovereignty, Inc. Three Inquiries in Politics and Enjoyment*, edited by William Mazzarella, Eric L. Santer, and Aaron Schuster, 113–60. Chicago: Chicago University Press.

McCurry, Justin. 2015. "Tokyo 2020 Olympics Logo Scrapped after Allegations of Plagiarism." *Guardian*, September 1, 2015. https://www.theguardian.com/world/2015/sep/01/tokyo-2020-olympics-logo-scrapped-after-allegations-of-plagiarism.

———. 2016. "Tokyo Olympic Stadium Architect Denies Copying Zaha Hadid Design." *Guardian*, January 15, 2016. https://www.theguardian.com/sport/2016/jan/15/tokyo-olympic-stadium-architect-denies-copying-zaha-hadid-design.

McGray, Douglas. 2002. "Japan's Gross National Cool." *Foreign Policy* 130 (1):44–54.

McLelland, Mark, ed. 2017a. *The End of Cool Japan: Ethical, Legal, and Cultural Challenges to Japanese Popular Culture*. Oxford: Routledge.

———. 2017b. "Introduction: Negotiating 'Cool Japan' in Research and Teaching." In *The End of Cool Japan*, edited by Mark McLelland, 17–46. Oxford: Routledge.

McLelland, Mark, Kazumi Nagaike, Katsuhiko Suganuma, and James Welker. 2015. *Boys Love Manga and Beyond: History, Culture, and Community in Japan*. Jackson: University of Mississippi Press.

McVeigh, Brian J. 1996. "Commodifying Affection, Authority and Gender in the Everyday Objects of Japan " *Journal of Material Culture* 1:291–312.

———. 1998. *The Nature of the Japanese State: Rationality and Rituality*. Oxfordshire: Routledge.

———. 2004. *Nationalisms of Japan: Managing and Mystifying Identity*. Asia/Pacific/Perspectives. Lanham, MD: Rowman & Littlefield.

METI (Ministry of Economy, Trade and Industry). 2005. *Dejitaru kontentsu hakushō* [Digital Content white paper]. Tokyo: Digital Content Association of Japan.

———. 2020a. *Kontentsu no sekai shijō Nihon shijō no gaikan* [Content industry international market and domestic market overview]. https://www.meti.go.jp/policy/mono_info_service/contents/downloadfiles/202002_contentsmarket.pdf.

———. 2020b. *Kūru Japan kikō ni tsuite* [A framework for Cool Japan]. https://www.meti.go.jp/policy/mono_info_service/mono/creative/2004CoolJapanfund2.pdf.

MEXT (Ministry of Education, Culture, Sports, Science and Technology). 2009. "Prioritized Financial Assistance for the Internationalization of Universities: Launching the Project for Establishing Core Universities for Internationalization (Global 30)." Press release. https://www.jsps.go.jp/english/e-kokusaika/data/00_mext2009.pdf.

———. 2012. "Selection for the FY2012 Project for Promotion of Global Human Resource Development." https://www.mext.go.jp/en/policy/education/highered/title02/detail02/sdetail02/sdetail02/1374093.htm.

———. 2014. "Top Global University Project." https://tgu.mext.go.jp/en/about/.

Miles, Elizabeth. 2019. "Manhood and the Burdens of Intimacy." In *Intimate Japan: Ethnographies of Closeness and Conflict*, edited by Alllison Alexy and Emma E. Cook, 148–63. Honolulu: University of Hawai'i Press.

Miller, Daniel. 2005. *Materiality*. Durham, NC: Duke University Press.

Miller, Laura. 2011a. "Cute Masquerade and the Pimping of Japan." *International Journal of Japanese Sociology* 20 (1):18–29.

———. 2011b. "Taking Girls Seriously in 'Cool Japan' Ideology." *Japan Studies Review* 15:97–106.

———. 2017. "Scholar Girl Meets Manga Maniac, Media Specialist, and Cultural Gatekeeper." In *The End of Cool Japan*, edited by Mark McLelland, 67–85. Oxford: Routledge.

Miller, Laura, and Jan Bardsley. 2005. *Bad Girls of Japan*. New York: Palgrave Macmillan.

Miller, Toby. 2002. "Cultural Citizenship." In *Handbook of Citizenship Studies*, edited by Engin Isin and Bryan Turner, 231–41. London: SAGE.

———. 2007. *Cultural Citizenship: Cosmopolitanism, Consumerism, and Television in a Neoliberal Age*. Philadelphia: Temple University Press.

Minami, Marie. 2019. "'Isshō Rorīta yamenai' 35-sai, Aoki Misako wa 'toshisōō no fasshon' no jubaku to tatakai" ["Never will I quit Lolita fashion": 35-year-old Aoki Misako's fight with the spell of "age-appropriate fashion"]. *Huffington Post*, February 20, 2019. https://www.huffingtonpost.jp/entry/misako-aoki_jp_5c6b83a8e4b0e8eb46b91a56.

Miranda, Carolina. 2014. "Hello Kitty Is Not a Cat, Plus More Reveals before Her L.A. Tour." *Los Angeles Times*, August 26, 2014. https://www.latimes.com/entertainment/arts/miranda/la-et-cam-hello-kitty-in-los-angeles-not-a-cat-20140826-column.html#page=1.

Miyadai, Shinji, Hideki Ishihara, and Mieko Ōtsuka. 1993. *Sabukaruchā shinwa kaitai: Shōjo, ongaku, manga, sei no 30 nen to komyunikēshon no genzai* [Dismantling the myth of subculture: Girls, music, manga, 30 years of sex, and communication in the contemporary]. Tokyo: Parco.

Miyadai, Shinji. 1995. *Owarinaki nichijō o ikiro! Oum kanzen kokufuku manyuaru* [Live an endless everyday: A manual for completely overcoming Aum]. Tokyo: Chikuma Shobō.

Miyadai, Shinji, Shion Kono, and Thomas Lamarre. 2011. "Transformation of Semantics in the History of Japanese Subcultures since 1992." *Mechademia: Second Arc* 6:231–58.

Miyazaki, Hayao. 2009. *Starting Point: 1979–1996*. Translated by Beth Cary and Frederik L. Schodt. San Francisco: Viz Media.

Miyazaki, Hirokazu. 2004. *The Method of Hope: Anthropology, Philosophy, and Fijian Knowledge*. Stanford, CA: Stanford University Press.

———. 2006. "Economy of Dreams: Hope in Global Capitalism and Its Critiques." *Cultural Anthropology* 21 (2):147–72.

———. 2009. "The Temporality of No Hope." In *Ethnographies of Neoliberalism*, edited by Carol J. Greenhouse, 238–50. Philadelphia: University of Pennsylvania Press.

———. 2013. *Arbitraging Japan: Dreams of Capitalism at the End of Finance*. Berkeley: University of California Press.

Miyoshi, Masao. 1991. *Off Center: Power and Culture Relations between Japan and the United States*. Cambridge, MA: Harvard University Press.

MOFA (Ministry of Foreign Affairs), Kokusai kōryū kenkyūkai [Research Council on International Cultural Relations]. 2003. *Arata na jidai no gaikō to kokusai kōryū no arata na yakuwari* [Foreign relations in a new era and a new role for cultural relations]. Accessed May 20, 2020. https://www.jpf.go.jp/j/about/survey/kkk/all.pdf.

———. 2008. "Inauguration Ceremony of Anime Ambassador." March 19, 2008. https://www.mofa.go.jp/announce/announce/2008/3/0319-3.html.

———. 2009. "Introduction of the (Kawaii) Cute Ambassadors." March 12, 2009. www.mofa.go.jp/announce/press/2009/3/0312.html.

———. 2017. "Pop-Culture Diplomacy." March 8, 2017. https://www.mofa.go.jp/policy/culture/exchange/pop/index.html.

Monden, Masafumi. 2013. "The 'Nationality' of Lolita Fashion." In *Asia through Art and Anthropology: Cultural Translation across Borders,* edited by Fuyubi Nakamura, Morgan Perkins, and Olivier Krischer, 165–78. London: Bloomsbury.

Mori, Yoshitaka. 2011. "The Pitfall Facing the Cool Japan Project: The Transnational Development of the Anime Industry under the Condition of Post-Fordism." *International Journal of Japanese Sociology* 20 (1):30–42.

Morinosuke, Kawaguchi. 2016. *Nihonjin mo shiranakatta Nihon no kokuryoku (sofuto pawā)* [The Soft Power of Japan That Even Japanese Don't Know]. Tokyo: Discover 21.

Muehlebach, Andrea. 2011. "On Affective Labor in Post-Fordist Italy." *Cultural Anthropology* 26 (1):59–82.

Murakami, Haruki. 1987. *Hear the Wind Sing.* Tranlsated by Alfred Birnbaum. Tokyo: Kodansha. (Originally published as *Kaze no uta o kike,* 1979).

———. 1989. *A Wild Sheep Chase.* Translated by Alfred Birnbaum. Tokyo: Kodansha. (Originally published as *Hitsuji o meguru bōken,* 1982).

———. 1985. *Sekai no owari to hādo-boirudo wandārando* [Hard-boiled wonderland and the end of the world]. Vol. 4 of *Murakami Haruki zensakuhin 1979–1989* [Complete works of Murakami Haruki 1979–1989]. Tokyo: Kōdansha.

———. 1991. *Hard-boiled Wonderland and the End of the World.* Translated by Alfred Birnbaum. Tokyo: Kodansha. (Originally published as *Sekai no owari to hādo-boirudo wandārando,* 1985).

———. 1997. *The Wind-up Bird Chronicle.* Translated by Jay Rubin. New York: Vintage Books. (Originally published as *Nejimakidori kuronikuru,* 1994–1995).

———. 2002. *Umibe no Kafuka* [Kafka on the shore]. Tokyo: Shinchōsha.

———. 2005. *Kafka on the Shore.* Translated by Philip Gabriel. New York: Alfred A. Knopf.

———. 2009. "Always on the Side of the Egg." *Haaretz News,* February 17, 2009. https://www.haaretz.com/israel-news/culture/1.5076881.

———. 2017. *Men without Women: Stories.* Translated by Philip Gabriel and Ted Goossen. London: Harvill Secker. (Originally published as *Onna no inai otokotachi,* 2014).

———. 2020. "A Feminist Critique of Murakami Novels, with Murakami Himself," interview by Mieko Kawakami. *Literary Hub,* April 7, 2020. (Excerpts from *Mimizuku wa kōkon ni tobitatsu: Kawakami Mieko kiku, Murakami Haruki kataru,* 2019.) https://lithub.com/a-feminist-critique-of-murakami-novels-with-murakami-himself/.

Murakami, Ryū. 2000. *Kibō no kuni no ekuzodasu* [Exodus in a country of hope]. Tokyo: Bungeishunju.

Murakami, Takashi. 2000. *Superflat*. Tokyo: Madra.

———. 2005. "'Earth in My Window' and 'Superflat Trilogy: Greetings, You Are Alive.'" In *Little Boy: The Arts of Japan's Exploding Subculture*, 99–149. New York: Japan Society.

Myers, Fred R. 1991. *Pintupi Country, Pintupi Self: Sentiment, Place, and Politics among Western Desert Aborigines*. Berkeley: University of California Press.

Nabokov, Vladimir Vladimirovich. [1955] 1989. *Lolita*. New York: Vintage.

Nagata, Kazuaki. 2010. "'Anime' Makes Japan Superpower." *Japan Times*, September 7, 2010. https://www.japantimes.co.jp/news/2010/09/07/reference/anime-makes-japan-superpower/#.XvDIyy2ZMWo.

Nakamura, Ichiya, and Megumi Onouchi. 2006. *Nihon no poppu pawā—sekai o kaeru kontentsu no jitsuzō* [Japan's pop power: The true image of world-changing content]. Tokyo: Nihon Keizai Shinbunsha.

National Personnel Authority. 2010. *Josei kokka kōmuin no saiyō, tōyō no genjō nado: Jinjiin, sankō shiryō III* [Female national public official employment and appointment conditions: Personnel affairs, reference document III]. https://www.jinji.go.jp/saiyoutouyou/sankoushiryou/III.pdf.

Navaro-Yashin, Yael. 2002. *Faces of the State: Secularism and Public Life in Turkey*. Princeton, NJ: Princeton University Press.

———. 2009. "Affective Space, Melancholic Objects: Ruination and the Production of Anthropological Knowledge." *Journal of the Royal Anthropological Institute* 15 (1):1–18.

———. 2012. *The Make-Believe Space: Affective Geography in a Postwar Polity*. Durham, NC: Duke University Press.

Neumann, Iver B. 2004. "Beware of Organicism: The Narrative Self of the State." *Review of International Studies* 30 (2):259–67.

Newell, Sasha. 2018. "The Affectiveness of Symbols: Materiality, Magicality, and the Limits of the Antisemiotic Turn." *Current Anthropology* 59 (1):1–22.

Ngai, Sianne. 2005. *Ugly Feelings*. Cambridge, MA: Harvard University Press.

NHK. 2011a. "Overcoming 'The Japan Syndrome.'" Accessed January 18, 2011. http://www.nhk.or.jp/pr/english/press/pdf/20110111.pdf.

———. 2011b. "Japan shindōrōmu o norikoero" [Overcoming the Japan syndrome]. Accessed January 18, 2011. http://www.nhk.or.jp/ohayou/special/20110117.html.

NHK World. 2009. "Nihongo" [Japanese]. *Cool Japan: Hakkutsu! Kakko ii Nippon* [Cool Japan: Excavation! Cool Japan]. Accessed August 12, 2020. https://www2.nhk.or.jp/archives/chronicle/pg/page010-01-01.

———. 2010a. "Cool Japan Program." https://www.nhk.jp/p/cooljapan/ts/P2RMMPW5JM/.

———. 2010b. "Cool Japan Program List." https://www.nhk.jp/p/cooljapan/ts/P2RMMPW5JM/list/.

———. 2010c. "Suimin" [Sleep]. *Cool Japan: Hakkutsu! Kakko ii Nippon* [Cool Japan: Excavation! Cool Japan]. Accessed August 12, 2020. https://www2.nhk.or.jp/archives/chronicle/pg/page010-01-01.

———. 2011. "The Aims of NHK World." NHK World. Accessed January 18, 2011. http://www3.nhk.or.jp/nhkworld/english/info/aboutnhkworld.html.

———. 2017. "Nipponjin e no daigimon 'naze Nihon no ie wa OO na no?'" [A big question for Japanese, "Why are Japanese homes . . . ?"]. *Cool Japan: Hakkutsu! Kakko ii Nippon* [Cool Japan: Excavation! Cool Japan]. Accessed August 12, 2020. https://www2.nhk.or.jp/archives/chronicle/pg/page010-01-01.

Nikkei Keizai Shinbun. 2020. "Tokyo Gorin 'saienki nai' IOC no kōtsu chōsei iinchō" [No second extension for the Tokyo Olympics, IOC Coates Adjustment Committee chairman]. *Nikkei Keizai Shinbun*, May 9, 2020. https://r.nikkei.com/article/DGXMZO589 17050Z00C20A5CZ8000?s=5.

Nozawa, Shunsuke. 2013. "Characterization." *Semiotic Review* 3. https://www.semioticreview.com/ojs/index.php/sr/article/view/16.

Nye, Joseph S. 1990a. *Bound to Lead: The Changing Nature of American Power*. New York: Basic Books.

———. 1990b. "Soft Power." *Foreign Policy* (80):153–71.

———. 2004. *Soft Power: The Means to Success in World Politics*. New York: Public Affairs.

———. 2017. "Soft Power: The Origins and Political Progress of a Concept." *Palgrave Communications* 3 (17008):1–3. https://doi.org/10.1057/palcomms.2017.8.

Occhi, Debra J. 2010. "Consuming Kyara 'Characters': Anthropomorphization and Marketing in Contemporary Japan." *Comparative Culture* 15:77–86.

———. 2012. "Wobbly Aesthetics, Performance, and Message: Comparing Japanese Kyara with Their Anthropomorphic Forebears." *Asian Ethnology* 71 (1):109–32.

Ōe, Kenzaburō. 1989. "Japan's Dual Identity: A Writer's Dilemma." In *Postmodernism and Japan*, edited by Masao Miyoshi and Harry Harootunian, 189–214. Durham, NC: Duke University Press.

Ogasawara, Yuko. 1998. *Office Ladies and Salaried Men: Power, Gender, and Work in Japanese Companies*. Berkeley: University of California Press.

Ogoura, Kazuo. 2006. "Sofuto pawā ron no shikaku" [The limits of soft power]. *Wochi Kochi* 11:60–65.

———. 2009. *Japan's Cultural Diplomacy*. Tokyo: Japan Foundation.

Ong, Aihwa, Virginia R. Dominguez, Jonathan Friedman, Nina Glick Schiller, Verena Stolcke, David Y. H. Wu, and Hu Ying. 1996. "Cultural Citizenship as Subject-Making: Immigrants Negotiate Racial and Cultural Boundaries in the United States [and Comments and Reply]." *Current Anthropology* 37 (5):737–62.

Oricon News. 2009. "Murakami Haruki 'iQ84' ga 09 nen saikō no deashi, uriage 35 manbu de hatsu tōjō ii, 2i dokusen" [The ultimate start to 2009 for Murakami Haruki's "iQ84": 350,000 copies sold, monopolizing the first and second ranking upon release]. *Oricon*, June 4, 2009. https://www.oricon.co.jp/news/66655/full/.

Orwell, George. [1949] 2003. *Nineteen Eighty-Four*. London: Penguin.

Otmazgin, Nissim Kadosh. 2008. "Contesting Soft Power: Japanese Popular Culture in East and Southeast Asia." *International Relations of the Asia-Pacific* 8 (1):73–101.

———. 2013. *Regionalizing Culture: The Political Economy of Japanese Popular Culture in Asia*. Honolulu: University of Hawai'i Press.

Ōtsuka, Eiji. 1989. "The Teenagers Cute Emperor." *Japan Echo* 26 (1):65–68.

———. 1991. *Shōjō minzokugaku* [An anthropology of girl culture]. Tokyo: Kōbunsha.

Oyama, Shinji. 2019. "In the Closet: Japanese Creative Industries and Their Reluctance to Forge Global and Transnational Linkages in ASEAN and East Asia." ERIA Discussion Paper no. 295. Economic Research Institute for ASEAN and East Asia. https://www.eria.org/publications/in-the-closet-japanese-creative-industries-and-their-reluctance-to-forge-global-and-transnational-linkages-in-asean-and-east-asia/.

Pink, Sarah. 2015. *Doing Sensory Ethnography*. London: Sage.

Rabinow, Paul. 2003. *Anthropos Today: Reflections on Modern Equipment*. Princeton, NJ: Princeton University Press.

Ramos-Zayas, Ana Yolanda. 2011. "Learning Affect/Embodying Race." In *A Companion to the Anthropology of the Body and Embodiment*, edited by Frances E. Mascia-Lees, 24–45. Malden, MA: Blackwell Publishing.

Rashid, Maria. 2020. *Dying to Serve: Militarism, Affect, and the Politics of Sacrifice in the Pakistan Army*. Stanford, CA: Stanford University Press.

Reed, Adam. 2018. "Literature and Reading." *Annual Review of Anthropology* 47 (1):33–45.

Rees, Tobias. 2018. *After Ethnos*. Durham, NC: Duke University Press.

Reis, Ria. 1998. "Resonating to Pain: Introspection as a Tool in Medical Anthropology 'at Home.'" *Anthropology & Medicine* 5 (3):295–310.

Reynolds, Isabel. 2009. "Japan Picks 'Schoolgirl' among Cute Ambassadors." Reuters, March 12, 2009. https://uk.reuters.com/article/us-japan-ambassadors-cute/japan-picks-schoolgirl-among-cute-ambassadors-idUKTRE52B4JC20090312.

Robbins, Joel. 2013. "Beyond the Suffering Subject: Toward an Anthropology of the Good." *Journal of the Royal Anthropological Institute* 19 (3):447–62.

Roberson, James, and Nobue Suzuki. 2003. *Men and Masculinities in Contemporary Japan: Dislocating the Salaryman Doxa*. London and New York: Routledge.

Roberts, Glenda. 1994. *Staying on the Line: Blue-Collar Women in Contemporary Japan*. Honolulu: University of Hawai'i Press.

Robertson, Jennifer. 1998. *Takarazuka: Sexual Politics and Popular Culture in Modern Japan*. Berkeley: University of California Press.

———. 2002. "Reflexivity Redux: A Pithy Polemic on 'Positionality.'" *Anthropological Quarterly* 75 (4):785–92.

RocketNews 24. 2015. "Gackt Lashes Out at Cool Japan: 'Almost No Results of Japanese Culture Exported Overseas.'" Japan Today, July 6, 2015. https://japantoday.com/category/entertainment/gackt-lashes-out-at-cool-japan-almost-no-results-of-japanese-culture-exported-overseas.

Roquet, Paul. 2016. *Ambient Media: Japanese Atmospheres of Self*. Minneapolis: University of Minnesota Press.

Rosaldo, Michelle Zimbalist. 1980. *Knowledge and Passion: Ilongot Notions of Self and Social Life*. Cambridge: Cambridge University Press.

Rosaldo, Renato. 1989. "Grief and a Headhunter's Rage." In *Culture and Truth: The Remaking of Social Analysis*, 1–21. Boston: Beacon Press

———, ed. 2003. *Cultural Citizenship in Island Southeast Asia: Nation and Belonging in the Hinterlands*. Berkeley: University of California Press.

Röttger-Rössler, Birgitt, and Jan Slaby. 2018. "Introduction: Affect in Relation." In *Affect in Relation—Families, Places, Technologies: Essays on Affectivity and Subject Formation in the 21st Century*, edited by Birgitt Röttger-Rössler and Jan Slaby, 1–28. New York: Routledge.

Rubin, Jay. 2003. *Haruki Murakami and the Music of Words*. London: Vintage.

Saitō, Kumiko. 2014. "Magic, *Shōjo*, and Metamorphosis: Magical Girl Anime and the Challenges of Changing Gender Identities in Japanese Society." *Journal of Asian Studies* 73 (1):143–64.

Sakai, Naoki. 1997. *Translation and Subjectivity: On Japan and Cultural Nationalism*. Minneapolis: University of Minnesota Press.

Sakurai, Takamasa. 2009a. *Anime bunka gaikō* [Anime diplomacy]. Tokyo: Chikuma Shinshō.

———. 2009b. *Sekai kawaii kakumei—naze kanojo-tachi wa 'Nihonjin ni naritai' to yobu no ka* [The global cute revolution: Why some girls say they want to become Japanese]. Tokyo: PHP Interface.

———. 2010a. *Nihon wa anime de saikō suru kuruma to kaden ga gaika o kasegu jidai wa owatta* [The revitalization of Japan through anime: The end of the era of growth through automobiles and electronics]. Tokyo: ASCII Media Works.

———. 2010b. *Garapagosuka suru Nihon* [The Japan that Galapagosizes]. Tokyo: Kodansha.

Saladin, Ronald. 2019. *Young Men and Masculinities in Japanese Media: (Un-) Conscious Hegemony*. Singapore: Palgrave Macmillan.

Sasaki, Norihiko. 2012. "Murakai Takashi 'kūru Japan wa aho sugiru'" [Murakami Takashi: "Cool Japan is Too Stupid"]. *Toyo Keizai*, December 7, 2012. https://toyokeizai.net/articles/-/12029?page=4.

Sassen, Saskia. 2007. *Sociology of Globalization*. New York: Norton.

Sato, Barbara. 2003. *The New Japanese Woman: Modernity, Media, and Women in Interwar Japan*. Durham, NC: Duke University Press.

Schachter, Stanley, and Jerome Singer. 1962. "Cognitive, Social and Physiological Determinants of Emotional States." *Psychological Review* 69:379–99.

Schudson, Michael. 2008. "The 'Lippmann-Dewey Debate' and the Invention of Walter Lippmann as an Anti-Democrat 1985–1996." *International Journal of Communication* 2:1031–42.

Seats, Michael. 2006. *Murakami Haruki: The Simulacrum in Contemporary Japanese Culture*. Lanham, MD: Lexington Books.

Sedgwick, Eve Kosofsky, Adam Frank, and Irving E. Alexander. 1995. *Shame and Its Sisters: A Silvan Tomkins Reader*. Durham, NC: Duke University Press.

Sedgwick, Mitchell. 2007. *Globalisation and Japanese Organisational Culture: An Ethnography of a Japanese Corporation in France*. London: Routledge.

Seyfert, Robert. 2012. "Beyond Personal Feelings and Collective Emotions: Toward a Theory of Social Affect." *Theory, Culture & Society* 29 (6):27–46.

Shamoon, Deborah. 2015. "The Superflat Space of Japanese Anime." In *Asian Cinema and the Use of Space*, edited by Lilian Chee and Edna Lim, 109–24. New York: Routledge.

Shigematsu, Hisashi. 2011. *Hai* [Ash]. Yokohama Red Brick Warehouse, Japan. Exhibition, June 5–11, 2009.

Shima, Nobuhiko. 2009. *Nihon no 'sekai shōhin' chikara* [Japan's global product power]. Tokyo: Shūeisha.

Shimamura, Mari. 1991. *Fanshī no kenkyū: Kawaii ga hito mono kane o shihai suru* [Fancy research: How cute controls people, objects, and money]. Tokyo: Nesco.

Shimizu, Yuichiro. 2013. *Kindai Nihon no kanryō: Ishin kanryō kara gakureki erīto e* [Bureaucracy in modern Japan: From the Meiji Restoration bureaucracy to the educational elite]. Tokyo: Chūkōshinsho.

———. 2020. *The Origins of the Modern Japanese Bureaucracy.* Translated by Amin Ghadimi. London: Bloomsbury Academic.

Silverberg, Miriam. 2009. *Erotic Grotesque Nonsense: The Mass Culture of Japanese Modern Times.* Berkeley: University of California Press.

Silvio, Teri. 2010. "Animation: The New Performance?" *Journal of Linguistic Anthropology* 20 (2):422–38.

———. 2019. *Puppets, Gods, and Brands: Theorizing the Age of Animation from Taiwan.* Honolulu: University of Hawai'i Press.

Slaby, Jan, Rainer Mühlhoff, and Philipp Wüschner. 2017. "Affective Arrangements." *Emotion Review* 11 (1):3–12.

Snow, Nancy. 2016. *Japan's Information War.* Scotts Valley, CA: CreateSpace Independent Publishing Platform.

Soga, Kengo. 2016. *Gendai Nihon no kanryōsei* [Modern Japanese bureaucracy]. Tokyo: Tokyo Daigaku Shuppankai.

Spinoza, Benedictus de. [1677] 1996. *Ethics.* Translated by Edwin Curley. London: Penguin Books.

Steinberg, Marc. 2004. "Otaku Consumption, Superflat Art and the Return to Edo." *Japan Forum* 16 (3):449–71.

———. 2009. "Anytime, Anywhere: Tetsuwan Atomu Stickers and the Emergence of Character Merchandizing." *Theory, Culture & Society* 26 (2–3):113–38.

Stewart, Kathleen. 2007. *Ordinary Affects.* Durham, NC: Duke University Press.

———. 2010. "Afterword: Worlding Refrains." In *The Affect Theory Reader*, edited by Melissa Gregg and Gregory J. Seigworth, 339–53. Durham, NC: Duke University Press.

Stodulka, Thomas. 2013. The Researchers' Affects. Research project, Freie Universität Berlin, 2013–2016. Accessed July 31, 2021. http://www.loe.fu-berlin.de/en/affekte-der-forscher/index.html.

———. 2015. "Emotion Work, Ethnography, and Survival Strategies on the Streets of Yogyakarta." *Medical Anthropology* 34 (1):84–97.

Stodulka, Thomas, Nasima Selim, and Dominik Mattes. 2018. "Affective Scholarship: Doing Anthropology with Epistemic Affects." *Ethos* 46 (4):519–36.

Stodulka, Thomas, Samia Dinkelaker, and Ferdiansyah Thajib, eds. 2019. *Affective Dimensions of Fieldwork and Ethnography*. Cham, Switz.: Springer.

Stolcke, Verena. 1995. "Talking Culture: New Boundaries, New Rhetorics of Exclusion in Europe." *Current Anthropology* 36 (1):1–24.

Stoler, Ann Laura. 2007. "Affective States." In *A Companion to the Anthropology of Politics*, edited by David Nugent and Joan Vincent, 4–20. Malden, MA: Blackwell.

———. 2008. *Along the Archival Grain: Epistemic Anxieties and Colonial Common Sense*. Princeton, NJ: Princeton University Press.

Storey, John. 2018. *Cultural Theory and Popular Culture: An Introduction*. London: Routledge.

Strecher, Matthew. 1998a. "Beyond 'Pure' Literature: Mimesis, Formula, and the Postmodern in the Fiction of Murakami Haruki." *Journal of Asian Studies* 57 (2):354–78.

———. 1998b. "Murakami Haruki: Japan's Coolest Writer Heats Up." *Japan Quarterly* 45 (1):61–69.

Sugiyama, Tomoyuki. 2006. *Kūru Japan—sekai ga kaitagaru Nihon* [Cool Japan: The Japan the world wants to buy]. Tokyo: Shōdensha.

Takahata, Isao. 2009. "Afterword: The Fireworks of Eros " In *Starting Point: 1979–1996, Written by Miyazaki Hayao*, 451–61. San Francisco: Viz Media.

Takeshita, Ikuko. 2018. "Tōkyō Gorin boranteia mondai, 11-mannin 'dōin' wa yarigai sakushu: Shikyū wa 1000 yen nomi, fuan na necchūshō taisaku" [Tokyo Olympic volunteer problem, 110,000 people-mobilization exploitation? Only 1000-yen payments, concern over heat stroke countermeasures]. *Business Insider*, September 25, 2018. https://www.businessinsider.jp/post-175616.

Tanaka, Yasuo. 1980. *Nantonaku, kurisutaru* [Somehow, crystal]. Tokyo: Shinchōsha.

Terada, Rei. 2003. *Feeling in Theory*. Cambridge, MA: Harvard University Press.

Thien, Deborah. 2005. "After or Beyond Feeling? A Consideration of Affect and Emotion in Geography." *Area* 37 (4):450–54.

Thrift, Nigel. 2004. "Intensities of Feeling: Towards a Spatial Politics of Affect." *Geografiska Annaler, Series B, Human Geography* 86 (1):57–78.

———. 2008. *Non-Representational Theory: Space, Politics, Affect*. New York: Routledge.

Tobin, Joseph. 2004. *Pikachu's Global Adventure: The Rise and Fall of Pokémon*. Durham, NC: Duke University Press.

Tolchin, Martin. 1988. "The Nation: 'Japan-Bashing' Becomes a Trade Bill Issue." *New York Times*, February 28, 1988. Accessed January 15, 2010. http://www.nytimes.com/1988/02/28/weekinreview/the-nation-japan-bashing-becomes-a-trade-bill-issue.html.

Tomkins, Silvan S. 2008. *Affect Imagery Consciousness*. New York: Springer.

Tomlinson, John. 1991. *Cultural Imperialism: A Critical Introduction*. Baltimore: Johns Hopkins University Press.

———. 1999. *Globalization and Culture*. Chicago: University of Chicago Press.

Tsang, Yat Him. 2011. "'Why Are We Set in This World?': Gender Representation in Murakami Haruki's Novels." MA thesis, Chinese University of Hong Kong.

Tsing, Anna Lowenhaupt. 2005. *Friction: An Ethnography of Global Connection*. Princeton, NJ: Princeton University Press.

Tsugata, Nobuyuki. 2004. *Nihon animēshon no chikara: 85 nen no rekishi o tsuranuku futatsu no jiku* [The power of Japanese animation: Rolling through eighty-five years of history on two axles]. Tokyo: NTT.

Tyler, Stephen A. 1986. "Post-Modern Ethnography." In *Writing Culture: The Poetics and Politics of Ethnography*, edited by James Clifford and George E. Marcus, 122–40. Berkeley: University of California Press.

Ueno, Chizuko. 1989. "Rorikon to yaoi-zoku ni mirai wa aru ka!? 90 nendai no sekkusu reboryūshon" [Do Lolicon and the Yaoi tribe have a future!? The sexual revolution of the 1990s]. In *Otaku no hon* [The book of otaku], edited by Shinji Ishii, 131–36. Tokyo: JICC Shuppankyoku.

———. 2010. *Onnagirai: Nippon no misojinī* [Women hating: Japanese misogyny]. Tokyo: Kinokuniya shoten.

United Nations. 2015. "International Day of Yoga, 21 June." Accessed May 15, 2020. https://www.un.org/en/events/yogaday/background.shtml.

Valaskivi, Katja. 2013. "A Brand New Future? Cool Japan and the Social Imaginary of the Branded Nation." *Japan Forum* 25 (4):485–504.

Vogel, Ezra F. [1979] 1981. *Japan as Number One: Lessons for America*. Cambridge, MA: Harvard University Press.

Wakeling, Emily Jane. 2011. "Girls Are Dancin': *Shōjo* Culture and Feminism in Contemporary Japanese Art." *New Voices* 5:130–46.

Warner, Michael. 2002. *Publics and Counterpublics*. New York; Cambridge, MA: Zone Books, distributed by MIT Press.

Watanabe, Yasushi, and David L McConnell. 2008. *Soft Power Superpowers: Cultural and National Assets of Japan and the United States*. Armonk, NY: M. E. Sharpe.

Weber, Max. 1949. *The Methodology of the Social Sciences*. Translated by Edward A. Shils and Henry A. Finch. Glencoe, IL: Free Press.

———. [1922] 1978. *Economy and Society: An Outline of Interpretive Sociology*. Berkeley: University of California Press.

Weiskel, Thomas 1976. *The Romantic Sublime: Studies in the Structure and Psychology of Transcendence*. Baltimore: Johns Hopkins University Press.

Welker, James. 2015. "A Brief History of *Shōnen'ai*, *Yaoi*, and Boys Love." In *Boys Love Manga and Beyond*, edited by Mark McLelland, Kazumi Nagaike, Katsuhiko Suganuma and James Welker, 42–75. Jackson: University of Mississippi Press.

Wendt, Alexander. 1999. *Social Theory of International Politics*. Cambridge: Cambridge University Press.

Westney, Eleanor 1987. *Imitation and Innovation: The Transfer of Western Organizational Patterns to Meiji Japan*. Cambridge, MA: Harvard University Press.

Wetherell, Margaret. 2012. *Affect and Emotion: A New Social Science Understanding*. Los Angeles: SAGE.

Whipple, Mark. 2005. "The Dewey-Lippmann Debate Today: Communication Distortions, Reflective Agency, and Participatory Democracy." *Sociological Theory* 23 (2):156–78.

White, Daniel. 2014. "Tears, Capital, Ethics: Television and the Public Sphere in Japan." In *The Political Economy of Affect and Emotion in East Asia*, edited by Jie Yang, 123–39. New York: Routledge.

———. 2017. "Affect: An Introduction." *Cultural Anthropology* 32 (2):175–80.

———. 2018. "Contemplating the Robotic Embrace." More Than Human Worlds. *NatureCulture*, June 20, 2018. https://www.natcult.net/contemplating-the-robotic-embrace/.

Wikan, Unni. 1990. *Managing Turbulent Hearts: A Balinese Formula for Living*. Chicago: University of Chicago Press.

Williams, Raymond. 1977. *Marxism and Literature*. Oxford: Oxford University Press.

Wittgenstein, Ludwig. [1953] 2009. *Philosophical Investigations*. Translated by G. E. M. Anscombe, P. M. S. Hacker, and Joachim Schulte. Chichester: Wiley-Blackwell.

Xinhua. 2019. "8 More Countries Set up Confucius Institutes or Classrooms in 2019." Xinhua Net, December 11, 2019. http://www.xinhuanet.com/english/2019-12/11/c_138623776.htm.

Yamada, Kenta. 2015. "Higashi Nihon daishinsai, Orinpikku, media: Kokueki to genron" [The great East Japan earthquake, Olympics, media: National interest and public opinion]. *Mass Communication Research* 86:39–62.

Yamane, Kazuma. 1986. *Hentai shōjo moji no kenkyū* [Anomalous teenage handwriting research]. Tokyo: Kodansha.

———. 1991. *Gyaru no kōzō* [The Structure of a Girl]. Tokyo: Sekai Bunkasha.

Yanagisako, Sylvia. 2002. "Asian Exclusion Acts." In *Learning Places: The Afterlives of Area Studies*, edited by Masao Miyoshi and Harry D. Harootunian, 175–89. Durham, NC: Duke University Press.

Yano, Christine R. 2002. *Tears of Longing: Nostalgia and the Nation in Japanese Popular Song*. Cambridge, MA: Harvard University Press.

———. 2013a. "Categorical Confusion: President Obama as a Case Study of Racialized Practices in Contemporary Japan." In *Race and Racism in Modern East Asia: Western and Eastern Constructions*, edited by Rotem Kowner and Demel Walter, 499–522. Leiden: Brill.

———. 2013b. *Pink Globalization: Hello Kitty's Trek across the Pacific*. Durham, NC: Duke University Press.

Yoda, Tomiko. 2006a. "A Roadmap to Millennial Japan." In *Japan After Japan: Social and Cultural Life from the Recessionary 1990s to the Present*, edited by Tomiko Yoda and Harry Harootunian, 16–53. Durham, NC: Duke University Press.

———. 2006b. "The Rise and Fall of Maternal Society: Gender, Labor, and Capital in Contemporary Japan." In *Japan after Japan: Social and Cultural Life from the Recessionary 1990s to the Present*, edited by Tomiko Yoda and Harry Harootunian, 239–74. Durham, NC: Duke University Press.

Yonezawa, Akiyoshi. 2008. "Facing Crisis: Soft Power and Higher Education in a Global Context." In *Soft Power Superpowers: Cultural and National Assets of Japan and the United States*, edited by Yasushi Watanabe and David L McConnell, 54–74. Armonk, NY: M. E. Sharpe.

Yúdice, George. 2003. *The Expediency of Culture: Uses of Culture in the Global Era*. Durham, NC: Duke University Press.

Zigon, Jarrett. 2008. *Morality: An Anthropological Perspective*. Oxford: Berg.

Index

Abe, Shinzō, 73, 101–3, 124, 130, 165; Abenomics and, 211n7
ACA (Agency for Cultural Affairs), 26, 39, 55–60
administration: of affect, 3–5, 20–28, 64–65, 88–89, 113–14, 136–40, 144, 168–71, 192–94; culture of, 49–60, 108–11
advisory councils (*shingikai*), 55–58
affect-emotion gap, 18–20, 64–65, 131, 173, 194, 201n28
affect, 3, 15–20, 168–71, 192–94; and affective types, 95–106; anthropology of, 199n23; and art, 131–43, 156–60; and bureaucracy, 4–5, 43–45, 197n7; circuitry of, 18, 200n27; critiques of, 17; and emotion, 3, 15–20, 199n23; ethnographic method and, 213n22; gaps, 16–20; and gender, 19–20, 24–28, 131–43, 187–92, 200n24; history and theory of, 200n24, 201n29, 206nn3, 4; labor and, 123–25, 202nn38, 4, 208n7; *meiwaku* and, 89–92; and nation-state, 60; transduction of, 20, 201n30
Allison, Anne 7, 144, 146, 169, 178, 205n6, 208n5
Ambassadors of Cute, 1–3, 115–43, 190

ambient literature, 182–83
American *Stiob*, 78–79
Anderson, Benedict, 5, 197n8
anime, 56, 132–37, 210n16. *See also* anime diplomacy
anime ambassador, 86–87
anime diplomacy, 86–89, 92–95, 107–11
Anpo jōyaku (US-Japan Mutual Cooperation and Security Treaty), 213n1
anxiety: administration of 3, 7–8, 21–24, 144–45; definition of, 23–24; gendering of, 126–27, 187–92; geopolitical, 3, 7, 85; hope and, 8, 12, 21, 84; Japanese words for (*fuan, fuantei, fuanshin*), 8, 153; politics of, 27–28, 85; precarity and, 7, 14, 27, 32, 144, 152, 168–69, 178; reflexivity and, 168–71; in relationship between Japan and West, 23, 125–27
Aoki, Misako, 1, 115, 118, 142
Asada, Akira, 205n8
assemblage and apparatus, 3, 165, 167–69, 196n4
Asō, Tarō, 36–38, 58, 130, 149, 204n22

banal nationalism (Michael Billig), 112–13

Basic Law on Intellectual Property (Chiteki zaisan kihon hō), 66
BBC (British Broadcasting Corporation),
13, 149–50, 188–89, 211n6
Billig, Michael, 112–13
bishōjo (cute girls). *See shōjo*
Boys Love (BL), 132, 209n13
British Council, 49–52
bundan (literary establishment), 176, 186
bureaucracy, 4–5; anthropology of, 197n7;
and bureaucrats, 5–6, 26, 43–45, 93–
106, 108–11, 126–29, 144–48, 202n37,
203n13, 204n19, 208n2

characterization, 88, 95–102; 199n22,
206n2, 209n10
China, 9, 38–40, 52, 61, 76, 83, 188
Choo, Kukhee, 21, 199n20, 204n20, 205n9
Confucius Institutes, 9, 212n12
content industries, 2, 13–14, 41–42, 66–68,
83–84, 154, 160–62; current status of
Japan's, 198n18
Content Policy Research Group (Kontentsu Seisaku Kenkyūkai), 41
Cool Britannia campaign, 12–13, 44, 76
Cool Japan (TV program), 14, 76–84
Cool Japan Fund, 14, 67, 199n20, 213n18
Cool Japan, 2–3, 12–15, 24, 33, 41–43, 76–
84, 163–65, 199n20, 201n35; critiques
of, 183, 186–87, 202n5; death/end of,
165, 202n5; education and, 163–68
cosplay, 87, 97, 107–8, 110–11, 197n9
COVID-19, 9, 189,
cruel optimism (Lauren Berlant), 23, 174
Csordas, Thomas, 19, 43, 203n11
cultural citizenship, 82, 84, 147
cultural diplomacy and policy 3, 49–52,
103–11, 151–53
cultural imperialism, 10
cultural nation (*bunka kokka*), 56, 66,
205n7
cultural resources, 10, 14, 56, 60, 104, 165

cute (*kawaii*), 24, 117–25, 129–35, 192,
209nn10–11; affects of, 140–43; history
of, 127–30; labor and, 123–25; in manga
132–35

Dewey, John, 4, 11, 16, 27, 147–48, 179–80,
196n5, 211nn3, 4; Lippmann-Dewey
debate, 196n5
Digital Content Association of Japan,
198n18
Digital Content Report (*Dejitaru kontentsu hakusho*), 198n18
Doraemon, 86–88, 206n1
DPJ (Democratic Party of Japan), 59–60,
204n22
Durkheim, Émile, 179, 193, 199n23

economy. See Japan: economy of
embodied states, 33–40, 203n8
emotion. *See* affect
Emperor Hirohito, 36–38
the endless everyday (Miyadai Shinji),
146–47, 211n2
ethics, 88, 92, 140–41, 181, 207n6
the everyday, 144–71; artists and content
producers and, 153–60; higher education and, 160–65; mass media and,
148–53; Miyadai Shinji and, 146–47,
211n2; Tosaka Jun and, 210n1

family resemblances (*Familienähnlichkeiten*, Ludwig Wittgenstein), 23,
201n34
Faubion, James, 181, 186–87, 193–94;
207n6
feeling. *See* affect
Field, Norma, 205n4, 214n11
fieldwork, 24–28
Fiske, John, 195n1
Foucault, Michele, 10, 92, 165, 181, 196n4,
201n31, 207n6
Freud, Sigmund, 177, 200n26

fuan (*fuanshin, fuantei*). *See* anxiety: Japanese words for

Fujiko, Fujio, 86–87, 206n1. *See also* Doraemon

Fujioka, Shizuka, 1, 115, 119, 142, 210n21

Galbraith, Patrick, 132–39, 216nn16, 19, 20

Garon, Sheldon, 43–44, 204n15

Gellner, Ernest, 159, 196n3

Genda Yūji, 146, 178, 201n33

gender, 2–3, 19–20, 24–28, 115–18, 121–43, 187–92, 209nn8–9

Gilroy, Paul, 177–78

girl culture, 115–17, 121–22, 131–32, 136, 208n1

globalization of education, 162–65

gross national cool, 13–14, 41–42, 56, 76

Hamano, Yasuki, 56–59

Hanada, Tatsurō, 145, 150

Harajuku-style fashion (*Harajuku-kei fasshon*), 1, 118, 120–21

Harootunian, Harry, 169, 210n1

Hayashi, Kaori, 145, 150, 204n19

Hello Kitty, 15, 129–30, 209nn10, 11

Herzfeld, Michael, 5, 159, 207n11

high school girls' fashion (*joshi kōsei fasshon*), 1, 119, 140

higher education, 47–48, 160–65

himote (unpopular men), 139–40, 210n19

hope, 8, 12, 21–23, 69, 139, 146, 169, 178, 188, 192, 201n33, 214n8

hypernormalization, 78–84

India, 9, 197n11

International public good (*kokusai kōkyōzai*), 104–5, 110

interpellation (Louis Althusser), 156, 212n10

Itō, Hiromi, 188, 192

Ivy, Marilyn, 22–23, 169

Iwabuchi, Koichi, 14, 21, 62, 148–51, 206n11

iyashi (healing), 52, 182, 192

Japan: disaster and, 188, 194; economy of, 6, 31–32, 61–62, 123–25, 198n18; history of, 22, 31–33, 43–47, 127–29, 210n1; as Japan Inc., 32, 167, 178; lost decades, 6, 32, 41, 211n7; modernity of, 45–49, 100–101, 204n16; national culture of, 3–5, 13–15, 21–24, 69–73, 195n2, 207n11; as number one, 45–47, 56; 62; as Pop-Culture Japan, 2–5, 14–22, 83, 100, 113–14; 173–74

Japan Expo, 120, 137–38

Japan Foundation, 1, 26, 49–54, 90–95; characterization and, 102–6; Murakami Haruki symposium sponsorship, 184–87; Pop-Culture Team and, 93–94, 119, 207n5

The Japan Syndrome 7–8, 151–52

jūnbungaku (pure literature), 81, 176

kata (form), 80–82, 206n13

Katayama, Tetsu, 205n7

kawaii taishi. *See* Ambassadors of Cute

kawaii. *See* cute

Kawakami, Mieko, 191–92, 214n15

Kelts, Roland, 202n5

Kimura, Yū, 1, 115, 118, 120, 123, 142

Kinsella, Sharon, 129–31, 209n12

kokutai (national body), 101, 207n10

Kusuda, Minoru, 36–38

Latour, Bruno, 147, 211n4

LDP (Liberal Democratic Party of Japan), 59, 188–89

Leheny, David, 13–14, 21–22, 26, 101, 201n35, 203n14

Lippmann, Walter, 196n5

Lolita Fashion (*Rorīta fasshon*), 1, 118, 142

lost decades, 6, 32, 41, 211n7

Lukács, Gabriella, 82, 124–25, 202n3, 208n7

Luoma-Aho, Mika, 203n8
Lutz, Catherine, 199n23

MacArthur, General Douglas, 36–38
manga, 11, 56, 58, 87, 97–98, 132–34, 137,
    164, 209n13, 210n16, 212n13. *See also*
    Doraemon
Marcus, George, 27
masculinity, 24–28, 78, 122–23, 126–29,
    132–34, 139–40, 190–92
mass media, 4, 77, 148–53
Massumi, Brian, 16–17, 19, 140, 200nn24,
    26, 207n8, 210n17
matters of concern (Bruno Latour), 147,
    211n4
Mazzarella, William, 64, 146, 203n10,
    206n12
McGray, Douglas, 12–15, 41–42, 56, 69, 77
McVeigh, Brian, 145, 147
meiwaku (disturbance), 89–92
melancholic belonging, 174–75, 177–80,
    187, 190–91
METI (Ministry of Economy, Trade and
    Industry), 13–14, 26, 67–70, 153–56,
    198n18
MEXT (Ministry of Education, Culture,
    Sports, Science and Technology),
    161–65, 212n14
Miller, Daniel, 203n10
Miller, Laura, 121, 127, 131, 135–36, 139,
    208n1, 213n20
minshū bunka (culture of the masses),
    195n2
Miyadai, Shinji, 146–47, 211n2
Miyazaki, Hirokazu, 178, 201n33, 214n8
Miyoshi, Masao, 175
moeru (to bud/burn), 133–35, 210n15
MOFA (Ministry of Foreign Affairs), 1–2,
    26, 86–88; Ambassadors of Cute and,
    115–17, 121–23, 136–39; anime diplo-
    macy and, 92–95; characterization and,
    95–102; Public Diplomacy Department

of, 2, 7, 12–13, 87, 93, 96–102, 122–23;
    security and, 94–101, 115–16
Monji, Kenjirō, 96–103, 106, 115–17
Motoya, Yukiko, 188
Murakami, Haruki, 175–87, 190–92, 213n4;
    administration of, 184–87; affect and,
    180–83; cosmopolitanism of, 175–77,
    180–83; gender and, 190–92; Japan
    Foundation and, 184–87; Jerusalem
    Prize, 184–85; melancholic belonging
    and, 177–80, 182–84
Murakami, Takashi, 129, 158, 183

Nantonaku kurisutaru (Somehow, Crystal),
    205n4, 214n11
nation branding, 3, 12–15, 61–85, 201n35,
    205n5; education and, 162–65; and
    logos, 63, 74–75, 205n8
nation-state, 4–5, 25, 39–40, 100, 145–46;
    affect and, 192–93; anthropology of,
    197n7; distinction between, 196n3;
    identity and, 60, 101, 112–14; ritual
    and, 145–48
national culture, 3–5, 13–15, 69–73, 195n2,
    207n11
national goods, 61–64, 69–73, 78
National Media Arts Center (Kokuritsu
    Media Geijutsu Sōgō Sentā), 58–60
Navaro, Yael, 25, 206n4
Neo-Japanesque Brand Promotion Coun-
    cil, 67–76
"New Japan Style" project (*Shin Nihon
    yōshiki*). *See* Neo-Japanesque Brand
    Promotion Council
NHK (Nihon Hōsō Kyōkai [Japan's public
    broadcaster]), 7–8, 38, 206n15; *Cool
    Japan* and, 76–84, 148–52
nijigen and *sanjigen* (two-dimensional and
    three-dimensional worlds), 133–34,
    210n16
Nixon shock, 35
Nostalgia, 21–23, 169, 173

Nye, Joseph, 6–9, 34, 62, 69, 106, 205n3, 211n5

Obama, Barack, 36–39, 57, 203n9
obligatory nationalism, 88–92, 109, 111–14, 185
Ōe, Kenzaburō, 176
Ogoura, Kazuo, 51–52, 54, 103–6, 109–10, 208n12
Olympics, 9, 103; Tokyo 2020, 188–90
otaku, 77, 101, 129, 131–36, 140, 209n14, 210n18
Overcoming Modernity (*Kindai no chōkoku*) symposium, 49, 204n18
Oyama, Shinji, 167, 198n18

Pacific War, 31–32, 46–47, 49, 99, 126, 158. *See also* World War II
pop-culture diplomacy, 1, 3, 6–8, 26–28, 87–88, 107–11, 113, 122–23, 139
Pop-Culture Japan, 2–5, 14–22, 67, 82–83, 87, 100, 113–14, 127, 130–31, 152, 173–74; future of, 192–94; gendering of, 123–27, 131–32, 187–92, 196n4
Pop-Culture Team. *See* Japan Foundation: Pop-Culture Team
popular culture, 3, 11, 15, 23–24; ethnographies of (Japanese), 212n17; globalization of, 165–68; in higher education, 160–65; politics and administration of, 52–53, 144–48, 151–53; theories of, 195nn1, 2
portable analytic (Dominic Boyer and Cymene Howe), 79, 206n10
precarity, 14, 27, 32, 144, 152, 168–69, 178
press clubs (*kisha kurabu*), 73, 148–49
public diplomacy, 50–53, 96–97, 102–5, 150–51; Department of, 2, 7, 12–13, 87, 93, 96–102, 122–23. *See also* anime diplomacy, cultural diplomacy
public and public sphere, 4–5, 76, 89–90, 102–5, 143, 145, 147–48, 150–51, 196n5, 204n19, 211nn3, 4

reflexivity, 165–71, 192–94, 213n21
Robertson, Jennifer, 195n2, 213n21
Roquet, Paul, 182–83, 192
Rubin, Jay, 175–76, 180

Sakai, Naoki, 44
Sakurai Takamasa, 120–21, 137, 207n7, 208nn13, 2
Satō, Eisaku, 36–38
Sawada, Tomoko, 188–89
Security, 53–54, 63, 85, 94–101, 115–16
Shibata, Motoyuki, 188
Shigematsu, Hisashi, 156–59
Shimizu, Yuichirō, 43–45, 203n13
shingikai. See advisory councils
shōjo (young women/girls), 119, 131–42, 210n20
soft power, 2–12; 31–60, 84, 123, 150–51, 163–65, 197n14, 198n17, 202n1, 205n3, 208n12, 211n5; in advisory councils, 55–58; criticism of, 100–106, 138; cute culture and, 138–39; and economy, 68–70; nation branding and, 68–69, 154–56; security and, 53–54, 85
soft power contradiction, 11–12
somatic modes of attention, 43, 203n11
South Korea, 6, 9, 52, 57, 59, 76, 154, 160–61
Stewart, Kathleen, 206n16
Storey, John, 195n1
Strategic Council on Intellectual Property (Chiteki Zaisan Senryaku Honbu), 66–67

taishū bungaku (popular literature), 176
taishū bunka (popular culture), 195n2
Takahashi, Hiroyuki Mitsume, cover, 2
Tanaka, Yasuo. *See Nantonaku kurisutaru*
Tokyo Contents Market and Licensing Asia, 153–56
Tokyo International Manga Museum, 212n13

Tomkins, Silvan, 200n24
Tosaka, Jun, 210n1
traditional culture (Japanese), 22–23, 66,
    70–75, 81, 130, 209n12

Ueno, Chizuko, 210n19
United Kingdom, 44, 49–52, 177. *See also*
    British Council
US-Japan relations, 33–40, 57, 61–62,
    68–69, 203n6, 204n16
ushinawareta jūnen. See Japan: lost decades

Vogel, Ezra. *See* Japan: as number one

washoku (Japanese food/cuisine), 201n35
Watanabe, Yasushi, 205n1

Weber, Max, 4–5; ideal type and, 95–96,
    197n6
Wetherell, Margaret, 19, 201n29
Womenomics (*ūmanomikusu*), 124, 208n6
World War II, 31–32, 49, 169. *See also*
    Pacific War
worlding and world making, 83, 206n16

Yano, Christine, 15, 80, 129, 203n9,
    206n13, 209n11
Yasukuni Shrine, 12, 198n19
Yoda, Tomiko, 127–28, 145, 147, 202n2,
    205n8
Yonezawa, Akiyoshi, 47–48
Yúdice, George, 10

CPSIA information can be obtained
at www.ICGtesting.com
Printed in the USA
JSHW030319270522
26288JS00003B/3